# OUR 351 SONS

# OUR 351 SONS

## HELPING YOUTH GROW BY
## LEARNING TO SERVE OTHERS

# JOHN & JAN GILLESPIE

### OUR LIFE VERSE — PROVERBS 3:5-6
*"Trust in the Lord with all your heart and lean not unto your own understanding. In all your ways acknowledge Him and He shall direct our paths."*

Published in association with The Fedd Agency, Inc., a literary agency.

Book Website: www.Our351Sons.com

John Direct: 920-427-9000
John@Our351Sons.com
Book Office: 2583 N. Millbrook Road. Appleton, WI 54914

Some names have been changed to protect the privacy of individuals.

Scripture taken from the New King James Version®. Copyright © 1982 by Thomas Nelson. Used by permission. All rights reserved.

ISBN: 978-1-943217-93-9
eISBN: 978-1-943217-94-6

Printed in the United States of America
First Edition 22 21 20 19 18 / 10 9 8 7 6 5 4 3 2

We dedicate this book to our sons Steve and Tim and their wives, Jerry Monson, Bart and Cherry Starr, Dal Wood, Terry Kohler, Chet Krause, and the hundreds of others that joined us on the Rawhide Boys Ranch team. And we acknowledge the continued blessings of our Lord.

# TABLE OF CONTENTS

# FOREWORD

## BY BART AND CHERRY STARR

## *Bart:*

During the past five decades, my wife, Cherry, and I have received numerous questions regarding what life was like as part of the championship-winning Packers during the 1960s. We are always grateful for those inquiries, yet those stories often overlook another profoundly important development that took place in that same period. This one carries on today with our support and gratitude, for reasons you will soon discover.

Early in the summer of 1965, a phone call at our Green Bay home from someone I did not know would start a sequence of events that would become our family passion for decades to come.

The caller identified himself as John Gillespie. He said that he and his wife, Jan, were embarking on an effort to help teenage men from broken homes, many of whom had been in trouble with the law. He asked if he and Jan could meet with Cherry and me to explain their dream and their vision of how we could make a difference.

Naturally, football was on our minds when that phone call came, because we were committed to returning to the championship years of the early 1960s. Summer camp was soon to begin, and our mind-set was focused. Yet the passion in John's voice prompted me to invite him and Jan to meet with us. He said they could be at our house within the hour, so I alerted Cherry that we were going to have guests. We sat in our living room and listened to their plans to turn a large estate and lodge into a nonprofit youth ranch.

## *Cherry:*

Bart and I had often discussed our desire to develop a program for youth at some point in our lives, expecting that it would be after his career in football had ended.

I remember sitting on our couch and getting excited as I listened to John and Jan's vision and approach to helping redirect the lives of at-risk young men. Their passion was compelling, and it was obvious they needed help. When Bart gave me a glance at the end of their presentation, I immediately gave him my nod of approval, and Bart took the next step. We have always been grateful for our decision to become part of John and Jan's dream. It quickly became a fulfill-ment of our dream as well.

## *Bart:*

Cherry and I knew the program needed the acceptance and support of the public. Early on, we involved many of the Green Bay Pack-ers players from the Super Bowl victory years. We even got Coach Lombardi to lend his help making contacts with some major donors.

We were fortunate that the National Football League backed us with promotional support and early financial gifts. The area press and public quickly took note of our old-fashioned approach to helping young men by motivating them when they were headed in the wrong direction. We received widespread state media coverage and even some national press.

Over the past fifty years, the dream of John and Jan Gillespie has developed into one of the most successful youth rehabilitation programs in the nation. Thousands of court-placed young men have redirected their lives at Rawhide Boys Ranch. Most have earned their high school diplomas, and many have gone on to receive college or technical school degrees. They've secured good jobs. Several have served our country through successful military careers. Most importantly, they've learned how to be good husbands and parents. Follow-up records of the alumni show that 85 percent of the boys who spend three months or longer at Rawhide never get in trouble with the law again. In the past decade our community counseling centers have offered practical support and training to thousands of families in need of help with teenage sons or daughters. The local public school system uses the special education program at Rawhide for many of its at-risk students.

This is an amazing story of the faith and passion of a couple with a dream.

How did it all happen? You're about to read about the struggles and successes after that first meeting at our home. Five decades after that first phone call, Rawhide Boys Ranch continues to be our main charitable focus, and John and Jan are very good friends. We suspect God may have had a role in the outcome of that initial meeting, for He knew this was something we wanted to become part of our lives.

We know you will be inspired by this couple as you read their story. They have motivated hundreds of others to adopt their vision and help develop the Rawhide Boys Ranch and to continue to impact the lives of youth and their families.

Cherry and I have had the privilege of being a part of the Gillespies' vision for fifty years. We feel blessed because of it, and we believe you will be blessed by reading about it.

# CHAPTER 1

# JERRY'S OVERNIGHT STAY

## *John:*

June twelfth, 1960, started out as a very typical Sunday for Jan and our three-year-old son, Steve. We had no idea that a very simple event would change the direction of our lives forever.

We were living in a rented farmhouse a few miles north of Appleton, Wisconsin. Before going to church, we fed a variety of animals, including our two horses, Prince and Danny Boy. To be more exact, they were Jan's horses that had become ours as a wedding gift of sorts. Her parents ran a commercial horse operation, so she had her pick of the herd. We also had two ponies, Peanuts and Popcorn, along with a collie (named Lassie, of course), a couple of barn cats, and two rabbits named Thumper and Flower. But our favorite pet was Andy, the naughty crow we had raised from a baby. He loved to play in the sandbox with our son, and many times took Steve's tiny trucks up to the roof, where he had a stash of stolen treasures in the gutter.

After the animals were all fed, we put on our Sunday clothes and piled into our Volkswagen Beetle for the short drive into Appleton. We worshiped at the small church Jan had grown up in, where her family all still attended.

At ten o'clock, half a dozen thirteen- and fourteen-year-old boys entered the classroom where I taught Sunday school. Five minutes into the lesson, one of the church members opened the door and brought in a young man I didn't recognize. He said, "This is Jerry. He's thirteen and lives near the church. I invited him to join your class."

I asked Jerry if his folks had brought him. "No, I just came over on my own." Jerry was very shy and listened politely without joining in the discussion. At the end of the class, he left with the other boys.

The next Sunday, Jerry was one of the first to arrive. The same scenario unfolded, with Jerry observing but not joining in. But this time, Jerry stayed behind after class ended.

"Do you have a question?" I asked.

Jerry said, "I was hoping I could come to your house this afternoon,"

Jan and I grew up in Christian homes where our parents were constantly inviting friends, or people who needed encouragement, to join us for a meal or even to stay overnight. I knew Jerry would be welcome to come home with us, so there was no need to clear this with Jan. "You are certainly welcome to spend the day, but we will have to check with your parents."

"I don't have a dad, and I already asked my mom. She said it was OK."

While Jan, Steve, and our guest waited in the car, I put a note on his mom's door. It explained who we were and that Jerry had told us he had permission to come to our house for the afternoon. The note included our phone number, and I added "If this is not all right, just call and we will bring him home." I ended my note saying that if we did not hear from her, we would bring him home about eight o'clock that evening.

## *Jan:*

It was early afternoon, and John and Jerry were brushing the horses and getting one of the ponies ready for Jerry to ride. Jerry's mom called and said that Jerry had gotten approval to visit us. "Where do you live? I'll bring him some clothes."

"Oh, he really doesn't need more clothes. He's dressed just fine."

His mom surprised me with her reply. "I'll bring some clothes. He may want to stay a few days."

I gave her directions, and then announced to John, "I think we're going to have a house guest."

His reply, as expected, was, "That's fine."

Within an hour, a car pulled into our driveway, and Andy greeted it by cawing a warning from his favorite perch on a branch over the driveway. At the same time, Lassie provided a ground-level greeting.

A lady accompanied by a young girl got out of the car. I assumed they were Jerry's mom and his sister. His mom carried a suitcase, and his sister struggled with a box that had shoe laces, shirtsleeves, and pant legs hanging down the side, ready to spill out at any moment. I opened the door, and they both came into the kitchen. I immediately noticed that the laces belonged to a pair of ice skates on top of the clothes. This was surprising, considering it was June and there was no ice, even in Wisconsin.

Jerry's mom told us a story that was hard to believe. "I'm Jerry's mom," she began. "Let me explain what's happening. I have three children. Jerry is thirteen, and he has a twelve-year old brother. This is my daughter, who is nine. I remarried two weeks ago, and my new husband gave me thirty days to find homes for any two of my three children. The Saint Joseph Children's Home in Green Bay has accepted Ronnie, but my husband will not pay any support, so they will not take Jerry. I'm going to keep my daughter. I encouraged Jerry to go over to the church to see if he could find someone to live with. I'm hoping he can live with you."

John and I did not take any time to discuss our response. How could there be any option other than putting our arms around this young boy who was being turned out of his home? Both of us assured her Jerry was welcome to stay, and his mom left him standing there next to his suitcase and box of clothes. We did our best to let him know we were happy to have him in our home and helped him take his things to his room. We knew Jerry needed to be loved and cared for, but we didn't know that he would be the first of 350 other sons, in addition to our two boys.

Jerry was a joy. He was a great "big brother" to Steve, and was always helpful and obedient. The end of summer was approaching, and we had to start thinking about school. John talked to our local school board, and they confirmed that Jerry's mom had approved his living with us. They agreed to waive the tuition for at least one year.

Jerry started school, but in mid-September we faced a surprise dilemma. I was home alone when a man appeared at the door, saying sternly that he was an investigator for the county welfare department.

He showed some credentials and then said, "Is it true you've been harboring an unrelated juvenile for more than seventy-eight days?"

I quickly figured out that "unrelated juvenile" meant Jerry. He had been with us about three months, so it would have been more than seventy-eight days. "Yes, but we are not harboring him. He's here with the permission of his mother."

The investigator's reply was blunt: "You're in violation of county law. You should have gotten a foster home license."

"No one is paying us to care for him. We are paying everything." I assumed someone thought we were doing this to make money.

"It has nothing to do with you being paid. You're breaking the law, and I am here to pick up the boy."

I asked if the county had talked to the mother and whether she would let Jerry move back home. Again, the response was shocking. "His mother said he cannot move back home, so we will place him in a licensed foster home."

"How can we get licensed?"

"You can't. You could actually be put in jail for what you have done." Of course, up until now we'd had no idea we were breaking a local law.

Luckily, Jerry was visiting my parents at their horse farm for the day, and I would not tell the investigator where he was. He became even more threatening with my refusal.

As soon as John returned, I anxiously explained the unnerving confrontation with the welfare inspector. We talked about whom we should contact to find out if they could really take Jerry away from us. John thought of someone he hoped might help.

# *John:*

I had met Gerald Lorge, our state senator, on several occasions, and I told Jan I would call him to see if he could help us. I looked up his home phone number and made the call. Senator Lorge answered the phone himself, and he seemed very interested in what had happened. He asked me several questions, showing encouragement. He concluded with, "John, I'll call the county welfare director. I know him well, and I'm sure we can work this out. By all means, do not let them take Jerry before we talk again."

This took place on Saturday. Senator Lorge called back Monday afternoon. "I talked to the county director, and everything you relayed to me is true. They seem to be on a vendetta to punish you for taking Jerry without contacting them first. Are you and Jan available tomorrow? I'll pick you both up and take you to meet with someone."

Early Tuesday morning Jan's mom came over and picked up Steve to stay with her for the day. Jerry boarded the bus for school. At eight o'clock Senator Lorge arrived in our driveway, and was greeted by Andy and Lassie, our welcoming team. We climbed into his car and headed south on US 41. For two hours we discussed what we were doing, our interest in helping needy youth, and his work with the government. I was reluctant to ask where we were going.

We arrived in Madison and pulled up to the impressive capitol building. We climbed a series of marble stairs, and to our surprise, our destination was the Lieutenant Governor's office. Senator Lorge spoke with the receptionist, mentioning a ten o'clock appointment. At this point the realization hit: we were going to be meeting with the Lieutenant Governor of Wisconsin.

Warren Knowles greeted Senator Lorge warmly. "Senator, is this the couple you called me about?"

We were invited to sit in black leather chairs around the table in the conference room, and Lieutenant Governor Knowles asked us to tell him our story. We explained the details of our confrontation with the county welfare inspector and his threats to take Jerry away. At the conclusion of our story, the Lieutenant Governor picked up the phone and said, "Wilbur, please come into my office right away." Wilbur Schmidt, the director of the Wisconsin Welfare Department, entered the office and sat down across the table from us., "This is John and Jan Gillespie," the Lieutenant Governor explained. "Their story is difficult to fathom. It involves an apparent lack of common sense by their county welfare agency. John and Jan, would you please share your story with Wilbur?"

We told the story one more time. At the conclusion, Lieutenant Governor Knowles said, "Wilbur, I want you to call the county and confirm the situation. It is important that we act in the best inter- est of Jerry. I want the Gillespies licensed as Wisconsin State Foster Home Parents by the end of today. I don't want Jerry removed from their home."

We drove the hundred miles back to Appleton, extremely grate- ful to Senator Lorge for what he had accomplished. It was a first- hand lesson in the operation of government, both the good and bad. When we pulled into our driveway, we were surprised to see the same county agent who had come to get Jerry a few days earlier waiting in his car. He wasn't smiling when he said, "I don't know how this happened." He handed me an envelope and then abruptly headed back to his car. I opened the envelope to find our Wisconsin Foster Home License.

Jerry lived with us almost two years before his mother divorced the stepfather and he could move back home. We had learned early on that his mom loved her three children very much, but she was struggling with serious issues herself. In desperation she reached out for someone to care for her. It was a good lesson for us to be slow to judge the actions of others, as we can never know the pain they may be going through.

The temporary home we provided for Jerry would lead to our founding the Rawhide Boys Ranch. Thousands of young men would follow to learn how they could have productive lives.

After living with us, Jerry eventually went on to serve in the army and saw combat in Vietnam. On his return, he became an active member of the Veterans of Foreign Wars (VFW), assisting at military funerals. He developed a successful car repair business and considers himself one of our sons. Now, in his sixties, he continues to be a passionate spokesperson for Rawhide Boys Ranch.

After Jerry moved home, and while we were still living in our small farmhouse, the Wisconsin Department of Corrections placed fifteen-year-old Ron Schuh with us. He had grown up with his Native American mother on the Oneida reservation near Green Bay. He had a history of truancy, alcohol abuse, and shoplifting. Despite his background, Ron quickly fit into our family and became an excellent big brother to Steve and our second son, Tim.

Our rented farmhouse had two modest bedrooms and one very small bedroom. Such an arrangement became far too small for us when we learned that Jan was expecting our second child. The search began for a larger house that would fit into our modest budget.

In December 1965, we made a dramatic move to a much larger home. Ron made the move with us to a home that was large enough to accommodate many more teenagers.

The chalet-style house had twenty-seven rooms, with eleven bedrooms and five and a half bathrooms. It sat on five hundred acres along the scenic Wolf River. We named the estate, and the program that would evolve there, Rawhide Boys Ranch. But at twenty-seven years of age, how did we think we were qualified to run a program for teenage boys with delinquent backgrounds?

We didn't know. But we had a passion to help youth in need of redirection, and we believed God would give us the guidance we would need.

Both Jan and I were blessed with parents whose compassionate hearts made them always willing to help others in need. We didn't know it at the time, but the wide range of charitable experiences they modeled for us would be the inspiration and preparation for the challenges and opportunities to come. The legacy of Rawhide Boys Ranch was founded on the values they instilled in us.

# CHAPTER 2
# EARLY EXPERIENCES

## *John:*

I was jolted awake at three o'clock in the morning as the fire station siren screamed its call to the volunteers who served our township. My dad was a charter member of the Grand Chute Volunteer Fire Department back in the days before the township even owned a fire truck. In two minutes I was out of bed and fully dressed. I could hear Mom outside my bedroom door saying, "Stanley, don't wake John. It's too early." But before my dad could reply, I rushed out into the hall, ready to join him on another fire call.

When we arrived at a fire, Dad would park our car in a safe location that faced the fire. Before he got out, he would look me in the eye and warn, "Remember, John, you must not get out of the car. I'll be back to check on you as soon as I can."

I would watch the men battle the blaze and wished I could help, but they don't let you do that when you're four years old. Many years later, I would be trained by the U.S. Army as a firefighter and serve as the fire marshal of the Army Airfield at Fort Belvoir, Virginia. This helped prepare me to serve as the fire chief of the Rawhide Fire Department, training local volunteers and the Rawhide boys to play a vital role supporting local departments in fighting forest and building fires. It would be only one of the many ways we would impart lessons about responsibility to the boys. There is no better motivation than knowing that your efforts can save others' property, or even their lives.

My parents gave me a host of opportunities to learn skills that would one day shape the way we developed the program at Rawhide. A key principle I learned was the importance of helping others in need, and Mom and Dad made it a point to involve me in their numerous acts of kindness. I went with them many times to call on sick neighbors, to buy groceries for poor families, or to round up cows that had wandered onto the road from a nearby farm. They also taught me the biblical principle of tithing, showing me how to give 10 percent of my earnings to our church.

My dad was the first employee hired by the founders of Integrity Mutual Insurance Company, and he also had his own agency under that company's umbrella. On weekends he worked with us on family projects, mainly our four-acre vegetable garden. During the week Mom, my younger brother, Dennis, and I did the planting, weeding, spraying, and harvesting. Our home and garden were nestled between a cemetery and two large farms, and we would occasionally borrow equipment from a farmer to pull behind our Farmall tractor, which Dad taught me to drive when I was eight. Before we returned any borrowed implement, Dad would always clean it completely, oil it, and repair any broken or loose parts. Sometimes he would touch-up the paint.

I remember helping him clean a manure spreader with a brush and garden hose one day. I asked him why it was necessary to clean a manure spreader. His answer was, "If you return borrowed items in better shape than when you got them, people won't hesitate to lend things to you again." This made an impression on me, and I shared this story many times with the boys at Rawhide as I taught them how to take proper care of the tools and equipment they used.

Since we had a long driveway, our tractor had a snowplow and tire chains for winter use. When it started to snow, my first thought was not sledding or making a snowman, it was being able to plow snow. When I was twelve, I started a snowplowing business serving a dozen neighbors. The money I earned was divided. Half went to my parents for gas and tractor costs. With the other half, I put 10 percent in the church offering and 10 percent into my bank account. I set half of what was left aside for practical items like clothes and school supplies and spent the balance on whatever I wanted.

At age twelve I began a summer produce route. Every Tuesday and Friday morning, Mom and I would load a trailer with freshly harvested fruit or vegetables such as strawberries, raspberries, onions, cabbage, lettuce, potatoes, sweet corn, and apples. For five hours I would stop at homes on my sales route. With World War II just ending, people were cautious about how they spent their money, but I was very dependable and showed up at each of the eighty homes on my route twice a week, and because my goods were priced a little lower than those at the local grocery store, my buyers saved money and became loyal customers.

My inherent desire to serve others would be joined at an early age by a desire to please one young lady in particular. In the '40s and into the '50s, the rural education system had a first-through-eighth-grade school located every few miles so students could all walk to school. School buses didn't exist in those days, and only rarely did parents drive their kids to school. My hike was exactly one mile, and in eight years I never missed a day, despite the challenging Wisconsin winters and chilling wet springs. Our neighbors had students who were older and we all walked together.

The school was heated with a basement coal furnace. One of the school board members, who owned a farm nearby, would start the furnace every morning before his six o'clock milking session. On a cold winter day, the big thermometer at the back of the classroom would not reach sixty degrees until about ten o'clock. We could keep our coats and mittens on until it hit that mark. That meant no writing assignments until then, only reading and recitation as we huddled in our winter clothing.

During my eight years at Woodlawn School, anywhere from thirty-five to fifty students would gather in the one room with one teacher for all the grades. We were more fortunate than some of the other area schools because we had an indoor "outhouse." It was a room with a toilet set over a big tank. It had a vent through the wall to outside, but it was still very aromatic.

Drinking water was carried from an outdoor hand pump, and the upper-class students were assigned the task of filling a bucket each morning and pouring it into a drink dispenser. Somehow, that pump always worked, even in below-zero weather.

On my first day in second grade a new student sat in front of me. She was a third-grader whose parents had purchased the farm next to the school. Her name was Janice Krull. Jan and I instantly became best friends, and we would later become partners for life.

## *Jan:*

John and I grew up in homes a mile apart. I lived with my parents, Ruth and Oliver Krull, in an apartment in downtown Appleton above my dad's pet store. My first job was giving fresh water to the canaries, rabbits, hamsters, and other animals in the store every morning. The pet store also sold a variety of garden plants and seeds. As time went on, I handled more responsibilities, including waiting on customers.

My mom worked in a knitting mill five days a week, and as an only child, I became my father's close companion and helper.

In 1941 my parents purchased a farm north of Appleton, right next to Woodlawn School, and my father started a horse business. He purchased wild horses from the Dakotas and had them shipped to Appleton by train, then hauled them in our truck to the ranch. As the fall rolled around, I was looking forward to the start of school. Little did I know the second-grade boy assigned to sit behind me would end up hanging around for the next seventy years.

I quickly became an accomplished rider, and when I was ten years old, my father would call on me to ride a "just broke" horse to show it off for potential buyers. If it was a horse I wanted to keep for myself, I made sure it didn't behave very well for our customers. I would use my leg on the side of the horse my father could not see and give it a little kick to make it act up.

My training and love for horses would prepare me to develop an "equine therapy" program at our boys ranch years later. We were practicing equine therapy at Rawhide even before that term became popular.

## *John:*

I liked horses, but riding them was not a high priority. However, because Jan was becoming my first girlfriend, horseback riding became part of my routine.

One day during recess, Jan said her father needed someone to clean their barn. The job would take about an hour and pay twenty-five cents. That was good money for a fifth-grader, and my parents said I could take the job. Reporting to Jan's father the next day after school, I was shown how to carefully rake the manure out of the sixteen box stalls, most with a "just broke" horse nervously moving around inside.

I liked the job. I cleaned each stall with the expected care, loaded the manure into a wheelbarrow, and wheeled it out the door and up a plank to the top of a horse manure pile. The job took about an hour. If Jan decided to help me, it took about half an hour longer. I took pride in doing a good job. On many evenings in the winter, before I could wheel out the manure, I had to shovel snow off the plank to get to the top of the pile. The manure was not loaded and spread on the fields until spring, so the pile grew to what seemed like a small mountain to a fifth-grader trying not to slip off an icy plank.

After a few months, I told Jan I thought I should get a raise to at least thirty-five cents a night to compensate for my perilous labors. One day in the spring, her father said, "John, when you're done with the box stalls, come and see me." I was sure I would get the raise I was lobbying for, but to my surprise, I was fired! Her father's words are still etched in my mind, making it one of the worst days of my early life. "John, Jan tells me you're being mean to the horses, and we can't have that. This will be your last night. Here's the money you have coming."

As I walked home, I thought, "Why would she lie to her father about me? What am I going to tell my parents?" As a fifth-grader fired from my first real job, I wondered whether this would affect my future employment opportunities.

I didn't say anything to my folks for two days. I found school friends to mess around with until the time I usually came home from cleaning the stable. But by that time, my firing started to make sense. I noticed that Jan was hanging around with Ronnie Hahn, the new barn guy, during recess. My firing had nothing to do with my work. I was a victim of sexual harassment! The funny thing is, the moment I realized the firing had nothing to do with my job performance, I felt better.

Ronnie had the job for the rest of the school year and for a month or so into the next year. Then something happened between them, and Jan asked if I would like the job back. She said Ronnie was just not working out.

Since I now realized the job was related to being Jan's boyfriend, I was glad to accept the stable-cleaning chores for a second time. But the revolving door of barn boys did not end there. Between fifth and eighth grades I was hired five times and fired four times. I did notice an interesting pattern with the revolving door: after each new boy was hired and let go, I was always hired back.

The last time, I quit on my own. I was starting ninth grade at Wilson Junior High, and I had football practice after school. No more time to shovel horse manure. Yet I had learned that I really liked Jan and her strong will. She knew how to get what she wanted and I was happy she wanted me.

I played football and worked summers as a lifeguard at the city swimming pool. I spent my spare time helping with our family truck garden, planting, harvesting, and selling produce. As a high school junior, I partnered with my cousin Jim Gillespie, scraping up enough money to buy a small landscape company. Jan continued to help her dad with the horse business. We dated, but we always seemed to break up in the summer. That was usually because Jan had found a short-term fling, so I would do the same.

She graduated from high school in 1953, and that summer she went to California for two months. She stayed with her aunt and uncle, who had two daughters near her age. She and her cousins attended a Bible camp for a week up in the mountains, and that week would impact our lives forever. Jan and her family were active in a small church, so she had a background in Christian teaching. But the Bible camp motivated her to become more devoted to her faith.

I was ready to start my senior year in high school, and it was a long summer with her gone and nothing to do but landscaping projects. One warm August evening after she returned, Jan invited me to come over. We found ourselves sitting on a swing set in the front yard. Working up the courage to ask if anything had changed in our relationship over the summer, I finally blurted, "Are you still my girlfriend?"

She replied in a serious tone. "I want to talk to you about that."

My first thought was she must have met a new guy, so I braced myself for the worst. Instead, she said, "I made a new commitment in my relationship with the Lord. We can continue to date only if you also know Jesus as your Savior."

My parents were also active in church, and I had heard Bible stories all my life. "Oh yes, I know Jesus personally." We kissed, and all was well.

However, on the mile walk home that dark night, I talked to Jesus all the way. I prayed, "Lord, I know you are the Son of God, and you died and rose from the dead for my sins. But I don't know if I have ever asked you to forgive my sins and to be my Savior. I am asking you that now." Since that night, I have known a growing confidence that God loves me and that my future with Him is secure in this life and the next.

College started for me in 1954, when I enrolled at the University of Wisconsin in Madison. My area of study was land planning and landscape architecture, aligning with my interest in the company that Jim and I had named Gillespie Gardens.

I grew up attending a Baptist church, so while attending the university, I qualified for a very inexpensive room at the Madison Baptist Student Center. They had a food co-op available to students in their men's and women's dorms, which saved me a lot of money. One day a notice appeared on our house bulletin board: Student volunteers were needed every Tuesday evening and would be driven half an hour away to a state-run girls' correctional facility. Each person would lead a Bible study for a small group of girls. I wondered aloud to my roommate if many of the girls would show up to study the Bible.

And in truth, a number of the hundred incarcerated teenage girls who showed up only did so because they knew University of Wisconsin guys would be leading the studies.

On that first night, a dozen of us from the Baptist Student Center nervously arrived at the girls' facility. We were given a few guidelines and then each assigned a staff person who led us to our respective rooms and stayed with us through the forty-five-minute class. I felt prepared because I had my lesson plan, but I didn't know what to expect.

The class really went well. Most of the girls did want to learn about God and the life of Jesus. Very few had any church or religious background, and they asked basic, sincere questions. After that first nervous evening, I looked forward to returning every Tuesday for the rest of the school year. I met with a revolving group of a dozen girls. Every few weeks one or two would leave the facility and one or two new ones would be added to my class.

As I led the classes, my understanding and compassion for youth whose lives lacked direction continued to grow. Looking back, I can see that God was preparing me for a future at Rawhide.

## *Jan:*

On June 15, 1957, I walked down the aisle to join my best friend, who was waiting for me at the front of the church. Our marriage occurred in the same year as Appleton's centennial celebration, and numerous men in the city, including our groomsmen, were getting into the spirit of the occasion by growing beards or mustaches. I was very concerned about what our wedding pictures would look like for the rest of our lives, so we decided to make lemonade out of lemons, planning an old-fashioned wedding. The men would wear tuxes with long tails, top hats, and canes. The gals would sport varied pastel hoop skirt dresses with big hats and matching parasols. And to top it off, we planned for a horse and buggy to take us from the church to the park for the reception. As you'd expect, my father was very willing to provide and drive the horse and buggy.

Before our wedding, John and I decided to select a life verse. We chose Proverbs 3:5-6: "Trust in the Lord with all your heart, and lean not on your own understanding; in all your ways acknowledge him, and he shall direct your paths." We wanted that verse to guide our life together and to honor God.

We had talked about our plans. John expected to be involved in landscaping and designing subdivisions and golf courses. I was con-fident that somehow horses would continue to be part of our lives.

## *John:*

I joined the Army's branch of the Reserve Officer Training Corp during my freshman year in college. As the ROTC advisor was going through the list of military occupational specialties, I stopped him when he came to Combat Engineers and asked what they do. He explained that they provide engineering support to combat units. They have an assortment of heavy construction equipment to build roads, airfields, small buildings, bridges, and landscaping. At the magic word, "landscaping," I stopped him and said, "That's for me. Sign me up."

I had finished second in my basic officer training class of one hundred, so I had my choice of an active-duty station. I selected Fort Belvoir, Virginia, just south of Washington, DC. My specialty was teaching heavy equipment operation, and demolitions. I continued in that role in a local Army Reserve Battalion for another eight years after completing active duty.

My cousin and partner, Jim, had done a great job maintaining the landscape business during my tour in the Army, and together we expanded our services to include government highway-beautification contracts. Our summer staff reached fifty people at times, and we employed a lot of "unemployable" workers. Despite a few issues, it was gratifying to help them out. On any given Friday, about 10 percent of our crew did not report for work, probably because they were getting ready to celebrate the weekend. On Mondays, the same 10 percent were recovering from the weekend, and we did not see them until Tuesday.

We also hired men from the local county jail work-release program. They turned out to be our most dependable employees, delivered to us every day in the county security van. We ended up getting involved in some of the personal lives of our summer help and provided support to their families.

Jan and I became active in a worldwide interdenominational

program called Youth for Christ (YFC). We directed the Appleton area chapter. Some of the activities included six-person Bible quiz teams, monthly citywide rallies, and special events. Since Jan and I knew unusual and challenging activities provide positive motivation to teenagers, we planned some "out-of-the-box" fun activities. One was a three-hundred-mile horseback ride in which Jan played a key role.

## *Jan:*

Truman "Tru" Robertson was a close friend of John and mine and the founder of Fort Wilderness, a wonderful youth and family camp in northern Wisconsin. He sat at our farmhouse kitchen table with us early in the summer of 1963. We were talking about the importance of challenging youth to set high standards and think outside the box. After three hours, we had sketched out plans to take fifty teenagers on a three-hundred-mile horseback ride across the state of Wisconsin. We would call the adventure "Teens on Parade." The theme would be "Challenging teens to be mentally, physically and spiritually fit in an age of space."

The ride was to take place in June 1964, because we knew we would need a full year to put together a volunteer support team and plan the detailed logistics of the adventure. I knew an average day's ride for novice riders would be twenty miles. From a quick look at a Wisconsin map, we figured the distance from Milwaukee to Fort Wilderness, located just north of Rhinelander, was 260 miles. The secondary roads we would want to follow would add another forty miles.

We contacted people with varied backgrounds to volunteer with the planning and drive the support vehicles accompanying the riders. I was to be the trail ride director and would ride Danny Boy on the trip. John's horse, Prince, would also come, but John made it clear that one of the teens would be riding him. John would be too busy to ride, as he would be the overall coordinator. I also knew riding a horse was not high on his priority list.

Vic Eliason, the state YFC director who later founded the national Christian radio network VCY America, took charge of recruiting the teenagers who would go on the ride. Tru was responsible to feed fifty teens and about a dozen adult volunteers both breakfast and lunch for fourteen days. They were all fed again at supper, along with several hundred additional people who purchased the meal in each of the communities where we camped overnight. The meal included an evening program, and the public was encouraged to attend through advance advertising.

Keith Thompson was responsible for feeding and watering the horses at each noon rest stop and at the overnight locations. He had to line up farriers who could work through the night at the half-way mark to re-shoe all the horses.

My father, was excited about our plans, and decided that a three-hundred-mile horseback ride should include a stagecoach. He purchased a full-sized replica of a Wells Fargo stagecoach and trained a four-horse team to pull it. He drove the stagecoach the whole trip, and at the end of the ride, he donated it to Fort Wilderness camp, where our ride ended.

The route took us north across most of the state, with stops every night at a community of at least one thousand people. John and I drove the route in advance to make sure each road had a wide shoulder for safety. In addition, we had to get advance permission at the locations where we would set up camp every night. We contacted a service organization along the route to promote local attendance at the nightly meal and program.

Fifty teens applied, which was the approximate number we

wanted. We had recruited teenagers who owned horses, but we also borrowed a few horses for those that did not have their own. The teens came from Youth for Christ chapters around the state, and a dozen or so had vocal or instrumental talents or public speaking experience. They were also interested in sharing their faith in the Lord. Using their talents, we designed a faith-based musical program with a country spin to perform at each of the fourteen communities where we would stay overnight along the route.

To fund the ride, we sold buffalo burger plate dinners at every evening event. The sponsoring service clubs sold advance meal tickets for $1.50 each. The meal was a real buffalo burger sandwich, beans, coleslaw, and dessert bars. Buffalo meat was still a novelty at the time, and the tickets sold very well.

In June 1964 we started out from a Milwaukee area park with fifty teenagers, more than thirty horses, half a dozen vehicles (including two with large safety signs and flashing lights to drive ahead and behind the line of horses), and a truck with a large horse trailer in case of a sick or lame horse. We had also borrowed a semi-tractor pulling a refrigerated trailer filled with tents, program supplies, a PA system, personal suitcases, extra tack, and food to provide an estimated ten thousand meals, which included a ton of ground buffalo meat. In the front of the semi-trailer was a six-by-eight-foot room where John and I would sleep on army cots. We ended up using those cots for about four hours a night during the two weeks of the ride.

We planned to arrive at four o'clock in the afternoon in every community, and the local sponsoring service club had promoted our arrival as a parade. We led the parade with a white Buick convertible with a speaker system playing country music and adorned with teenage guys and girls in western clothing. Behind the lead convertible were the horses and riders, the Wells Fargo stagecoach, and then the support vehicles. The semi-trailer had a large sign advertising that everyone was invited to the evening meal and program.

The ride went without a hitch, other than a few saddle sores on some of the teens. It received a lot of press coverage. Near the middle of the trip, a team of people showed up from the state humane society to check the horses. They found no problems and gave every horse a passing grade.

The service clubs had done a good job selling advance tickets for the dinner in every community, and we fed anywhere from 500 to 1,200 guests. Each stop was at an athletic field or park where we had permission to stay overnight. Most had bleachers and a stage area for the program.

The program was a huge hit, drawing large crowds of local teenagers. At the end of each evening's show, the crowd often stayed more than an hour visiting with the riders and performers, even asking some for their autographs. The teens were able to share their faith in a fun and effective way.

Many of them found their faith greatly deepened. Five decades later, we still hear from some of them, saying that they were never the same after their experience with "Teens on Parade." It gave them more confidence to face future challenges and to trust that God would give them direction. As for us, it reinforced our belief that teenagers could be motivated through big challenges and bonding with horses. At Rawhide we would continue that philosophy, teaching the boys to care for and enjoy the animals.

## *John:*

During the many years I was involved in the YFC program, I had become a good friend of the national vice president, Jay Kessler. One day, Jay asked to meet and share a cup of coffee. To my surprise, he asked me to work full time with YFC. He offered me a position as a regional vice president in charge of Wisconsin and four surrounding states. The job would provide a very good salary, a car, and an expense account, but the work would entail traveling throughout the region and being away from home three nights a week.

It was a heady offer, and I knew I could do and enjoy the job. I presented it to Jan with a positive spin. After I completed my sales pitch, Jan calmly asked, "How much would you be gone?"

"I will be home four nights a week," I assured her.

"So you would be gone three nights a week. I'm not excited about that at all."

"Well, let's pray about it."

"No," she quickly replied. "I will not pray about it. I did not marry you to be a half-time husband and father."

Jan's refusal to even consider the position frustrated me. I didn't realize that when I was saying, "Let's pray about it," what I was really doing was telling her was, "This is what I think God wants." I wasn't really asking what she wanted. The truth was, I wanted the job.

I was already working long hours in my site-planning design business and the Army Reserve. At home, Ron was living with us and we were expecting our second son.

I had been married long enough to know I could not make a major decision like this without Jan's agreement and support. This was one of many times we referred to the verses we adopted at our marriage, not leaning on our own understanding, but letting God direct our path. After two weeks of mostly silent grumbling, I called Jay to tell him that the time was not right for me to accept the YFC job.

Little did I realize that God was at work in our lives, and just around the corner would come His much bigger project. In fact, Jan and I would devote the rest of our lives to it.

# CHAPTER 3
# RAWHIDE BOYS RANCH IS BORN

*John:*

A week after I turned down the YFC job, a gentleman called and said he had seen my land planning business ad in the Yellow Pages. He wanted to meet with me about a proposal to design a subdivision for his five-hundred-acre property. He sounded elderly and was difficult to understand as I took his name and address. His house and property were twenty miles away on the Wolf River. I put the note on my desk and didn't follow up right away. He called back in two weeks, and this time he insisted that I come to see him. I explained to Jan that I had to meet a possible client and invited her to ride along. We headed for a remote location in the country outside of New London. We had no idea the meeting would change the course of our lives.

It was a beautiful fall day as Jan and I made the drive with our three-year-old son, Tim. Ray Carlson's directions were complicated, and we did not have Google Maps in 1965. Luckily, I had carefully written down his directions. His final comment was very interesting: "Follow Weiland Road three miles to a driveway on the left. Be careful, because one hundred feet past the driveway, the road becomes a boat landing, and without warning it runs into the Wolf River."

As we drove, the beautiful countryside alternated between scattered farms and dense woodlands. Because of the sandy soil in this part of the state, white birch and pine trees abounded, and potato fields were plentiful. We arrived at a driveway with impressive ten-foot stone pillars on either side. We could see the river just past the driveway, and we continued one hundred feet to the end of the road to have a look. And yes, the road ran into the river and disappeared.

The Wolf River, a few hundred feet wide at this point, was dotted with fishing boats. This scenic waterway, a great fishing river, winds its way down from northern Wisconsin. A walleye pike run takes place as the ice goes out each spring. This is followed by a white bass run, which peaks in the middle of May.

As we started up the driveway, I thought this would be a great location for a subdivision except that it was definitely in the middle of nowhere.

Then, to our amazement, an impressive three-story Swiss chalet-style lodge appeared, sitting back from a bend of the river. As we pulled up to the building, Mr. Carlson came out and welcomed us. Introductions were made, and he asked us to call him Ray. We expressed our admiration for his home, and he asked if we would like to see the inside. We said yes!

The inside was every bit as appealing as the outside. It had twenty-seven rooms, all finished in knotty pine: eleven bedrooms, five and a half bathrooms, three huge stone fireplaces, two living rooms, a third-floor gym/game room, and a finished basement. Ray explained that he had sponsored a craftsman and his son from Europe, and they had lived at the home for almost three years doing extensive remodeling work. His plan had been to use it as a business retreat and training center, but the venture had not been successful.

Ray was in his late seventies, and now he just wanted to sell the home and land. He hoped a subdivision plan for the hundred cleared acres and quarter-mile of river frontage would help sales. Dense woods and some swamp covered the rest of the land. It was habitat for one of the largest deer herds in the state. He told us the property and home were listed with a real estate firm at two hundred thousand. He had an offer, but it was somewhat below his asking price, and he did not want to accept it.

Our tour included a room filled with antique furnishings, where we paused to enjoy the view through picture windows looking out on the river. As I stood looking at the Norman Rockwell scene, I said, almost to myself, "Oh, my. This would make a great boys' home."

"Why did you say that?" Ray's question sounded almost demanding.

I explained our passion for taking in teenage boys who were from dysfunctional families or who were in trouble with the law. We had been praying we could find a larger, affordable house.

After a few more probing questions, Ray said, "If this property and home could be used for disadvantaged youth, I would be willing to sell it for $87,500."

At this point, the conversation took a major change in direction. "Why are you quoting us less than half your current asking price?" I asked.

He went on to explain. "I want to buy a four-unit apartment building near Lawrence University in Appleton, live in one of the units, and rent out the other three. The price of the apartment building is $87,500. With the building paid off, I will be able to live comfortably. My military and business pensions will take care of living expenses. I would love to see this become a boys home."

I looked at Jan, wondering if it could be possible that this offer might be part of our dream to help more boys? Our life verses in Proverbs did say that all things are possible when God is involved.

I asked Ray if he could give us a week before accepting a purchase offer to see if we could put together a financial package. He paused a moment before asking us to provide a nonrefundable earnest payment to show we were serious. After another pause, he said, "$500 will buy you seven days." But we did not have $500.

## *Jan:*

After a polite thank you, John and I left and drove to see my father. We explained what we had seen and its potential to be a boys home. We asked him if we could borrow $500. Dad went into his home office and came out with five hundred-dollar bills. "This is not a loan," he declared. "It's a gift."

We thanked him and immediately made the half-hour return trip to the Carlson home. Ray was impressed because we had left him only an hour earlier. He was very excited about the possibility of his home and property being used to help youth.

We had no money to purchase the property. John's land planning and landscape business was barely paying our bills, and we still had college loans to pay off. We had no interest in personally owning the property or making any money for our efforts to help youth. John expected to continue his land-planning business to provide our income, and we talked about setting up a nonprofit corporation as the best way to raise funds to purchase the home and property.

# *John:*

I had become friends with numerous community business leaders, and I called half a dozen to explain the potential the property had as a youth home. Everyone I met with expressed polite support, patted me on the back, and said "good luck." None were willing to get involved. We remained empty-handed, and the week was almost over. We needed more time, so we headed back to meet with Ray Carlson, who was still very hopeful that his property could become a youth home. However, he was concerned about the possibility of losing a buyer. There was also the possibility of his current offer being raised to a point he would have to accept it. He offered to give us four more weeks to see if we could raise the money, but the extension would cost another $2,000.

Some months earlier, I had been talking with an acquaintance when he mentioned meeting Paul Patz, the founder of the Patz Corporation, a barn cleaner systems company in Pound, Wisconsin. He had told me Mr. Patz had an interest in youth and hoped to someday develop a college program to train students for the Christian ministry. I called the Patz Company, and when I reached Mr. Patz, I outlined our dream for a youth program. He scheduled a meeting for us to see him the following day.

We headed north on the seventy-mile drive. I had taken some pictures of the lodge and grounds, and I had put together a three-ring binder outlining our vision for a program for teenage boys. Jan and I asked God to help Mr. Patz see how this program could help youth. He greeted us at the door of his modest company office and cordially invited us to tell him our story. He listened intently as we shared our vision to help teenage boys and showed him the binder. He asked a few questions during our fifteen-minute presentation and then sat back in his chair, thinking, for what seemed like a very long time.

His minute of contemplation came to a decisive end. "John and Jan, here is what I will do. I will give you a check for $2,000 right now on this condition: If God blesses your plan, and this can be set up as a successful nonprofit program for youth, this will be a gift. If it does not succeed, then at some point you must agree to pay it back, but there will be no interest." We quickly agreed.

As we headed out of town, we stopped at the first pay phone booth we saw. We called Mr. Carlson to let him know we had raised the earnest money for the next month.

We realized we needed a lot of publicity to share our plans to help youth. Using the pictures of the beautiful lodge seemed the way to start. I headed to downtown Appleton for a meeting with Victor Minahan, the publisher of the Appleton Post Crescent. He was very supportive of the plan and agreed to send a reporter and photographer to do a feature story about the proposed youth project.

The next morning we met at the Carlson property with a reporter and photographer. We spent over an hour sharing our vision for a program for disadvantaged teenage boys. Two days later, a half-page feature story with pictures appeared in the regional section of the paper. Thousands of people read it, and it opened the door to numerous invitations to share our story at service club and church meetings.

On a few of those occasions, someone would come to me at the end of a presentation and say, "You should try to meet with Bart and Cherry Starr." They had heard Bart say that he and Cherry might start a program for underprivileged youth after football. I mentioned this to Jan, and she said, "Call Bart, and see if we can meet with him and his wife."

The year was 1965. Under Vince Lombardi's coaching and Bart Starr's leadership as their quarterback, the Green Bay Packers were about to become the NFL champions with a decisive win over the Cleveland Browns. They would eventually go on to win Super Bowl I and II, and Bart would be selected Most Valuable Player of both games.

I was not excited at all by Jan's suggestion. "You don't just pick up the phone and call someone like Bart Starr. I'm trying to find someone who knows him well enough to introduce us so I can ask for a meeting."

"Just call him," she insisted. "If God is going to bless this venture, He will bless your phone call."

# Reaching for the Starrs

Time was slipping away. We were in the middle of the third week of the month we had been allotted. For probably the sixth time, Jan suggested I just call the Starrs. With some exasperation I told her I had asked a few people if they had the Starrs' phone number, and no one did.

"Just call information," she said.

"He will have an unlisted number," I countered.

"How do you know that if you don't try?"

Annoyed by her persistence, I picked up the phone and dialed zero. An operator asked the number I wanted, and I said Bart Starr in Green Bay, Wisconsin. In a few seconds she said, "Here is the number."

Hanging up the phone, I announced sheepishly that I had gotten their number. She was not surprised. "Great! Give him a call."

I was twenty-seven years old at the time, and Bart was a few months older. He was my hero, partly because he was a great quarterback, but even more because of his family and spiritual values. With considerable nervousness, I dialed the number.

A man answered simply. "Hello."

"Is this the Starr residence?" The man said it was. "Is Mr. Starr available?"

"No. There's no Mr. Starr here. But Bart is here." So I asked if I could please speak to him, and the same voice replied, "I'm Bart."

Somewhat awkwardly, I explained our dream. I told him what we had heard about him and Cherry possibly having a similar interest in helping youth. I followed with, "Would it be possible to meet with you and your wife at some point?"

"Of course. Do you want to come to our house in Green Bay right now?"

I hung up the phone in amazement and told Jan. Again, she showed no surprise. "OK, great. Let's go."

We dropped Steve and Tim off with Jan's parents and drove to Green Bay. On the thirty-minute drive, I reflected on my less-than-stellar football career. An avid Green Bay Packer fan, I had made the University of Wisconsin Badger team as a freshman walk-on. My memories of my freshmen year consisted of being run over numerous times by Alan "The Horse" Ameche, a senior who would go on to achieve fame as a Baltimore Colt. I was invited to return in my sophomore year, but an injury in spring practice brought my playing days to an end.

We arrived at the Starrs' house, a modest, one-story home, and rang the doorbell. Bart opened the door, introduced himself, and led us into the kitchen, where Cherry was making supper. After Bart introduced us, I said we would make our stay brief so we would not interfere with their dinner plans. Cherry, in her southern drawl, said, "If y'all make your visit brief, you will definitely interfere with our dinner plans because you're eating with us."

I was instantly impressed with the Starrs' hospitality. After getting a call from someone they had never met, Bart had invited us to visit and Cherry started making dinner, assuming we would join them. For good reason, Bart and Cherry have a legendary reputation for generosity and hospitality in Wisconsin and beyond.

Bart suggested we move to the living room to hear the full details of what we wanted to do. I explained that I had a three-ring binder with pictures and concepts of the youth program we envisioned, and I asked if we could sit together on their couch so they could both see the booklet.

I started through the pages, first explaining why we had selected the name "Rawhide" for the program. We wanted a name that young men sent to us by a juvenile court could talk about with pride. Typical names like "Sunny Hill Children's Home" did not excite us at all. We wanted a rugged name that did not immediately identify what we were about. One of my favorite television programs growing up was *Rawhide*, starring Clint Eastwood, and after listing a few dozen possibilities, it was settled. Rawhide is leather in its unfinished form, like the young men we would be working with. The full name would be Rawhide Boys Ranch. When we used just the term Rawhide, it sounded cool and generated immediate interest. The response was always, "What is Rawhide?" The name opened many opportunities to explain what we were doing.

"I love the name," Cherry remarked.

Next in our booklet were pictures of the outside and inside of the lodge. I explained that we expected to live like a traditional family, with the foster boys having the same rules as our own sons. At the end of that part of the explanation, Cherry said, "Bart, that's what we talked about—how a youth home should be run."

I explained that a strong work ethic would be taught and modeled. The boys would be given responsibilities appropriate for their ages, with rewards for good effort and a positive attitude. At the end of that page, Cherry said, "Bart, that's what we expect of our boys."

We went on to share that, because of our Christian beliefs, our home would have faith-based values, but we did not want the boys to feel pressured to accept our religious views or practices. They would be asked to be respectful during prayer before meals, but they would be allowed to just sit quietly with their eyes open. They would be encouraged to go to church with us or to a church of their family's choice. For the third time, Cherry commented, "Bart, that's exactly what we believe."

At this point Bart put his hand on my presentation book. I still had three pages to go. He grinned at Cherry and said quietly, "Cherry, please do not tip our hand until we hear the bottom line."

Things were looking pretty good up to this point. I was hopeful they would be willing to help us in some way. Sure enough, when I completed the presentation, Bart said, "What do you want from us?"

"Everything. I don't know how to set up a nonprofit corporation. We need help in getting the county and state social service departments to consider licensing us, and most of all, we need name recognition to raise the money needed to purchase the lodge and property."

At that point, Bart turned toward Cherry, and I saw her give a silent nod of approval. Bart turned back to us and said, "I guess we're on board."

Our meal with Bart and Cherry was delightful. We spent the

time visiting about our lives and theirs. We both had two boys about the same ages. Bart Jr. was their oldest, and Bret was four years younger. The more we talked, the more we realized how much we had in common, including our Christian faith. We talked some football. I admitted that my claim to fame of getting run over by Alan Ameche was definitely not close to Bart's football success. We had both married strong-willed, beautiful women who loved animals. And, of course, we shared an interest in helping youth.

The next day, we sent out a press release to all the local newspapers and radio stations and the three Green Bay television stations. The announcement that Bart and Cherry Starr had agreed to partner with us totally changed people's reactions. Our dream went from being a long shot to a real possibility. New doors were opened for talking to groups and setting up meetings to ask for financial support. Even though raising meaningful funds continued to be difficult for the next few years, we were on our way.

# The Move to Rawhide

The numerous stories area newspapers and television and radio stations ran about the new charity Bart and Cherry Starr were supporting created increased interest from churches, foundations, service clubs, law enforcement offices, and social service agencies. Requests came in almost daily to attend meetings and meet with community leaders to share our intentions for the Rawhide program.

Mr. Carlson joined this group of interested citizens. He was so excited about the newfound use for his estate that he allowed us to move in with only a land contract agreement. The plan required us to pay $2,000 a month. Yet at this point we were not incorporated as a nonprofit charity. This made raising any meaningful donations difficult.

In early December 1965, with anticipation and a good measure of blind faith, we gave up our rental farm house, took our oldest son, Steven, out of second grade, loaded our belongings and our sons, including our foster son Ron, and headed for the Carlson property, which would soon become Rawhide Boys Ranch.

Oh yes, included in the move were Prince and Danny Boy (our two horses), Peanuts and Popcorn (our boys' ponies), a collie named Lassie, and the two rabbits (Thumper and Flower).

Our pet crow, Andy, had disappeared a month earlier, or I am sure we would have taken him along also.

Both Jan and I grew up with a love for pets, and we knew first-hand the benefits they had for children. We expected to involve the boys at Rawhide with dogs, cats, and horses. Little did we know that our menagerie would expand to pet skunks, raccoons, parrots, fox, sheep, goats, and even pet pigs.

For Rawhide to be recognized as a nonprofit organization by the federal government, we had to set up a Board of Directors. It took dozens of presentations to finally find our first seven board members. My appreciation goes out to that first group for the many hours they put in at long monthly meetings advising Jan and me on program plans and sharing concerns about the never-ending financial struggles.

I felt that the director of a charity, and especially a founder, should not be a voting board member but should answer to the board. That led to times when I was not sure the board was doing the right thing, but their collective wisdom provided the best decisions for the growth of Rawhide.

The first Rawhide board members each agreed to cosign personal collateral, and some even pledged their own homes, to guarantee an initial startup loan. Their belief in Jan and me, and in the future potential of Rawhide, gave us extra time to continue our effort to build a base of financial supporters. Our thanks to Sanford Paulson, Jim Wendorf, Harry Levenhagen, Dr. Gilbert James, Vince Derscheid, Robert Wuerch, and Clyde Stephenson for serving on the original board.

We chose a Saturday morning in May 1966 for a public auction of thousands of dollars' worth of antique furniture, which was included in the purchase of the lodge. We placed ads in newspapers several weeks ahead of time and printed and posted handbills listing all the items. Holding the sale entailed moving about a hundred items, from pictures to furniture, onto the lawn. A month ahead of time we had arranged for a dozen teens from a local youth group to arrive by six o'clock the morning of the auction, and move all the items to the lawn.

At eight o'clock the Friday night before the auction, I called the youth director to confirm the number of teens to expect. I panicked when the youth leader's wife exclaimed, "He was not able to get anyone to help, and he has gone fishing."

I anxiously started to call a few people who we thought might be able to help, but the first four calls were unsuccessful. One of the people gave me two names of Appleton Junior Chamber of Commerce (J.C.) officers. They were both Jerrys: Jerry Long and Jerry Shoepke. I was told one was the president and the other the vice president. I looked in the phone book and found Jerry Long's number. I called, and his wife, Gladys, told me he was at a J.C. event. She gave me the phone number where they were meeting. By now it was approaching ten o'clock, and the prospects of getting any help did not look good.

The phone rang several times before someone answered. In the background, I could hear what sounded like a party. I asked for either of the Jerrys. After hearing a few loud yells for "Jerry Long!" he came to the phone. I explained our dilemma, telling him of our desperate need for help. He had read about Rawhide in the local newspaper, so my call had some credibility.

"I need six to ten people at six in the morning to move furniture," I explained.

"How do we get to Rawhide?" he asked.

It is a very complicated route, and with the party going on, I was not very hopeful he was going to remember the directions. I asked if he could write them down. He said, "No, just tell me." I proceeded to give him the directions I had recited many times in the past, but never in a situation as vital as this.

As soon as I finished the travel details, Jerry said, "OK. We'll be there," and he hung up. I knew he didn't write anything down. I hung up the phone, turned to Jan, and said, "I don't think we're going to get any help. We will just have to get up at five with Ron and Steve and do the best we can hauling out the things ourselves."

But at exactly six o'clock, three cars came down the driveway, horns blaring. The first was a convertible with the top down, filled with a half dozen people with arms waving. Their mini-parade was a very welcome sight.

Both Jerrys introduced themselves and said, "Put us to work."

I said "Oh, my gosh. Did you guys get any sleep?"

They both laughed and said that after my call they asked for volunteers, and everyone decided it would be better to just keep the party going and head out as soon as it became daylight. They figured if anyone went to bed, they might not get up until noon.

For the next hour, the J.C. members carefully moved everything into the yard, ready for the auction crowd that started showing up ahead of nine o'clock. We were ready for the bidders thanks to the Appleton Jaycees.

Their support did not end with that superb Saturday morning effort. They went on to help Rawhide with numerous fund-raising and promotion events in the years to come. Through the efforts of both Jerrys and the entire Appleton J.C. chapter, the boys ranch was adopted as one of the Wisconsin J.C.'s state projects. That meant fund-raising support from chapters across the entire state.

# Left Guard Luncheon

In early December 1966, we faced another financial deadline. When we moved to Rawhide, the land contract with Mr. Carlson had called for us to make a $2,000 payment every month. We were four months behind making any payments, and he could not wait any longer. He gave us until December 20, or we would have to move out.

Rawhide board chairman Jim Wendorf and I met with Harold Adams, the president of Appleton's First National Bank. We spelled out the potential to help youth, the ideal facility we had found, and our financial situation. After an hour, Mr. Adams said that in order for the bank to put the Rawhide facility on a traditional mortgage, they would require a down payment of $20,000.

I had kept the Starrs aware of our month-to-month struggles, and they were also concerned, but Bart was busy leading the Packers through a successful 1966 season. It would conclude with the Pack going twelve and two and winning the first-ever Super Bowl by beating the Kansas City Chiefs 35-10. But without a miracle that it would take to raise $20,000, the Rawhide dream was about to end.

I prepared a letter to Bart and Cherry. It started out with the date, inside address, and "Dear Bart and Cherry." Then in the middle of the page, in gigantic letters, it said, "HELP." At the bottom the page was, "Urgently Yours, John and Jan Gillespie."

Cherry opens all the mail at the Starr home and sorts items that need to be handled by Bart. But when she opened the HELP letter, her reaction was different. Cherry called the Packer office and asked that Bart call her as soon as practice was over. She almost never did that unless the situation was urgent, so when he got the message he called immediately. Cherry asked if he was coming right home.

He said, "Yes, what's up?"

"There is a letter here you have to respond to right away."

Bart asked what it said.

"Just come home and read it for yourself."

When Bart finished reading the letter, which took all of five seconds, Cherry sternly said, "Bart, we have to do something to save this program."

Bart thought for another five seconds and said, "I have an idea. Tomorrow I'm going to ask Coach Lombardi if I can address the team to enlist their help."

Vince Lombardi was already aware of Bart's involvement with Rawhide, and when he learned of the financial challenges, he gave his approval for Bart to share our need with the other players. Bart then approached teammate Fuzzy Thurston, who owned a popular eatery in Appleton called The Left Guard, asking if he would foot the bill for a Tuesday noon luncheon. Tuesdays were the team's day off. Fuzzy quickly agreed, and the date was set for December 20, the very day the $20,000 had to be raised.

Bart shared with the team our dream to help young men and the financial deadline we faced. He invited the players to attend the luncheon and bring potential donors with them. Bart had not asked for a commitment who would attend, so as we gathered for the luncheon, we had no idea who would show up.

We were very impressed as players and guests started streaming through the door into the private dining room: Henry Jordan, Zeke Bratkowski, Boyd Dowler, Jerry Kramer, Fuzzy Thurston, Carroll Dale, Dave Hathcock, Elijah Pitts, and of course, Bart Starr. They were all players whose names would be etched in football history as part of the first Super Bowl victory. Also in attendance were Ray Carlson and Harold Adams from the bank.

A friend of Bart's, Ralph Lewis, was the program host, and he called on Jan and me to share what we were already doing and our plans for future expansion of the Rawhide program. Bart followed with a thank you to Fuzzy for hosting the luncheon and to the players and others for attending. He mentioned that by five o'clock that day we needed to raise $20,000 or the program would close. As was Bart's way, it was a very gentle request. He didn't want to put pressure on anyone. At the end of his five minutes of comments, he said that anyone wanting to make a contribution could bring it to him at the end of the luncheon. Bart said if the Rawhide program did not continue, the gifts would be returned. More than a dozen guests and players handed Bart checks. He thanked each person but did not look at how much had been given.

When the room was almost empty, one guest approached Bart and asked if it was appropriate for him to learn how much we had collected. Bart said of course, and we started totaling the gifts. They ranged from $100 to $1,000. In all, they totaled $14,000.

The man who had asked to learn the total, Julius "J.O." Johnson, owner of a local sewer contracting company, said, "I'll give you the other $6,000."

We watched in humble gratitude as he wrote out his check. We took all of the checks and drove to the First National Bank in downtown Appleton. At last the Rawhide property had a mortgage. We finished signing papers two hours ahead of the deadline, and we believed we had just participated in a miracle.

The facility now had a secure mortgage, and we could make the manageable monthly payments, but fund-raising would be my ongoing responsibility and challenge. We laid out a budget to present to the Rawhide Board of Directors for approval. It did not include wages for Jan and me. We did not expect and did not receive any income for the first year, although we did get our meals and lodging.

In reviewing the proposed budget, the board made an addition. If all of the bills were paid by the end of the year, Jan and I would receive $3,000. The year ended with all but one of the bills paid. We had fallen behind in bank payments on the mortgage. However, the board still approved paying us $1,500 each. Given our fourteen-hour workdays, the salary worked out to about thirty cents an hour, and that was just fine with us. At the end of the next year we received the same income. Being paid was never a concern. In the third year, the board put us on a modest monthly salary that continued for the next three decades.

The year 1966 was a life-changing time for Jan and me. Our search for more space resulted in finding a twenty-seven-room home large enough for our family and another eight to ten teenagers. Rawhide Boys Ranch grew from the spark of an idea fanned by generosity to a flame ready to warm the hearts of boys in need of guidance and love. Yes, it needed tending, but because Bart and Cherry Starr agreed to partner with us, providing the name recognition we did not have, it was burning brightly. Our dream was indeed becoming a reality.

# CHAPTER 4
# EXPECTATIONS & MEMORIES

## *John:*

In 1966, Jan and I received state certification as group home parents, allowing us to care for as many as eight young men at a time. After several years of working with teenagers and having Jerry and Ron live with us, we were very comfortable setting clear guidelines for young men. What we expected of the boys came easy for us since it was the same as what our parents had expected of Jan and me.

As knowledge about the ranch increased, the boys started coming, some unexpectedly. Ron Schuh had been placed with us prior to starting Rawhide, and he was already well established as a member of our family. He was excited about making the move from our crowded farmhouse to, as he called it, the mansion. Ron was a big help in terms of the physical demands of the move and a positive mentor to the new boys as they arrived.

That process did not take long. In January, David Wilson joined our household. He was seventeen when the state social services department placed him with us. David had a short temper, and he had been involved in numerous fights with peers, parents, and even the police. For the first few months, he defied our direction as well, but eventually he settled in and became cooperative. A year after David turned eighteen he moved home. The state licensing agent confided in us that David had been a high-risk test case to see if we were really qualified to work with difficult young men. "You passed the test."

Frigid February brought Don Sellick. He was fifteen years old when he just showed up at our front door at ten o'clock one evening. It was snowing, and the young teenager was cold and wet. We invited him in and hustled him into some dry clothes. When we asked him who had dropped him off, he said he had walked from a town that was twelve miles away. He had read about Rawhide in the paper, and he braved a snowstorm to get away from his abusive father. We contacted social services in the morning, and because they had considerable previous contact with the family, they approved Don's staying with us until they could complete an investigation. Within a few days, the county asked if he could stay with us. He was delighted, as were we.

In the same month we gained Fred Mason. He was thirteen, and he looked even younger, weighing only a hundred pounds. However, he wasn't small in spirit. At the time, Fred was using alcohol to excess, refusing to attend school, and running away from home. He had lived with his mother on the Oneida Indian Reservation just west of Green Bay. He had no idea who his father was. Fred kept our house very lively with his constant prattle and pranks. Most were funny, but some were very irritating, especially to the other boys.

In March, Dean Brown became our fifth boy. He came to live

with us in an unusual way. We got a call around three o'clock one morning from a local police department. They said they had responded to a domestic violence call. When they arrived, they found a fourteen-year-old-boy who had been beaten up by an intoxicated stepfather. They explained that the hospital had examined the boy, and he was uninjured, but they had nowhere to put him except in a jail cell. They asked if they could bring him to stay for the night. We quickly said of course. After a home study was conducted, the county officially placed Dean with us. Other than running away several times to escape his abusive home, he had not been in any trouble.

On April 15, Ben Frasier, age fifteen, arrived for what we thought was a two-hour preplacement visit. A Wisconsin county worker called to ask if they could bring Ben for us to consider whether we would accept him. He was living in a dysfunctional home and had been picked up after stealing his fourth car. When Ben arrived a couple days later, we asked the police officer who brought him for his history report and placement orders.

He was surprised. "They just gave me Ben and said to take him to Rawhide."

I explained that we first had to conduct a preplacement interview. "It will take about two hours, and you can head back with him."

The officer didn't care about our procedures. "My orders are to drop him off here, so I am leaving." He marched back to his patrol car and left.

We contacted the county the next day to obtain the court order and find out who his social worker was. After being transferred to three different departments, I was told they could not find any paperwork on a Ben Frasier. They would check and get back to us. Two weeks went by without a word. I made another call, only to be told they had no record of ever sending this boy to us. Ben had no family we could contact.

After several months we gave up and accepted that Ben must have been a placement from God. He lived with us for more than two years, and we never did get a penny from his county. Money was never the reason we wanted to care for boys, and he was only the first of several over the next three decades we would take in without promise of payment. We just made sure there was always food on the table for everyone.

In May, Larry Eckes arrived. The oldest boy of nine children, he was fifteen years old when his parents separated and placed his eight siblings together in a foster home. Larry didn't have a history of delinquency, and he was a nice boy from the start. He developed an interest in vehicles and assisted our maintenance man with caring for our small fleet of a car, two donated trucks, and two tractors. Larry's interest developed into a lifetime passion.

In July, Martin Rogers, our eighth boy, arrived. Sixteen at the time, he was a big kid raised in a family that was in constant turmoil. He was skipping school and failing, but he was not a serious disciplinary problem. His social worker felt Martin had a great deal of potential, but he needed to be removed from his chaotic home. He settled in quickly after arriving and was almost immediately a help in encouraging the other boys to get along and cooperate.

We were now at our license limit of eight youth for a group home. Eight was a full house, and it was very lively. We estimated that the average time they would stay with us was two years, and we were looking forward to many months of working with all of them. At no point did we forget our own two sons. They liked the idea of having so many new big brothers, and we made sure that they were not lost in the demands of a very busy schedule. We made a point of spending some special private time with them every day.

Our new family had taken shape. Ron, his seven new brothers, our two boys, Jan, and I made an even dozen around the table.

As Jan and I combined clear guidelines with lots of praise and appreciation, the boys quickly began to like being part of their new family. They were used to being corrected in public by parents, police, and teachers, and rarely praised for anything. Our motto was "Praise in public; correct in private." Every one of them tested the boundaries, but once they realized they couldn't intimidate us, they developed a sense of security they never had before.

# Expectations Explained

Some boys with unique problems were not suited for Rawhide. Jan and I developed a placement procedure to evaluate each referral. Before a boy was accepted, he would be brought to the ranch for at least a two-hour visit by his social worker, probation officer, or parent. Even though each boy thought we were deciding whether to accept him, the visit was arranged only after the authorities had approved his placement and we had reviewed his past behavior and decided he would be accepted no matter what his attitude was on the visit.

We interviewed each boy and asked if he saw the need to change the direction in which his life was heading. We explained the basic rules, expectations, and activities he would experience if he came to live with us. Many of the boys were angry and did not want to be parted from their friends. But when they saw the ranch facilities, met some of the boys, and realized they would be involved in fun activities, they often decided that coming to Rawhide might not be that bad. However, they kept on their tough-guy faces and didn't let anyone know how they felt at the time. After all, we might reject them just as all the other parental figures in their lives had.

Our initial meeting with David Wilson, the first boy placed with us after we moved in, is an example of how we conducted preplacement interviews. After he had completed an initial tour of the home, shop, barn, and waterfront, we sat down to go over what we would expect of him.

"David, if you decide to come to live with us, you'll have a lot of opportunities to learn new vocational skills, and to have a lot of fun. As you saw, we have horses, boats, a swimming lake, and great fishing to enjoy, if you follow the rules. The first thing we expect is that you will get a haircut, shave off your mustache, and take out your earring."

"What's wrong with my hair and my earring?"

"There is nothing wrong with either," I explained, "but you will be attending the area high school and be involved in numerous community events and work projects with us. We live in a very conservative rural area, and adults unfortunately make first-impression judgments based on appearance. Your long hair and earring, not to mention the fact that you come from a youth home, will put you at an immediate disadvantage. You won't be accepted as the real person you are." That point struck home with him.

His next question was, "Can my friends come to visit me?"

"For the first thirty days after you move in, you will not be allowed to contact friends or family. Your mother already knows this is what we expect. After a month we want you to have contact with your mother, but you can't call friends until you have been here a few months and are doing well. At that point, your social worker will tell us which friends you can contact."

He was not pleased, but he seemed to understand the precaution. After all, his friends had helped him get into trouble.

I went on to explain that he had to take care of his room. His roommate would be Ron Schuh, with whom he had already spent time on the tour. He would be assigned work jobs just like the rest of the boys. The house had an hour of supervised study time five nights a week after supper, and discipline would be handed out for infractions. The word "discipline" caught David's attention.

I explained, "We do not allow swearing, stealing, bullying, or fighting. We also do not want boys to brag about offenses from their life prior to coming to Rawhide."

"So what happens if I do something against your rules?"

"Well, for minor offenses you will lose your privilege to be involved in some or all of our recreational activities. For more serious offenses, you might be restricted to the living unit, and you will have to be accompanied by Jan or me anytime you are outside, other than attending school."

"What happens if I run away?" he asked with some hostility.

"David, there are no fences at Rawhide, except for the horses. If you run away, you will be picked up and brought back. We will sit down and talk about why you ran away, if you did anything illegal while you were gone, and if you want to come back. For infractions like stealing, lying, fighting, or running away, you will be required to join our physical fitness block program."

This caught David's interest. "What is a fitness block program?"

"We have a pile of fifty cement blocks in the open field you can see out the dining room window behind us. They weigh twenty pounds each, and they have to be moved three hundred feet, the length of a football field, to the stake you can see close to the woods.

"The number of times you have to move the pile back and forth is determined by the seriousness of your offense and your willingness to accept your discipline.

"Ultimately, it comes down to this. If you want to change, and if you are willing to trust us to know how to help you change, you will benefit from staying at Rawhide. At some point if you continue to refuse to obey the rules and accept discipline, your county will have to choose a different place for you to live. Usually, that somewhere has more rules and restrictions. You'll probably be sent to a secure lockup facility. We don't want that to happen, and I don't think you do either."

I finished the interview by saying, "David, based on our short time together, we have decided that if you want to come to live with us, you are welcome. I hope I have clearly explained some of the rules and benefits. We want you to tell us your decision within two weeks. "Do you have any questions I can answer?"

"Not really. I'll give it some thought."

"David, it was nice meeting you. If you think of more questions you want to ask us to help with making your decision, you can call Jan or me directly."

David had seen enough to decide he wanted to come. Quite a few boys shared later that their initial impression of being sent to a ranch was not positive. As they drove into Rawhide, winding through several miles of woods down bumpy country roads, they were dead set against wanting to stay. But as the tour proceeded and they realized that Rawhide was offering a chance for a new start—and as they learned about all the fun activities they could do—they changed their minds. Every boy understood that being able to come to Rawhide meant making a verbal commitment that they would work on making changes. By the end of the visit, most of the boys were pleased to learn they would be accepted.

# *Jan:*

Knowing that move-in day was an emotional time for every boy, we made sure they felt welcome immediately and were kept busy. Once we had carried their personal items to their bedroom, I went through a clothing inventory list to see if they had an adequate supply of work and dress clothes and other items they would need. Of course, I also checked to see if they had brought any unapproved items with them.

Most boys look forward to their first day at Rawhide with apprehension. But not Fred Mason. He had no intention of waiting. The day after Fred's preplacement visit, his social worker called us to say, "I got a call from Fred Mason this morning. He said he wants to go to Rawhide today. I told him he can't go today, as I have to call you and see how his visit went yesterday. Fred told me the visit went great and you said it was OK for him to come live with you. He really wants to come today."

"The visit did go well," I said. "You can bring Fred anytime. Even today."

"Well, I guess I can have someone bring him this afternoon."

Fred arrived early that afternoon, very excited to be moving in. John asked the police officer who brought him whether he had a suitcase or any personal items.

"I asked the same question when I picked him up at the detention center. They said his mother told them he did not have any clothes. So I guess you will have to figure that out."

The officer left, and we welcomed Fred to our home. Unlike any of the other first-day arrivals, he was grinning from ear-to-ear.

John and I invited him to sit down at the dining room table with a pitcher of lemonade. We had Don Sellick join as well. Even though

Don had only been with us a few weeks, we thought they would be good roommates for one another. We had previously alerted Don, who was also a Native American, that this was our plan. We got his assurance that he would welcome the opportunity to help a new roommate learn the rules.

I started with a review of check-in day. "Fred, we usually start with an inventory of clothing to see what additional items you may need. Since you have no other clothing and personal items, we are going to have a great shopping trip. But first we will stop at the barbershop for a haircut. You probably remember from the conversation we had when we met why we want all the guys to be well-groomed.

"Sure, I remember," Fred answered. "But I have never been to a real barber. My mother would cut my hair a couple times a year."

The haircut went without a hitch, and the shopping trip was a treat. Fred said, "I have never bought new clothes from a store. I would get used stuff from a secondhand store once in a while, and they usually smelled bad." We picked out three pair of jeans, some T-shirts, a few short- and long-sleeve shirts, underwear, socks, handkerchiefs, belts, a pair of tennis shoes, a pair of dress shoes, work boots, a work jacket, and leather work gloves. It was winter, so we included a warm hooded jacket.

The three of us, Fred, Don, and I, were able to haul all the clothes to the car in one trip. It was actually a donated 1956 Cadillac hearse, our only vehicle other than our personal VW Bug. We put Fred's clothing stash in the back of the hearse, expecting all three of us to ride in the front, the way we had come to town. Don climbed in next to me, but Fred stood by the hearse door and said, "Would it be OK if I rode in the back by my clothes?"

"Of course," I said. "Climb in, and keep an eye on them."

After arriving back at the ranch, Don and I helped Fred take the tags off his new clothes and put them in dresser drawers and in the closet. He was very grateful. The new style of grooming and more conservative wardrobe was a look most boys found they enjoyed only after they had a month or so to adjust to the change. Not Fred. He loved "his new look" from day one.

By now it was late afternoon and, as is the custom the day a new boy arrives, we all loaded up in the hearse for a trip to town for pizza. This was a chance for the new boy to get to know everyone in a relaxed activity.

# Building Team Spirit
## *John:*

So what is it like living with a group of young men with such diverse sets of attitudes and backgrounds? We never had any dull days. We had to monitor and counsel as a lot of problems surfaced.

A few months after matching Don and Fred as roommates, we realized they were not getting along. Don had a Menominee Tribe mother. Fred had an Oneida Tribe mother. When we sat down with Don, he complained, "Fred is constantly cutting down my Menominee background and boasting about how much better his tribe is." When we consulted with Fred, we heard the same story, except Fred said, "Don is constantly telling me the Oneidas are a bunch of losers. I'm tired of it."

John and I brought them together to resolve the tension. Neither was willing to try, so we announced we would bring this up after dinner to hear the opinion of all the guys. They went along with that. At dinner, the group criticized both their attitudes, so we felt the next step would be to separate them as roommates.

This was not unusual. When a new boy arrived, we matched him with a roommate we thought would be a good influence on him. But a few times a year we allowed the boys to make roommate change suggestions. We would tell the guys we wanted their confidential suggestion for a new roommate. They would all list their first, second, and third choices on a slip of paper. Some boys put down the roommate they currently had as their first choice, but others wanted to change. Then John and I would sit down with the lists and try to accommodate each boy's first, second, or third choices. We were usually able to make the room changes to satisfy everyone. In this case, we were in for a surprise. Don listed Fred as his first choice! Fred listed Don as his second choice, so we left them together, and they were able to work out their differences.

For most boys it was the first time an adult had ever sat down and encouraged them to share their pain and their hopes. They did not open up right away. Most moved in with a chip on their shoulder and a cocky attitude to hide their fears and disappointments. It was our job to win their trust by showing respect and appreciation while still making clear that we were in charge.

There were no fights during that first year, and over the years to follow a physical conflict between boys occurred only once every two or three years. But as we settled down with a full house in August of 1966, we had no idea that another 343 teenage guys would move through our home over the next thirty-five years. We loved every one of them, and after only a few weeks, or in rare cases a few months, they realized they were living in a home where they were appreciated. They found they could quickly earn our trust. This was a new experience for most of the boys.

# Together Around the Table

## *Jan:*

John and I grew up in homes where we looked forward to meals. What we enjoyed most was the chance for the entire family to sit down and talk together. My father had a great sense of humor, and he was always making jokes or pulling pranks.

Most of the boys sent to live with us came from families that seldom or never sat down together, so the family members had little positive interaction. In many cases there was not enough food to eat either. We wanted the boys at Rawhide to have as much as they wanted, and we made sure mealtime was fun and relaxing. We never scolded at the table, although I took many opportunities to teach them table manners. Eat slowly; take your elbows off the table; use a napkin, not your sleeve; cover your mouth when you cough; and don't burp or pass gas. Yet these were garden-variety infractions. John and I always discussed true discipline issues with the boys privately at another time. Our philosophy remained, as always, "Praise in public; correct in private."

The food was not always fancy, but we served it with flair. I would typically introduce a noodle dish loaded with leftovers by saying, "Tonight we are having Bake-dish Surprise!"

We had a lot of fun at the table, and some of the stunts we pulled off caught the boys by surprise. One of the memorable events involved some blueberry pies I had just baked. They were about thirty minutes out of the oven when I went to the head of the table, where John sat, and held out one of the pies in front of him to observe.

In a challenging voice, John said, "Very nice. What do you intend to do with it now?" I raised it like I was going to put it in his face. His daring reply was, "You don't have the nerve."

Without any thought to the consequences, I hit him square in the face with the still-very-warm pie. I was so surprised I'd really done it that I instantly ran from the room.

The boys sat in stunned disbelief. Based on their past experiences, often with parents that had quick tempers, they expected John to explode in anger. Yet he just sat quietly wiping pie from his face and eyes while taking a taste. His first words were, "Hey, guys, this is great pie."

Every morning started with a hearty breakfast. For the first two years, I had no housekeeping help, so the boys, John, and I all had meal responsibilities. Breakfast was ready by six thirty on school days. As boys came down from their rooms, they would select their food from the serving counter to eat at the table. The school bus would stop twenty feet from the dining room door every morning at just after seven o'clock.

The bus driver was Angie Schneider, a neighbor and a good friend who helped us in various ways over the years. She was very comfortable with the boys, and having raised sons herself, she had no problem making sure our guys acted appropriately on her bus. If they didn't, she told us about it the same day. Our second-grade son, Steve, took the same bus and was dropped off at the grade school in nearby Readfield.

The house was very calm for nine hours with all the boys gone except our four-year-old son, Tim. They all showed up again at four o'clock as the same bus delivered eight hungry teenagers plus Steve. They piled into the dining room to devour the snack that was always set out for them.

On Saturday mornings during the school year and every day during the summer, the breakfast routine varied somewhat. Two of the boys who were trained to do so would feed the growing horse herd and return to the house for breakfast by eight. From nine to noon there were chores for everyone. Rooms were cleaned, laundry was collected, and other household or grounds-cleaning projects were tackled.

Daily chores provided us with opportunities to teach the boys how to be good workers, and they quickly developed pride in their jobs. They also were able to earn money based on how well they did, and this allowed us to teach some basic money-management practices.

I should mention one ongoing ritual that saved an endless amount of trouble. Getting the boys to pick up after themselves was a never-ending challenge. Finally, I asked John to put a hinged cover with a padlock on a fifty-five-gallon metal barrel. After the barrel was painted, we set it in a corner of the living room. After supper I invited everyone to gather around the barrel. I unlocked the padlock, opened the cover, and explained that any clothes or other personal items I found lying around the house from the day before would be locked in the barrel.

On Saturday at noon, I would open the barrel, and anyone could get their items back—for ten cents an item. If that item were needed for school or right away for any other reason, I would charge an additional ten cents as my "special unlocking fee." The system worked well. Almost daily, someone would say, "Have you seen my blue jacket?"

"Probably went in the barrel," I would reply. "We'll see on Saturday." All the money collected went into our house party fund. I should note that I treated John just like any other member of the family. His stuff ended up in the barrel too, and the boys loved it when he had to buy something back.

At the beginning of meals, John or I opened with a short prayer of thanks. At the end of the prayer, the meal began. All the serving dishes moved to the left until they had gone full circle. Once the plates were filled, all eyes turned to me. Only after I picked up my fork could everyone start to eat. This was new for the boys, but it allowed each meal to start in a very orderly way. Also, the respect they showed for me was a first step in learning to respect each other as well.

To have seconds, they had to ask for any dish that was not within arm's reach. "Please pass the potatoes," or whatever it was they wanted. Interestingly, sometimes a new boy would refuse to say the magic word, and he had to settle for only what he could reach.

Dinner was the big meal of the day, and after eating, just sitting and talking was a valuable part of the boys' experience of traditional family life. Conversations among the group would go on for half an hour and many times even longer.

During the school year, most of the conversations revolved around the events of the day at New London High School or questions about life at Rawhide. Our boys learned they could bring up any subject without being criticized or embarrassed.

For example, after one meal David asked, "What should I do when students at school tease me about being a friend of Bart Starr? Two boys in particular give me a hard time almost every day. I don't know why they do that."

Larry was the first to respond. "They're just jealous, and you should ignore it."

"You should ask why it bothers them that you are a friend of Bart's," Dean added.

Many of their high school classmates envied the boys because Bart and Cherry's involvement at the ranch was featured in the paper so often. Another problem came up when the boys would mention specific names of Packer players who had visited the ranch recently. Many students did not believe them. That problem was resolved one weekend when several players came out to bow hunt for deer and stayed for supper. The New London Press had a reporter in attendance, and the next week a front-page story appeared. The article featured the hunt and a photo showed right guard Jerry Kramer, defensive back Doug Hart, offensive tackle Steve Wright, tight end Allen Brown, and taxi squad player Larry Moore all sitting around a table with the boys, enjoying dessert. Students at school now believed them, and even their teachers were impressed. The ranch guys had attained near-celebrity status.

On occasion we would go around the table and have the boys share the best thing about their day or one encouraging thing they had learned. Sometimes we asked them to say something nice about the person sitting to their left or what would they do if they won $100,000. We would make notes of what they said so we could follow up privately with various boys.

At one meal, one of the boys was upset with Fred for spilling something on the table. "If you're going to be a pig," he said, "why don't you go back to the reservation?"

Fred was Native American, and the comment hurt. At the table we required the boy who made the comment to apologize, and we met with him privately later to talk about why and how his comment was cruel. We also met privately with Fred and encouraged him to be proud of his heritage.

When everyone was excused, I would go upstairs to our apartment area and spend an hour or more with our two sons. They had to know that they were a part of our family inside our bigger Rawhide family. Trying to maintain balance was an ongoing challenge. We tried to give them the encouragement they needed, and it was important that they never felt left out.

John organized meal cleanup into efficient teams, allowing the boys to choose different tasks. Ron and David handled putting the food away, and Fred and Don cleared dishes off the table and scraped the food before stacking them in the kitchen. Ben and Dean loaded the dishwasher and hand-washed pans and kettles; Martin was responsible for wiping the table, sweeping the floor, and taking out the trash bags. Larry was John's assistant and could supervise the process if John was not present. He would work along with the various crews, following John's example of helping rather than just supervising.

The process was not always as orderly as it sounds. In our first year, we were confronted with the mystery of several large frying pans and kettles that went missing. I asked the boys where they could be, and no one knew. It was a very dry fall, and the river level had dropped about three feet from its normal low point. One day I was looking at the channel that was fifty feet from the kitchen door, watching two otters sliding down the bank into the water. All of a sudden, I noticed a kettle stuck to the part of the bank that was now above the water. I called John, and we headed to the channel. To our amazement, we discovered half a dozen pans and kettles peeking out of the water.

We gathered the boys together and asked them to come with us to the edge of the channel. We asked them if they knew how all the kitchen items could have gotten there. Sheepishly, they admitted that sometimes when a pan had food baked on it, it somehow ended up being tossed in the channel.

As the story emerged, we learned that almost all the boys had been required to throw an item away, so if they were caught, they were all involved. The subterfuge was almost comical, but we couldn't let it pass. John and I met privately, and although we didn't like group discipline, we felt that this time everyone needed to pay a penalty.

We set aside three hours the next Saturday afternoon, and instead of having recreation time, the boys helped me clean all the cupboards in the kitchen. First, they had to remove the plates, pans, kettles, and the food items. Everything was taken off the shelves and out of the drawers and set on the dining room table. Then the boys wiped down every shelf and drawer and put everything neatly back in place. The job took more than two hours, but the discipline turned out to be very beneficial. I worked alongside the boys, and we had a good time.

The boys were embarrassed at having been caught throwing out utensils. They knew the punishment was fair, and the fact that I worked with them made it a positive learning experience. No utensils went missing again.

An hour of study time was scheduled on Sunday through Thursday evenings during the school year. Half an hour after dinner cleanup was finished, everyone returned to the table with their schoolwork. They could bring water or a soda, and if they didn't have schoolwork, we would ask them to write a letter to their family or give them reading projects. John or I would sit at the table the entire hour to answer academic questions and to work on our own schedules and reports. The boys soon learned that, if they had to sit there for an hour anyway, they might just as well be doing their homework.

Going to class with homework done was a new experience for most of the boys, and they liked the feeling. Plus, it was an opportunity to acquire the practice of being prepared along with the other new things they were learning. They were amazed to see that they were getting passing grades, another new experience.

The study hour was over by nine o'clock, leaving an hour and a half for relaxing, visiting, or recreation before going to their rooms by ten thirty. However, bedtime was flexible. If we were involved in a productive conversation or maybe even an intense game of Monopoly, the boys could have extra time before going to their rooms.

Eating out was a good bonding time for everyone. The boys liked being part of a group going out on the town. On Friday nights we would go to any of the dozens of area fish fries, pizza places, or burger joints. Then we might take in a movie, a sporting event, or other activity that was of interest to the boys. These events were both a reward for good behavior and a disappointment for boys on restriction who had to stay at the ranch. The loss of privileges was a great motivator.

Birthdays were special occasions. The birthday boy would tell me what he wanted for his special meal. Then we would decorate the dining room, and he would always get some presents. Usually we gave him one significant present and half a dozen lessor presents, such as a bag of M&M's, a Packer magazine, or a bottle of mouthwash.

For his birthday, Ron told me he wanted a six-course dinner. So the meal started with a spicy tomato juice cocktail. Next were chips and dip. Course three was shrimp and sauce followed by salad. The main course consisted of grilled garlic bread and lasagna. Course six was banana splits. We were touched when Ron told us it was the first birthday party he'd ever had. When their birthdays came around, most of the other boys said the same. They loved being the center of everyone's attention, and a number have told us that it became an example they took with them when they had families of their own.

# Union Negotiations

*John:*

One of the most interesting after-dinner conversations took our home of teenage boys into the realm of corporate negotiations. When we asked if anyone had questions or comments, all eyes turned to Peter Zukas, a sixteen-year-old who was attending New London High School. We were very impressed with Peter's leadership abilities, and he had surprised everyone by being elected president of his senior class. That made him the unofficial president of our boys at Rawhide.

Peter took out a folded piece of paper from his pocket. "We have just completed a course in our social studies class about the founding and purpose of unions." He paused a few seconds, and continued with bold confidence. "We have decided to set up our own union, and we have drawn up a list of ten union demands we want approved."

Jan and I were impressed with the preparation he and the other boys had put into the subject, and we were enjoying what Peter, the new union president, had to say. We could agree with or at least negotiate most of the demands, but some would require more discussion. Peter started with, "We want a ten-cent an hour pay raise, and we want to sleep a half hour later on school days." The very creative teenage wish list went on. But the last was a demand I knew Jan would not accept. They wanted to get rid of Jan's rule that each guy had to have seven pairs of dirty underwear each week in their laundry. Jan and our housekeeper shared the duty of laundering their clothes and kept a running count of all the skivvies. The boys thought that was unrealistic. They wanted to decide for themselves whether a pair of underwear was good enough to wear more than one day.

At the end of the ten demands, I said, "That's an impressive list, and it's certainly worth discussing. Let's go through them one-by-one and see what we can agree on."

At that point Peter announced, "These demands are not negotiable. We have decided that if they are not all approved, we are prepared to go on strike."

The room went silent as the boys wondered what our response would be.

## *Jan:*

I could see that John appreciated the guys' willingness to present us with a list of bold demands; however, I didn't want him to give in quickly to their requests. We worked well as a team, but the guys knew John was more of a softy. I calmly said, "No problem. If you are not willing to negotiate, then I will go on strike also. You will be on your own getting on the school bus in the morning, making your own meals, and cleaning up the kitchen." I told the guys to let us know when they were ready to negotiate, and we would be very willing to see what we could agree on. Then I got up, left the table, and went up the stairs to our apartment, where I sat down to think about whether I really should have appointed myself as the union buster. Everyone else left the table, and the strike was under way.

I was impressed with the boys' unified spirit, but I was not sure how it would play out. John came up later and asked me who was going to put the food away and take care of the table full of dirty dishes. "Let's just wait and see where this goes," I said.

We spent the evening as if nothing had happened, and we came down later only to put the food away. The dirty dishes stayed on the table and kitchen counters where everyone had left them. As we interacted with the guys that evening, the talk was polite but superficial. There was no more talk about the union demands.

The next morning, everything remained as we had left it the night before. The only difference was that the food had dried solid on the plates and pans. John and I made breakfast for ourselves and Steve and Tim, but nothing for the guys. When the boys came into the kitchen, we told them to feel free to make themselves some breakfast. Most had cereal and just pushed the dirty dishes aside to find room to eat. The dishes stayed on the table or were piled in the sink. Some of the boys didn't eat. Amazingly, they all were dressed fairly well when they headed out to get on the school bus.

The stalemate continued on their return from school. I didn't have their traditional snack set out, and no supper was prepared. Once again, we made a meal for our immediate family, and the guys had to play catch-as-catch-can in terms of what to eat. Once again, no one did any cleanup.

This went on for three days, and you can imagine what the kitchen looked like. The garbage can was filled to overflowing and started to smell.

On the third night, about midnight, we could hear dishes clinking amid the sounds of the kitchen being cleaned. We had a hard time not peeking over the railing to see what was going on, but in the morning we entered a spotless kitchen, as if nothing had ever happened.

I proceeded to make a big breakfast of scrambled eggs and sausages for everyone. Right on time, all the boys came down nicely dressed for school, and they entered the dining room as a group. Everyone made superficial talk during the meal, and at the end everyone helped take the plates to the kitchen and stack them up to be washed. The bus pulled in, and they all left for the day.

That evening, when we were done eating dinner, I asked Peter if the guys would like to talk about their list of union demands. His reply was, "Not really. I think we are OK with the rules as they are."

We really did want to negotiate so the guys could learn more about the union process, but nothing further was ever said about the three-day strike. Several of those same boys went on in later life to work as union members, and one became a union steward. I think all of them look back fondly on their first attempt at unionization.

We had many other interesting after-dinner discussions, but the most important lesson the boys gained was how rewarding it was to enjoy a meal followed by a sharing time. The boys, and others to follow, told us they went on to establish a tradition of eating at least one meal a day with their future families.

# A Christmas Blessing

## *John:*

Shortly after the Left Guard luncheon when the funds were raised to secure the Rawhide property, Bart and Cherry invited the boys to visit them at their home in Green Bay. They all promised me they would be on their best behavior.

Bart opened the door with a big smile and invited us into the living room. We formed an impromptu line, and Bart shook the boys' hands and asked a few questions of each. Fred Mason, our little live wire who had grown up on the Oneida reservation a few miles from the Starrs' home, was standing next to me at the end of the line. I noticed Fred's leg shaking, and I said, "Are you nervous?"

"I sure am."

"Well, you know, Bart's just a man."

In a very serious voice, Fred said softly, "So is the Pope."

When Bart got to him, Fred did just fine. By then Cherry had joined the greeting line. Cherry loved every one of the boys even before she met them, but I think Fred became one of her favorites.

# *Jan:*

As we approached Christmas 1966 with a house full of eight boys plus our family, John and I knew we would have a very limited budget. We had reviewed our current financial situation and realized we could not spend money for a special Christmas dinner, and we would have to limit presents for the boys to about five dollars each.

In the year since our move to Rawhide, we had been losing ground paying bills. The monthly mortgage payment was current, and community support was encouraging, but we were very concerned about spending any money that was not necessary. Terry or Mike McPeak, owners of McPeak Dairy, delivered our milk, eggs, butter, and other dairy products once a week, but we were six months behind on our account "Don't worry," they said. "We want to help with what you are doing. We're not in a position to donate the dairy products, but we can sure wait until you can pay us."

Milt Fannon, owner of Fannon Standard Oil Products, was another wonderfully supportive vendor. Milt delivered heating oil and gasoline for our bulk tanks. John would apologize at almost every delivery, and Milt's answer was always the same: "John, I believe in what you and Jan are doing, and someday you will be able to pay me. Don't worry about it."

In any case, we wanted the celebration of Christmas to focus on the birth of our Lord—not on a meal and gifts.

It was the day before Christmas; I was in the dining room when a station wagon pulled up by the front door. "John, come quickly,"

I called. "Bart and Cherry are here."

We greeted them at the door, and after exchanging hugs, Cherry said, "Jan, we put some food together for you and the boys. I hope that's OK."

"That's wonderful."

"Could a couple of boys help unload the car?" Bart asked.

Ron was just coming back from feeding the horses with Don and Fred, and they volunteered to help. The first thing Bart handed Fred was a twenty-five-pound turkey. Fred took it from Bart and then grunted. "I think I need some help with this thing." Fred weighed only a hundred pounds, and the big bird was a challenge for him to carry.

The turkey was just the start. Next came a large ham, regular and sweet potatoes, two heads of cauliflower, a container of stuffing, cranberry sauce, a bag of apples and oranges, and, best of all, an apple and a peach pie that Cherry had baked. By now all the other boys had gathered around the car, watching the unloading process with great interest.

When everything was inside, we all sat around the dining room table chatting with Bart and Cherry. After ten minutes, they said they had to leave to get back to Green Bay. When they got up all the boys gave them hugs. As Cherry hugged me she slipped something in my hand and whispered, "Here is some money in case you need help with presents for the boys." It was a check for $400, which meant we could add fifty dollars per boy to the five-dollar limit we had set.

After lunch John and I excused ourselves and told the boys they would be on their own for a couple of hours. We headed to Treasure Island, which was a huge one-stop shopping mall. As John and I traveled the twenty miles to Appleton, we talked about the things each boy would like. We laid out a plan to get each boy a major gift and two smaller items, like winter jackets, gloves, radios, and especially some Green Bay Packer gear and pictures. If a boy had not been a Packer fan when he came to live with us, he was one by now.

We had soon bought all the items on the list, but John was a little concerned about one present I had picked up. It was a three-foot tall teddy bear for Fred. I had a feeling he needed a special friend.

When I explained that we were from Rawhide, the store manager said they would wrap all the presents for us at no charge. With the help of three clerks, we carried out the mountain of gifts that filled the station wagon.

When we arrived home, John went in to ask for help unloading the car. Several of the boys hauled in the gifts and set them under and around the Christmas tree. Before long everyone had gathered in the living room, excited about the huge assortment of beautifully wrapped presents.

We had originally planned to have a modest Christmas Eve meal and open presents on Christmas morning. That plan ended when one of the boys said, "We can't wait until tomorrow morning to open presents. Can we please open them now?" Everyone in the group, including John, supported that request.

We headed to the kitchen to set out a soup and sandwich meal that the boys ate with lightning speed. Everyone's goal was to open the presents. All the boys volunteered to do the cleanup, and that was done in record time, too.

We adjourned to the living room. With the tree lights glowing over the three-dozen presents, the main event was about to start. John led us in a prayer of thanksgiving and then explained that presents would be opened one at a time, so we all could enjoy everyone's gifts.

We decided the order of selecting presents would be determined by where everyone was seated, starting to the left of the tree and moving around the room. It was a delightful scene, watching each boy search through the larger boxes first to find his name, and then opening his present. Some boys unwrapped their presents very carefully, while the other boys encouraged them to hurry. More than an hour had passed before the last gift was taken from under the tree.

After all the presents were opened, I asked if any of the boys wanted to share anything they were grateful for. Every boy shared that they had never had a Christmas like this before.

"I don't remember ever getting a Christmas present," Dean said.

"All I remember of Christmas at my house was dad being drunk—if he was even there," Don added.

But the most touching comment came from Fred. "I want to thank Bart and Cherry for the money to buy our presents. I want to tell Cherry I got a teddy bear, but I don't know if I want to tell Bart. I'm not sure he would understand."

John had expressed his concern that the other boys would tease Fred about having a teddy bear, but that never happened. He loved that bear, and occasionally when we were all sitting in the living room watching TV, he would fetch the bear from his room and sit with it. A few times one of the other boys would ask if they could have the bear sit by them. Sometimes that was OK with Fred, and sometimes it was not. What was touching was that most of the boys had missed growing up in a home with love and approval, much less a teddy bear.

## *John:*

Jan and I scheduled a few hours on New Year's Day, to review our first year. Our belief was confirmed that an effective way to teach young men how to want to change their attitudes and how to become loving husbands and fathers was for them to actually live for a time in a loving family.

"We envisioned establishing a family atmosphere just like the homes we grew up in, and it had happened, even better than we expected," Jan said, and I agreed. Our philosophy of being houseparents and living full-time with young men from dysfunctional homes had produced the closeness and role-modeling we had hoped for. Most of the boys would be with us into a second year, giving us more time to teach a variety of things they needed to know to be successful in life.

Our house of eight boys had bonded like they were actual brothers, and they were appreciative of being part of our family. They had grown to the point of sharing their emotions, and they were even comfortable letting us give them a hug and say we loved them. As each of the boys would leave, a new boy would arrive to take his place. The process of integrating every new boy into the family took extra effort on our part and plenty of help from the other boys. But that was the challenge and the goal.

It is important for parents to realize the importance of building family unity with the parent(s) in control. Children, and especially teenagers, resist authority. They always want more freedom, but parents must set and enforce rules with calm firmness. That's the principle we followed with each of our 351 boys.

# CHAPTER 5
# ENJOYING WORK

*John:*

Jan and I learned the value of hard work from the example of our parents. She grew up working in her parents' pet shop, and I worked with my parents on our four-acre vegetable garden. By working alongside them, Jan and I learned how to accept our various tasks with a positive attitude, and that training served us well in the years to come.

This was the approach we planned to use at Rawhide. We would work directly with the boys, and as we hired staff members, we would have them do the same thing.

Maintaining the Rawhide home and grounds was a high priority, because the routines helped the boys develop pride in their work. In addition to daily responsibilities, every Saturday morning was room-cleaning time. It's true that charity begins at home, and we applied that maxim to the boys' cleanliness as well. It was their first step in gaining respect for themselves. Before breakfast two boys would head for the stable to feed the horses. After breakfast the boys changed their sheets, brought down their laundry, dusted and vacuumed, made sure all their clothes were in a dresser or closet, and cleaned their bathrooms. Two boys shared each room, and when they felt their cleaning effort was complete, they asked Jan to make an inspection. Once they understood her high standards, they usually passed the first time. Once all the bedrooms met with her approval, the boys tackled other areas of the house.

The whole house was spic and span by noon, and everyone sat down for a light lunch followed by outdoor projects. In the summer there was grass to cut, boats to scrub, vehicles to wash, box stalls to clean, and a variety of other grounds work to be done. We developed a merit-based ranking system based on attitude and job performance. Two of the higher-ranking boys would be "on-call" to take visitors on a tour of the facilities.

Our goal at Rawhide was to create opportunities for the boys to learn responsibility, the value of hard work, and the skills they would need to be successful. My background in land planning and construction gave me the ability to develop a creative master plan for the five-hundred-acre property. It included a frontier street with building fronts resembling the Old West. A series of boys homes would be located in the woods and along a quarter mile of frontage on the Wolf River. A private lake would be dug to provide a safe swimming area.

After fifty years, most of the original plan has been completed. But as intended, the plan keeps expanding. I designed a detailed plan precisely because we never wanted the work to be complete. Construction and maintenance would teach the boys the value of good workmanship and provide the satisfaction of seeing the results of their efforts. The process always remained the same: adult staff working shoulder-to-shoulder with the boys as they partnered together on various projects.

Over the years this philosophy has worked wonderfully, as the boys and staff have worked together and taken pride in their accomplishments. Jan and I knew it was important to find just the right kind of people to help us. They had to have the necessary technical skills, along with the desire to share their skills with the boys. A positive and caring attitude was essential.

# Henry, Our First Volunteer

At seven o'clock one morning during the second week after we moved in, there was a knock at the door. I answered the door, and a rugged gentleman in his sixties greeted me with, "Are you Gillespie?"

"Yes, I am, but please call me John."

"I've been reading about how you want to help kids. I'm Henry Moeller, and I own the first farm on the right just beyond the second bend. I want to work for you."

"We do need help, but we don't have money to hire staff. "

"Did you hear me say anything about money?" Henry countered. "I will plan to be here Monday, Wednesday, and Friday mornings at eight o'clock. You just put me to work."

With that brief meeting, Henry had hired himself to work with us for no pay. Like clockwork at eight o'clock, three mornings a week, Henry showed up to start with a cup of coffee while we talked about the projects for the day. At noon he went home by car, or sometimes on one of his horses, to do his own noontime chores. He came back in the afternoon to continue his volunteer support.

Henry worked without pay for almost two years before we were able to pay him a small hourly wage. "We are so grateful for your help," I said. "Why did you help us all this time even though we couldn't pay you?"

Henry looked me in the eye and said, "I've had a tough life, and learning to work hard without complaining got me several good jobs. Now it's my turn to pay this back by helping boys learn how to be good workers. I just hope I can make a difference in some of their lives."

Henry was not exaggerating about having had a tough time as a child himself. He had left home at seven years of age to live with and work for a neighbor, because his own family could not afford to keep him. He dropped out of school as a third-grader and went on to a variety of jobs, including bulldozer operator building roads for the county. Then he was a foreman on a Western ranch driving cattle by horseback hundreds of miles to market, and later a home and barn builder. Now he had a small farm, doing all the fieldwork with just horses. He would hitch his matched team of four white horses to various implements to work the land, harvest the crops, and even plow snow.

Henry was an ideal volunteer, providing help with facility maintenance, developing the grounds, and putting up rustic buildings. He was especially good at teaching construction skills and helping the boys learn to enjoy work.

One of my favorite Henry stories happened on a weekend when a United States Army Reserve construction company was working at Rawhide. I had been the training officer in Company C of the 291 Engineer Battalion, and I was able to get approval for our unit to train one weekend at Rawhide. We had all 130 men plus our unit's D-6 Caterpillar bulldozer and a motor grader to use. Everyone was soon hard at work building roads through the woods. In midmorning two bulldozer operators from the unit walked a quarter of a mile to find me.

"Is there a problem with the dozer?" I asked.

"Well, sort of," one of the men said. "An old guy in bib overalls stopped us and said we were not doing it properly. He asked us to get down and said that he didn't need us anymore. He climbed up and started operating the dozer, so we just left."

"OK," I said, trying not to laugh. "Come with me."

We got in a Jeep and drove to where Henry was doing a great job pushing down trees to build the road with the Army bulldozer. As tactfully as possible, I explained to him that I knew he was able to do a much better job than the reservists, but learning to operate the dozer was part of their training. He would have to let them do the best they could. He reluctantly agreed, but first he gave them some tips on how to be more productive breaking open the trail. He would prove to be an unending source of advice for the boys at Rawhide. We couldn't have asked for a better teacher and example for our boys.

Henry and our foster son, Ron, got along famously as maintenance partners. Ron liked the horses, and he especially liked working with Henry to build a small barn and paddock area for the two horses and two ponies we had brought with us to Rawhide.

Starting in 1967, almost every year one of the neighbors would donate an old barn that we would tear down for the lumber. This became a summer-long project, with the boys climbing into the back of our donated truck a few days every week to drive to the barn site. Jan would help the boys pack a cooler with water, sodas, and sandwiches for their noon meal. With Henry supervising, the boys would remove the weathered boards that could be safely reached from short ladders. Henry would remove the boards higher than ten feet above the ground. The boys would carefully pull out the nails and pile the lumber into the back of the truck. It was hard work, but they thought tearing down a barn was cool. And work could be fun.

Once all the siding boards were removed, Henry would chainsaw a V-notch almost through the twelve-inch, upright timbers. With everyone standing a safe distance away, he would then pull down the barn with a long cable attached to the truck. Once the structure had fallen to the ground, the boys could safely remove the roof shingles, clean up the rafters and large beams, and haul everything back to Rawhide. We used the lumber from the first two barns we tore down to build an equipment shed and a large barn with a big hayloft. Again, Henry and the boys did all the work.

Henry was demanding and a little gruff on the surface, but Ron and dozens of other teenagers loved him. They worked hard and learned to appreciate a comment from Henry at quitting time. It might be as simple as, "You did a good job today." Hardly any of the boys had ever had a male mentor who taught them practical skills and provided encouragement and respect.

Henry would continue to work for Rawhide for fifteen years. When Jan and I get together with alumni who lived with us in the '60s and '70s, the topic of Henry usually comes up. They make comments about how tough he was to work for, how much they respected him, and how he prepared them for the future. Of the first two-dozen boys sent to live with us, six enlisted in the Army, Marines, or Navy. Every one of them excelled in the military, and they all said boot camp was, in some ways, easier than working with Henry. They all credit him with the good work ethic that has been part of their lives ever since.

# Caring for Horses

*Jan:*

As visitors noticed we had only two horses, people started offering to donate others. When this happened I would ask about the age, temperament, and training of the horse. If it seemed like the horse would be safe for the boys, I would make an appointment to visit and ride the horse. Most were excellent, but some didn't pass the test, and I politely declined those. By the end of our first year, we had half a dozen additional horses, a donkey, and two naughty goats. It was time to build a full-sized barn, and we would do just that the following year.

I was able to quickly assess the personalities of new boys, and if they had an interest in horses, I would assign them to one with a similar personality. Caring for the horses, including feeding, cleaning, and grooming them, was an opportunity for the boys to learn dependable work habits and the importance of attending to the needs of animals.

All the box stalls had to be cleaned and new bedding put in every day, 365 days a year. It was a job the boys liked. We used a trailer made from the back of a pickup truck to hold the manure from the dozen horses housed in the barn. The tractor would come in through a big sliding door at one end of the barn and exit at the other end. With two boys cleaning and one driving the tractor, it took about thirty minutes to clean the barn and paddock. Then the two shovel guys would climb on the trailer and ride to the ever-growing manure pile. Once the trailer was empty, the next job was to fill it with a small load of dry shavings from a storage shed. After another fifteen-minute trip through the barn, all the stalls were bedded.

Driving the old, donated Ford tractor was a coveted responsibility, and we would select the most responsible boy for the job. John put new drivers through a demanding driving safety course. Martin Rodgers was very responsible and became our first driver. He had spent a couple of summers on his grandfather's farm, where he drove a tractor much like ours. A boy authorized to operate the tractor was careful to drive slowly and cautiously, knowing that if he was caught doing anything improper, he would lose his driving privileges for a month. No one wanted that to happen. We didn't watch them constantly, but we would often secretly observe as they made the block-long trip to unload at the manure pile.

I made sure the boys understood the importance of giving proper care to the horses and other animals. If there was ever a question of who eats first, the boys or the horses, the horses always won. The boys never had a problem with this rule.

The horses had to have their hooves trimmed about every three months, and some of them needed to have shoes put on. That involved using a professional farrier, and we hired one named Marty Forman, who enjoyed working with the boys. They would bring him a list that I had prepared, noting which horses needed various things done to their hooves. Then, the boys would bring the horses from their stalls and hold them for Marty. He loved talking with the boys and showing them what he was doing. The ranch dogs, including a Saint Bernard named Oliver and a Great Dane named Dino, also loved trimming day. They found the trimmings off the horses' hooves to be a wonderful delicacy. They would pick up a piece of hoof and take it outside the front of the barn, lie down, and chew it with delight until it was gone.

Marty was a colorful character and a great promoter. In addition to graduating from farrier school, he had a college degree in journalism and was the editor of a local weekly newspaper. One of the

events he sponsored was a chicken-flying contest, and on one occasion he was able to get the original Colonel Sanders to attend. The
boys enjoyed getting their picture taken with the colonel.

The miles of logging trails provided an excellent opportunity
for other staff members and me to take the guys on trail rides. A
donated Mack semi-tractor and a large horse van allowed us to haul
hay bales provided by area farmers. We could also load up to a doz-
en horses to take part in organized trail rides, which often included
a hundred or more horses and riders. Many were weekend events,
allowing us to camp out on Saturday night. The organization sponsoring the ride would provide a big food tent and a western-style
cookout. There was always a country band. The boys didn't usually
like country music much when they first came to live with us, but we
converted most of them to at least tolerate it.

Everyone was assigned responsibilities during these outings, such
as setting up our sleeping tents, keeping our camp area clean, taking
pictures, or helping with food preparation. And, of course, everyone
had to make sure his horse was brushed, fed, and watered.

The guys liked the trail rides for a variety of reasons. They especially liked these outings because there were teenage girls on the
rides, a lot of them. I had the guys all dressed sharp, they rode well,
and the Rawhide horses were always in excellent shape.

The boys all quickly learned to enjoy riding, and most loved it.
Of special note is Roger, a boy sent to us with some previous riding experience. We assigned a registered paint horse to him, and he
asked if he could compete in our county's 4-H horse show. By this
time our son, Tim, was beginning to show a horse he personally
owned, and he took Roger under his wing. He taught Roger how to
compete in pleasure classes, like western riding, showmanship, and
trail. They both did very well at the county fair, winning ribbons in

every class they entered. Roger was hooked. He and Tim went on to compete in several horse shows over the next year, and they developed an extensive winning record.

## The Early Ranch Vehicle Fleet
*John:*

During the first few years, Rawhide had a small fleet of old donated vehicles consisting of a pickup, a bigger truck for general hauling, and a forty-year-old Ford tractor. We also had a 1956 black Cadillac hearse donated by Chuck Woolery and Elkin Thomas, a singing duo that visited Rawhide once a year for many years. Jan and I owned a Volkswagen Bug, but the hearse was the only vehicle that could transport all the boys at one time. People would look on in wonderment when we arrived at a restaurant, movie theater, store, recreation event, or church, and eight teenage guys piled out. We were not trying to attract attention, but we surely did.

The vehicles were the responsibility of Henry and me. I had worked a few years during college at a full-service garage in Madison. My job there was to remove and install rebuilt engines, so I picked up a range of automotive skills.

A few weeks after Larry Eckes, our seventh boy, came to live with us, Henry noticed he had an interest in tinkering with the vehicles. Henry asked if he would like to help check fluid levels, change oil, replace light bulbs, keep the cars washed, and take care of other basic maintenance. Larry agreed and soon came to regard the aging fleet as his personal responsibility. He was soon helping Henry with more technical tasks, like changing starters, replacing water pumps, and fixing mufflers. Larry went on to a lifetime automotive career, which started with his days at Rawhide.

# Boys Making Their Own Beds . . . Literally

During my first year in college, I shared a small bedroom in the Baptist Student Center with my cousin David Zuelhke and Austin Cotton, a close friend from Appleton. With three single beds and three dressers, we only had about two feet between each bed.

I designed a creative triple bunk that would give us extra space. Under the cover of darkness, we started moving in all the lumber we would need, including four-by-four timbers for the corner posts. The structure we built would have made Frank Lloyd Wright proud. The top bed was seven feet above the floor, with stairs leading to its own four-foot-square landing complete with safety railing and a built-in desk. The middle bed was positioned ninety degrees opposite the top one, jutting out into the room. The bottom bed was about eighteen inches off the floor. Each bed provided about three feet of headroom.

After seeing our bed, the other twenty-five guys living in the center wanted us to build replicas in their rooms. But when the house manager found out about our bed project, we took a stern scolding for proceeding without approval. We were able to keep our new beds on the condition that we would avoid any future construction projects. When I came back for my sophomore year, I was flattered to see that the center leadership had equipped every room with the beds of my design.

After our second boy arrived, I sat down with Ron and David and said, "On Monday the two of you will be making your own bed."

"I have been making my bed since I arrived last week," David replied.

"Actually, you will be working with Henry, and he will help you make a very different type of double bunk bed for your room. I think you will enjoy it and maybe learn some carpentry skills."

With lumber already on hand, Henry and the two boys built the bed in a single day. We did the same every time we had two more boys arrive, and the bunk beds resembled the one I had designed for my college room with the famous deck attached to the top bunk.

When we took visitors on a tour of the home, they made numerous requests for a sketch of the beds. Some even offered to purchase a bed if we would build it for them. A few years later, we did market the bed units in double or triple configuration and built and sold several. The boys received excellent carpentry training, but the lumber was expensive, and so much labor was involved in building the beds and then delivering and installing them that we lost money on every sale.

# *Jan:*

We purchased top-quality, hospital-type innerspring mattresses that were about nine inches thick and very comfortable. They rested on sturdy plywood bases built into the bed units. During one of the first of many surprise visits by a state social service inspector, John was gone, so it was my task to show him around. When we got to the bedrooms, he was impressed with our creative bunk beds but showed me the licensing manual, which required each bed to have a set of springs under a mattress. He said we did not have springs, and they would have to be installed. I explained that the springs were in the mattresses, but he would not waiver from the manual's instructions. We had ninety days to correct the problem.

We were able to make purchases from a government surplus warehouse, where nonprofit organizations could buy things at a very low cost. We found twelve sets of bedspring sections for a dollar each. They were intended to be used with separate legs and had thin metal frames around each spring set, making them only half an inch thick. We hauled them home and placed one under each mattress.

On the inspector's next unannounced visit three months later, John was gone again, so I took him on another tour of the home. When we came to the first boy's bedroom, I showed him the springs we had put under each mattress, just lying on the plywood. He laughed and said there was nothing in the manual that said the springs had to serve any purpose. We passed the inspection.

We always kept the home clean and well maintained. If a window shade got a small rip, we didn't tape it up; we replaced it. If a boy's desk chair was loose, we glued it tight. If a light bulb burned out, we replaced it the same day. This created an environment that was very different from the homes many of the boys had grown up in and from the many youth care programs Jan and I visited. Ripped shades, loose chairs, and burnt-out light bulbs were the norm, not the exception. At Rawhide boys learned to value their home and the entire ranch. That helped them take pride in themselves as well.

## *John:*

Old habits die hard though, and not everything went smoothly. One of our boys, Sam, had been living with us less than a month when he carved his initials in the side of the support timber of his bunk bed. His roommate, Larry, discreetly alerted us to what Sam had done, and Jan made believe she found it on her routine Saturday morning room check. She told me, and I went to inspect the damage. I calmly asked Sam why he had done this. His reply was a shrug of his shoulders. "I was bored."

I told Sam he would have to fix it.

I asked him to accompany me to the woodshop, and we had a

short lesson on using sandpaper. I asked him to get me a scrap piece of four-by-four from the surplus lumber bin.

"What's a four-by-four?" he asked.

"It is the size of the timber used in your bed where you carved your initials," I explained.

He found a two-foot piece without any difficulty. We clamped it in the workbench wood vise, and I drew his initials with a black marking pen.

I explained to Sam that he could remove the initials from his bedpost with sandpaper. "I'll show you how to do it." The first sheet of sandpaper was coarse, and I had him feel it. "This is rated forty grit. It is coarse, and you use this first to sand down the area where you put your initials." I went on to explain that he would have to sand about a three-inch area to get the letters completely out. I then folded the paper four times into a usable size, and had him put on some leather gloves and start sanding for a few minutes. As the sandpaper started to fill with wood and lose some of the grit, we refolded to a new area of the paper. I then handed him a half dozen sheets of the forty-grit paper to take back to his room.

The next sheet was an eighty-grit piece, and I explained that, after all the letters were removed, he would use this to get a nice, smooth surface before we varnished the sanded area. I explained that he could take as long as he wanted to remove the letters, but he would be restricted from all recreational activities and required to do the evening dishes by himself every day until the damage was repaired. I handed him two sheets of the eighty-grit paper.

My short class on sanding wood ended with a talk about how much we appreciated the nice buildings we had and wanted everyone to take good care of them. I looked Sam in the eye, asked if he understood everything, and inquired whether he had any questions.

He had none. I gave him a hug that I don't think he was expecting.

It was noon when we returned to the house and ate lunch. At the end of the meal, I announced that our new family member had volunteered to do the dishes, and everyone else could be excused. This was met with a round of applause and a few pats on the back from guys sitting near him. He finished clearing the table and did the dishes in about an hour. Saturday noon is much simpler than the evening meals. With sandpaper in hand, Sam headed to his room, armed with his leather gloves and his new knowledge about sandpaper.

Realizing that boys react differently to discipline, especially the first time, Jan and I made sure that one of us stayed in the house that afternoon. About once an hour, one of us made a trip down the hall past Sam's room with a quick glance to make sure he was still at work. He was, sanding all the time. A house rule was that if a boy is on restriction, his bedroom door must be open at all times, including through the night.

About four o'clock that day, Sam came to me saying, "I think I have it sanded." We went to his room, and he had indeed done a very good job. I complimented him and said we would varnish it Monday. I knew the incident had made a good impression on him when he asked, "Is it OK for me to keep one sheet of the forty-grit and the eighty-grit sandpaper?"

"You sure can."

# Daily Achievement Scores

By the end of our first year, Jan and I developed a job performance system that is still in place more than fifty years later. At the end of every work or study day, each boy was rated from one to five, with five being best, in four performance areas:

* Use of time
* Quality of work
* Clean up
* Attitude

The staff person working with the boys would add positive and negative comments on the bottom of each rating sheet. Twenty was a perfect score; however, they had an option to reach twenty-one. There was a Bible verse of the week, usually a verse from Proverbs about being a diligent worker or having a positive attitude. Anyone who could recite the verse would get an extra point. Boys were not pressured to learn the verse, as a twenty score was considered outstanding.

Each boy brought his score sheets with him after his day of job training and gave them to Jan or me prior to supper. At the end of the evening meal, as we sat around the table, we complimented each boy who had received positive scores and comments. If a boy had a poor work day we would talk to him privately at a later time and discuss what he could do to improve. The boys worked hard to get this daily "well-done." Here again we were using positive reinforcement to build their confidence to help them learn to make positive choices in their lives.

Every summer we would have a few college students who worked for us as interns. Some of them started out thinking their status as "educated" young men would make them special with Henry. However, Henry regarded them as a challenge: he wanted his crew of teenage boys to outwork the college guys, and they always did. His self-imposed "intern probation status" lasted only a couple of weeks, and then he accepted all of them as part of his team.

One day I got a phone call from a fraternity leader at Lawrence University in Appleton. He asked if we would take eight freshman pledges for a workday the following Saturday. "I think so, but let me call you back in an hour," I said. I went to Henry and said, "A university wants us to take eight students and put them to work for a very demanding day as part of their pledge initiation. Should we do it, and would you be willing to work on Saturday to supervise?"

With a grin Henry said, "Bring 'em on. My guys will outwork them easy."

A commercial logging crew had cut down hundreds of eight-foot pine logs from four to eight inches in diameter and piled them in the woods. We didn't allow them to make a new road to get them out, but we had agreed to haul them out by hand so they could pick them up with their boom trucks. This would be a great project for the pledges to work on.

Henry and I met with our boys and explained what would happen. "The college fraternity upperclassmen want us to work the buns off the freshman," I explained. "Would you guys like to have a competition to see who can move out the most pulp logs during a full work day?"

"You bet," was the boys' reply. They were eager to outperform the college students!

At seven thirty on Saturday morning, two vans pulled up with the eight pledges and five fraternity members as observers. The pledges were in tennis shoes and t-shirts with no gloves. Our eight guys were dressed in work boots, long-sleeve shirts, and leather gloves.

After introductions, during which the fraternity freshmen were not particularly polite, we explained that this would be a competition against the ranch guys. "Whatever makes you happy," one of the freshmen commented sarcastically. We all headed to the woods and explained that the pulp logs would be hauled out and stacked into two piles, one for each team, in order to determine the winner.

Henry, who supervised the project, had previously briefed our boys as to what might happen. "The college guys will probably start running with the logs, but don't be intimidated by that. Let them run. You guys just set a steady pace, because they can't run for eight hours. They will probably wear out by noon."

This was exactly what happened. By ten o'clock the pledges were exhausted, and one was throwing up. Several had blisters. I had a cooler of cold water I offered to the fraternity observers to share with their pledges. "Oh, no. We have warm water for them," they replied. "And for lunch they can only have bread and water." I did have extra gloves along, and they allowed the pledges to use them.

By the end of the pledges' fifteen-minute lunch break, half of them were sleeping and had to be awaken to get them back to work. By noon the Rawhide guys had hauled double the logs of the pledges, and the contest was all but over. By three in the afternoon, all the pledges gave up entirely and refused to work anymore. We all walked back to the parking lot for them to load up and head back to the university. Our guys tried to shake hands with the pledges, but the older boys' hands were in such bad shape that none of them would shake. Plus these young guys at this rehab center had humiliated them.

I have no idea whether their dismal performance had an impact on passing their pledge challenges, but it sure was a great day for the Rawhide guys!

The ranking system we developed was a big help in motivating the guys to enjoy hard work. The system provided specific privileges and restrictions for each rank, and the ranks were as follows:

- **Dogie:** A dogie is a calf that needs to be watched to make sure it doesn't get itself into trouble. In our ranking system, when dogies were on a work crew, on field trips, or in other activities, they had to be with a staff or a high-ranking guy all the time. Their job training pay was ten cents an hour.

- **Line Rider**: This characterized a boy riding the fence. Sometimes he was doing great; sometimes not so great. He had some privileges, but they were under fairly close supervision of a staff person or higher-ranking guy. Daily job scores had to average at least twelve points. Pay was twenty-five cents an hour.

- **Wrangler:** This was a boy who was very dependable and could be by himself around the ranch. Jobs scores had to average at least fourteen points. Pay was fifty cents an hour.

- **Trail Boss:** This was someone who was very dependable and could be responsible for lower-ranked guys. Job score averages had to be at least sixteen points. Pay was seventy-five cents or more an hour.

- **Foreman:** This was a very esteemed rank, and in many ways a foreman was considered one of our junior staff. Job scores had to average at least eighteen points. Pay was one dollar or more per hour.

To move up in rank, each boy had to submit a written request explaining why he deserved a promotion. Requests were reviewed each week at a meeting we called our Ranch Council. The first year the council consisted of Jan, Henry, and me. We added other staff to the council as we grew. A boy's general attitude was evaluated, and his daily job training scores and staff comments over the past two weeks were reviewed.

After the meeting, we would privately inform each boy of the Ranch Council decision. If the promotion wasn't approved, we would share what the council thought the boy should improve to advance in the future. Boys were motivated to move up in rank to earn the additional pay and freedom, but more important was the sense of achievement that came with the promotion.

# The Boys Learned to Be Gentlemen
*Jan:*

John and I expected the guys to be polite and courteous to others. When we came to the table for dinner, everyone stood behind his chair, and a boy next to me would pull out my chair and help me to be seated. Then everyone sat down. As we've mentioned, no one ate until everyone was served and I had taken the first bite. I never opened the car door. One of the boys or John would open it for me. These courtesy requirements were new to the guys, so if they forgot, I would just stand next to the passenger door and wait. After a few seconds, John or one of the boys would jump out of the car to open my door.

We also stressed to look people in the eye and extend a hand for a firm handshake when meeting them for the first time. Then give your name, and ask theirs. We encouraged the boys to work on word association to remember people's names.

On one occasion, the new Wisconsin governor, Warren Knowles, came to the ranch. Fred Mason, a fourteen-year-old, met the governor and talked with him for a few minutes. Three months later, our guys were helping serve food at a Republican corn roast in a nearby town. The governor came through the food line and stopped in front of Fred. He paused for a few seconds, then pointed his finger at Fred before saying, "You're Fred Mason, right?"

The governor was pleased with himself to have remembered this young man's name. Without skipping a beat, Fred pointed back and said, "Well, I remember your name too, sir. It's Governor Knowles."

"Yep, that's right," the governor said with a grin.

The governor's two aides broke into laughter at seeing the governor upstaged by a polite teenager.

# Visitor Tours

On Saturday afternoons unexpected visitors would drop in to see what Rawhide was all about. Higher-ranking boys would be "on call" to meet the guests along with Jan or me, and then the boys would take the visitors on a tour. We always had two boys go together for safety. It wasn't the boys we were concerned about, but the possibility of visitors being inappropriate.

The guys were proud to conduct these tours, and they made favorable impressions. Plus, it was more fun than doing yard work or other afternoon ranch chores. We did not tell the guests that their tour guides were boys who had been placed with us by the courts, but that always came up.

Here is a typical conversation. I introduced the boys to an older couple. Let's call them Bill and Sarah Smith.

"Bill and Sarah, thank you for visiting Rawhide Ranch. I would like you to meet Dean and Ben. They will take you on a thirty-minute walking tour of the grounds. Is that OK?"

"Oh that would be nice," said Sarah. "Hello, boys."

"It's nice meeting you, Mr. and Mrs. Smith," Ben answered.

"We're looking forward to our tour, but please call us Bill and Sarah," said Bill.

Dean started the tour. "The first thing we will see is the stable. The guys are taught to care for the horses and learn to ride them."

"When we drove in, I saw two horses and a donkey in the open field by the entrance. Do they run away?" asked Sarah.

"Oh, no," Ben replied. "We let a couple horses out of the corral every day, and they never leave the grounds. The donkey always goes out with them. They love the fresh grass."

"Where are the boys from who are sent to live here?" asked Sarah. At some point in every tour, the guests asked something along those lines.

"Well, Ben and I are two of the boys sent here," Dean replied. "We arrived last spring, and we now are both at the second highest rank: "Trail Boss." There is a lot of responsibility at that rank."

The tour continued into the stable, then on to the equipment shed and down to the channel by the river where the boats were tied up. The tour ended back at the lodge, where John and I met up again with Bill and Sarah. We thanked the tour guides and dismissed them. Then we sat down at the dining room table with coffee or sodas.

The first comments from every guest were the same as we had heard from Bill and Sarah. "John and Jan, we were impressed with the tour of the facility, but we especially enjoyed meeting Ben and Dean. They are very courteous young men. We don't know why they were sent here, but what a wonderful place for them to get help turning their lives around."

The boys took hundreds of guests on tours, and hearing their comments never got old. It reminded John and me that we were helping young men with troubled backgrounds prepare for promising futures.

After the guests left, John and I would always compliment the boys for doing a wonderful job on the tour. We would tell them how proud we were to have them living with us and helping us run the ranch. The guys would grin with pride, knowing they had done a good a job.

# CHAPTER 6

# PLAY WITH A PURPOSE

## *John:*

The twenty-seven-room lodge is situated on a scenic bend of the Wolf River, with the five-hundred-acre ranch located on an ideal spot for boating twenty miles up and down the river. This meant a variety of the boys' activities involved the water, so we had to make sure they were all good swimmers.

The river is 225 miles long, starting in northern Wisconsin and running past the boys ranch and eventually into Lake Winnebago. At that point it flows into the Fox River, and then Lake Michigan at Green Bay. So technically you could take a boat from Rawhide to the Atlantic Ocean. But it would be a very long trip.

When we moved to Rawhide, we found one old, wooden boat with a set of oars and life preserver cushions. This was all Fred and Don needed to keep them happy. Both of these Native Americans boys had spent many hours fishing during their days living on their reservations. We got them fishing licenses and, with guidelines, they were soon able to take the boat a short distance up the river to Colic Slough, a safe place to fish away from the current and boat traffic on the river.

In the spring as the ice is melting, there is a walleye run, as the females swim upriver to spawn. The weather is usually chilly, and only passionate fishermen brave the temperature to sit in a boat or fish along the bank. Next comes the famous white bass run that starts in mid-May. They are not large fish, but when fifty or more were filleted, they provided a substantial meal for our whole family. During the peak of the run, a fish can be caught every few minutes, sometimes even on a hook with no worm.

Throughout the state, and especially in northern Wisconsin, fishing is very popular. Each winter we planned a trip with all the boys to the Mepps Lure Company in Antigo, Wisconsin. The Shelden family, owners of the famous fishing lure company, adopted Rawhide as one of their favorite charities. The guys were fascinated by the process of making tens of thousands of various lures for sale around the world. The visit included a tour of the factory and a nice luncheon meal, and then each of the boys got a few lure samples they could use on their Wolf River fishing ventures.

# Colic Slough

By our second year, we had two donated fourteen-foot aluminum boats, an older ten-horsepower Mercury outboard motor, and a pontoon boat. Bob Lang, an area businessman, donated a houseboat he had built called the Little Toot. It was big enough for us to load up all the guys and even some of their friends for short trips or a full day on the water.

By this time Don and Fred had proven they were dependable,

and they had finished a course in boater safety. One warm summer day, they went fishing in one of the boats with the unpredictable Mercury motor. They put on their life jackets and headed to Colic Slough.

As they entered the slough, their motor stopped. They paddled over to a large houseboat that was equipped with twin one-hundred-horsepower Evinrude motors, the largest motors made at that time. A man and, as the boys described her, a very pretty lady, came to the railing of the houseboat and asked what the problem was. Don asked if they could borrow a pair of pliers and screwdriver to get their motor started. The man loaned them the tools, but then he gave them a hard time about their Mercury motor. "If you had an Evinrude motor, you wouldn't have broken down."

They told the man they were from the Rawhide Boys Ranch and the Mercury motor was donated. They were glad to have it, but they added, "If you'd like us to have an Evinrude motor, you can sure donate one."

Don and Fred knew we expected them to treat everyone with respect, so they made sure to tell us they were very polite about how they made their request. I suspect they thought their comment about donating a motor might have been over the line.

We didn't think any more of the event until a week later, when a personal letter arrived from Mr. Ralph Evinrude, CEO of the Evinrude Corporation. He related how impressed he and his wife, radio and film star Francis Langford, were with the two young men who introduced themselves on the river. His letter went on to say, "The boys expressed great pride in living at Rawhide and boldly suggested that I might want to consider donating an Evinrude motor to the ranch. I want to take them up on their suggestion, and I have directed my shipping department to send six new 9.9 horsepower

Evinrude outboard motors to Rawhide. They should arrive in about two weeks."

We gathered the boys together and read the letter. Don and Fred got some pats on the back for being polite to Mr. and Mrs. Evinrude!

Another blessing from the Evinrudes came a few years later with the donation of six new snowmobiles and a 120 horsepower inboard/outboard ski boat. Evinrude is a real Wisconsin success story, and it was very generous of the company to play a special role helping Rawhide in those early years.

# Softball

Softball was a favorite summer activity for boys. However, they had no idea that they would have the opportunity to play against a professional women's team. Wilbur and Dorothy Pfeifer, friends of Jan's and mine, lived in Fond du Lac, Wisconsin. They owned a trucking company and sponsored a very successful semiprofessional girls softball team, which traveled and competed nationally.

The Pfeifers visited the ranch and offered to bring their team to Rawhide for an intersquad practice on our softball field. I suggested we make up a story to explain why more than a dozen attractive girls in their twenties were coming to visit. We agreed to tell the boys they were employees of the Wilbur Pfeifer Trucking Company, and that was technically true. Without knowing what they were getting into, the boys agreed to be good hosts and looked forward to the Saturday visit.

The girls arrived in casual clothes with no talk or outward appearance to suggest that they were a national championship team. After a tour, which every one of our boys insisted on being part of, there was an hour before an outdoor cookout would start. On cue, one of the girls casually asked the boys if they would like to play softball before lunch. After an enthusiastic yes, one of the boys suggested they split up with half the boys and half the girls on each team. But the spokesperson for the team said, "How about if we girls play against you guys?"

After a few comments from the boys, who didn't think that would be fair at all, they agreed. As the girls went to their cars to get their softball gloves, the boys assured me they would play politely and not embarrass their guests.

As the girls returned from the cars with not only softball gloves but also spiked shoes, some of the guys started thinking winning might not be as easy as they thought. After a coin flip, which the boys won, they chose to let the girls bat first. That was a big mistake. After the entire nine-member starting team for the girls had batted around, with half of them hitting home runs over our short out-field fence, the guys knew they had been set up. Everyone enjoyed a big laugh before the sides were divided and the game continued. Thankfully, the girls had suggested it be a slow-pitch game. If it had been fast-pitch, which was the girls' game, I doubt if any of our guys would have hit a single pitch.

# Snowmobiling

On the five-hundred-acre Rawhide grounds, several miles of old log-ging trails run along the river and through wooded forest, ideal for hiking, cross-country skiing, and snowmobiling. We had two older snowmobiles, plus the six new snowmobiles the Evinrude Company had donated. The boys were all trained in how to operate the ma-chines, and a staff member always accompanied them on the rides.

Snowmobiles provided many hours of fun, as well as some good mechanical training. The machines were brought into the heated shop every few weeks, and a staff member and the boys examined them for loose parts, worn belts, and routine maintenance.

# Skiing

As soon as the first snow arrived, we would gather the boys on a small hill at the ranch to learn how to walk with skis, do a side pass up a hill, and master a simple snowplow to turn and stop. Nordic Mountain Ski Resort was a great hill located twenty miles from the ranch. As soon as it opened every winter, we loaded up the guys and headed for their first ski outing, courtesy of Nordic Mountain. They learned quickly, and by the end of the first day they were skiing down every slope with only an occasional wipeout.

Our son Tim became an expert skier even before he reached his teenage years and enjoyed teaching the boys. He developed a close relationship with Roger Devenport, one of our guys his age. The duo would compete down the challenging black diamond runs to see who could look the coolest "catching air" as they raced over the moguls.

My college roommate, Dave Lunberg, went on to own and expand the popular White Cap Mountain Ski Resort in Wisconsin, near the Upper Michigan border. Dave and his wife, Evie, invited Jan and me to bring our two sons and our first ten foster boys to White Cap for four days of midweek skiing. We drove the three hours to the resort, where we enjoyed lodging, skiing, and great meals, all courtesy of Dave and Evie. Our boys had skied a dozen times at our local hill before arriving at White Cap, so they were all ready for the new challenge.

Since the first invitation in 1967, the Lunbergs have generously

PLAY WITH A PURPOSE

hosted the Rawhide boys annually for a ski outing the last week of February. As Rawhide continued to grow, the number of boys and their home staff rose to about eighty skiers a year, and they all enjoyed free skiing at White Cap.

Dave has said that in fifty years, they have never had a disciplinary incident with the boys. Many other skiers have told Dave and Evie about the nice group they met on the hill, and they were always surprised to learn it was a group from a youth correctional program.

# Summer Camp

In the '60s and '70s, we ran a weeklong summer camp for nonresidential boys who were sent to us by police departments or juvenile agencies. Forty boys arrived every Sunday throughout the summer for a week of teamwork and intense competition.

The boys were assigned to four groups of ten each, and each group lived with two counselors in the woods, in what we called "outposts." Each outpost had a twenty-by-twenty foot concrete pad covered by a tent. It was large enough for each person to have a folding cot and a footlocker for clothes and personal items. Their eating area included an antique wood stove, a grill, two picnic tables, a five-gallon water dispenser, and a refrigerator that was without power and cooled with ice that was delivered daily. Last, but certainly not least, each outpost had an outhouse.

The senior counselor for an outpost was usually a schoolteacher with experience working with aggressive teens. Each of them would work for at least part of the summer. The junior counselor was usually a college student studying for a career in teaching or youth work, preferably with an athletic background. Most of them would work the whole summer.

The outposts had different names, and the campers quickly developed great pride in their names as they wore their matching shirts and carried their banner with them throughout the day. One outpost was called the Renegades, complete with matching red t-shirts and sweatshirts; another was called the Vigilantes, in black; the Mustangs wore blue; and last, the Sphinx, in gold. These may not have been the most positive names, but the guys loved them.

Each outpost had a matching banner on an eight-foot wooden staff. Rawhide had professional silk-screen equipment, and during the winter the staff and boys would prepare t-shirts, sweatshirts, and banners for the outposts.

Summer camp was designed to teach the boys to work together as a team and help each other. To reinforce that message, the scoring was based on how well the team did as a group, not how well an individual did. One of the first rules was to protect their outpost banner. If it was left unattended, day or night, another outpost could steal it and be awarded points. So at least one team member had to be assigned to carry the banner with them at all times. Every morning food and ice were delivered to each outpost. There was a daily menu, but the counselors and boys prepared the food. At noon the camp director inspected each outpost for cleanliness, creative improvements to the campsite, and proper storage of food.

Two or three competitive events, in which outposts could earn points, took place every day. The events included racing hydroplane boats with ten-horsepower motors through a timed course on the Wolf River, driving a bulldozer through an obstacle course, blasting a barrel on a cable with hoses from the ranch fire truck, or racing on foot through a half-mile course that included a dozen difficult obstacles.

For transportation, each outpost was assigned an old car with the trunk cover removed. The counselors would use the car to transport their group from their outposts far back in the woods to the competition areas each day. The boys were told that about mid-week there would be a race among the four outpost cars. On Wednesday all four cars were set in place at the end of a hundred-acre field, with the boys waiting with excitement for the start. But their excitement was greatly dimmed when they were told the cars' engines could not be started, and each team had to push their car to the finish line. But push they did, with the hope that they could win points and a blue ribbon to add to their flagstaff.

Each evening there was a roundup in a big circus tent. It started with awarding ribbons for the day's competition. The first-place outpost got a blue ribbon, second got red, third got white, and fourth got pink. The outpost flagstaffs had preattached screw eyes where two dozen ribbons could be attached, creating an attractive pole as the week progressed.

The competition among outposts became intense. One week, one of our outposts had nothing but pink, last-place ribbons, on their flagstaff by the middle of the week. The group had set a goal to win only pink ribbons, but when the other teams saw what they were doing, they were determined not to let it happen. Thus, a competition to see who could come in last swept through the other three outpost teams. It was humorous to watch each team trying to be the most terrible at the competition. Regardless of their goals, our goal was accomplished. The boys were working together as a team to reach a goal, no matter how strange it might have been.

Each roundup included a program emphasizing the personal values necessary for a successful life. This included practical tips for living with teachings from the Bible and the example of Jesus's life, as well as how Jesus's death and resurrection promise eternal life for those who accept the Lord as our Savior. Most of the boys had never heard this message of salvation before, and they always had a lot of questions after the program.

# A Camp with Lifelong Benefits

One of our best senior counselors—even though he came for just one week each year—was Dave Rich, a Racine County probation agent. Dave had a caseload of ninety adjudicated delinquent teenagers, and each year he selected ten of his toughest cases, brought them to Rawhide, and lived with them for the week. The following story about one of his guys provides an example of the effectiveness of a week of camping.

Even though he was only sixteen, Mike Lensby had a long juvenile record. His father was a former Marine sergeant and ran his home as if he were still in the military. Mike received numerous beatings with a belt, sometimes for infractions as minor as calling his sister a dummy.

Running away became a way to escape from the abuse, and staying with friends who were not good influences led to an early record of fights, drugs, alcohol, burglary, and car theft. After Mike repeatedly broke the terms of his court-ordered probation, the Racine County juvenile judge directed him to attend Rawhide's one-week program under the supervision of his probation officer, Dave Rich. Mike was loaded in the van for the trip to Rawhide. He was determined to make the most of the camp but certainly not to work on any of his problems. His plan was to drop out of high school, having completed his junior year with mostly failing grades.

To his surprise, he actually enjoyed camp and excelled in the competition. He even had some serious conversations with Dave about options for changing the direction of his life. We had the option of keeping one boy out of forty from each week to stay on for the rest of the summer as a staff helper. That gave us more time to work with those who had shown great potential for change during the camp week. We gave Mike the invitation to stay on, and he quickly accepted.

After he did a great job the rest of the summer, we asked him if he wanted to come back the next summer as paid support staff. He said he would. At that point I said, "Mike, there is one catch. You have to finish your senior year and graduate."

After a long pause, Mike said, "I'll have to think about that."

Mike did graduate and came back for the next summer, and as we expected, he did a great job. At the end I asked him, "How would you like to come back next summer as a paid junior counselor for the whole summer in the outposts?"

Again he responded with an enthusiastic yes. I followed with, "There is a catch. You have to enroll in college this fall and get at least passing grades in your freshman year."

Again Mike responded with, "Oh boy. I will really have to think about this."

Mike did get passing grades in college, went on to get his bachelor's degree in marketing, and became our camp director in charge of the entire camp program for several years after he graduated.

Seeing the complete turnaround in Mike (and also in several other boys he brought to the summer camp), Dave was very impressed with the success of Rawhide. We were impressed with him as well, and we asked him and his wife Jeannine if they would consider moving to the ranch as full-time houseparents. They agreed, and they worked with us for several years.

# A Week of Change

Another dramatic success story about a camper in the one-week summer program features a young man named Steve Bender. His journey in life had started to fall apart many years earlier as a conflict developed with his dad. Both had quick tempers, and Steve was the recipient of numerous beatings with a belt. Tensions grew, and his father became more abusive as Steve reached his teen years. He began failing in school, and getting into fights, and on numerous occasions, he ran away to stay with friends.

Steve was referred to the Winnebago County Social Service Agency. They tried a foster home, but that only lasted a few weeks. Shortly afterward, they made the decision to send Steve to Rawhide's one-week camp program to see if that would help.

In addition to learning how to start making better decisions, Steve learned how God could become a part of his life. Even though his parents did not go to church, his mother had wanted her three children to attend Sunday school. She dropped them off at a nearby church every Sunday and picked them up. Steve had heard Bible stories, but never understood that he could have a personal relationship with God by accepting Jesus.

By the middle of the week, as Steve was sitting around the outpost campfire talking to a counselor, he said, "I want to accept Jesus as my Savior." They bowed their heads. Steve said a simple prayer, and the first step for his new life with the Lord began.

He went back for his junior year in high school, and he graduated on time by taking extra courses. The next few years, Steve worked in a mill, all the time thinking he could do more with his life. He enlisted in the Air Force and served a four-year tour as an aircraft repair inspector.

On his first leave, he was wearing his dress blue uniform when his father picked him up at the airport. For the first time, he could tell his dad was proud of him, and their relationship took a positive turn from that point on.

Today, Steve and his wife Sandy have a beautiful home nestled on six acres of wooded land where their children and grandchildren love to visit. Steve is an active member of the American Legion and the AMVETS organization. Steve and Sandy are active in their local church and enjoy helping others in need.

A very proud moment for Steve came in 2006, when he was asked to become the first alumnus to serve on the twelve-member Rawhide board of directors. To date, he has served for more than ten years, helping oversee the program that helped him turn his life around.

When I met with Steve at his house to record his story in detail, the first thing he showed me was the certificate he had received during the Friday night awards program at the end of his week at camp. Every camper received the same one at the end of his week. Steve's was framed and still hangs on his living room wall, over forty years later, as a reminder of the week his life started to change. It is dated July 21, 1972.

Sometimes a week may be all that is needed to set a teenager on a positive path. Numerous young men point to their week at camp as a turning point in their lives.

# CHAPTER 7
# OUR CUP RUNNETH OVER

*John:*

When a boy was placed with us, it was understood that we were making a commitment to accept and work with his whole family, regardless of the challenges they were going through. As we got to know the families, which many times consisted of a mother, her boyfriend, and the boy's siblings, we asked if they were involved with a local church. Usually they were not. Then we asked if it would be all right for their son to attend church with the rest of the group, along with their houseparents. On rare occasions, when the parent(s) had a denominational preference, we made arrangements for their son to attend a church of that denomination accompanied by one of our staff.

A good church is a place where people can find acceptance regardless of their backgrounds or current struggles. They can often receive encouragement and counseling to give them the freedom to be honest about things they are facing, and if they choose, they can find help turning to God. Also, engagement with active church youth programs helps give the boys a healthy environment for building relationships with other teens. Parents need the help of other adults, such as church youth leaders who can influence their children through the challenging teenage years.

The reason the boys accepted going to church with us was that this was only one part of our Sunday routine. Jan and I planned ahead of time what we would do after church, without sharing the plan with the boys. We just told them if they needed to bring a swimming suit or a change of clothes with them. Following the service, we went to eat at places that served ample portions for not much money. Lunch was followed by an afternoon outing, such as the beach, civic event, concert, county fair, or movie. When we arrived home the guys talked about the fun they had. A new boy who had decided not to go, knew he had missed out on a great time.

## *Jan:*

My brothers, sister, and I attended a small church where my parents served in a leadership role. John started attending prior to our engagement, and after we were married, we both volunteered to work with the church's youth group. The members were thrilled when we launched Rawhide Boys Ranch, but the excitement faded one Sunday morning when we arrived at church with just a few of our first group of boys.

The church had a youth group made up of a half dozen attractive high school girls and a few boys. The girls were very friendly, and our foster boys enthusiastically returned their attention. The boys were all in favor of returning the next Sunday.

A few parents came up to us after the service to share their concerns about how this arrangement would work out. Two of the men in leadership asked if they could meet with John and me early the next week to discuss an idea they had to make our boys feel more "comfortable" during Sunday school.

One of the leaders asked if we planned to bring all the foster boys to church most Sundays. The question seemed a bit strange. Our little church encouraged everyone to come every Sunday. To our answer in the affirmative, he replied, "Our leaders met, and we understand that most of your boys have little knowledge of the Bible. We don't want them to be embarrassed in a class with the teenagers from our church families. One of our members has a large home only a few blocks from the church, and he has agreed that your boys can meet there during the Sunday school hour for a special class. We will provide a teacher, but we want at least one of you to be present with the boys."

We were shocked. Our boys were not going to be allowed to be in a class with the other teens, and the reason certainly was not their lack of biblical knowledge. These boys who had suffered so many rejections in life were being shunned by the very people who were supposed to show God's love.

This was my church. I had attended there for twenty-five years. My father was an elder and one of the major financial donors. I felt the rejection of our boys was a rejection of me. The wound was so deep that it would be a few years before I would let myself trust another church.

John and I decided we would start looking for a church where everyone in our expanded family would be welcome.

# *John:*

Jan and I made a list of four churches we would visit, and we planned to ask our foster boys to give us their impressions of each one. The first three Sundays and the first three churches did not impress any of us. No one greeted us when we arrived, and no one talked to us when we left. We left each service feeling that we didn't matter to anyone else.

But on our fourth church visit, something happened. That Sunday we drove thirty miles to Calvary Bible Church in Neenah, Wisconsin. It was located in an older building in a residential area near the center of the city. We parked the hearse out of sight of the main entrance. We climbed the stairs to a small entry area, and a young pastor reached out to shake hands with Jan and me, Steve, Tim, and each of our six foster boys. "I'm Elden Davis, the pastor here," he said. "And who are you guys?"

I explained, "We are from a youth program called Rawhide Boys Ranch, and we are just visiting for the day."

He paused and said, "I have read about Rawhide in the paper. Would you be able to wait a few minutes after the service so I can talk with you?"

The service was friendly, with pleasant music and a very down-to-earth, practical sermon from Pastor Davis. After the closing hymn, we walked to the back of the sanctuary to wait for the pastor. Once most of the congregation had shaken his hand and left, he approached us and said, "If you have a couple of hours, I have a plan. My wife and I would like to take you and Jan and your sons out to eat. Three of our member families with teenage boys would each like to take two boys each to their homes for lunch. We will all meet back at the church at three o'clock this afternoon. Would that be OK?"

The boys nodded their heads with cautious approval.

We had a delightful lunch with Elden and his wife. We learned that he probably should have been placed at Rawhide as a teenager. His honesty about his past was refreshing, and we found ourselves drawn to his genuine concern for the boys and us. We met back at the church to collect our tribe of six teenagers and learned that they had all had a great time, too. Their opinion was unanimous. They all asked if we could go to this church every Sunday!

# A Pastor's Visit

A few weeks later, I mentioned to Jan my desire to invite Pastor Davis and his wife to the ranch for a meal. "That's fine," she said, "but I have to be away."

I wondered aloud. "Be away? We haven't set a date yet."

"Whenever the date is, I have to be away."

This was the first time I realized how deeply Jan had been hurt by the rejection from her family's church. She wasn't about to spend a casual meal getting to know a new pastor and building her hope of acceptance, only to be wounded again. She agreed to prepare a meal, but would then take the evening off and go shopping.

We set a date, and Jan prepared a meal of spaghetti and meat sauce with a salad and French bread. I briefed the boys that Pastor Elden's nickname was P.D. (for Pastor Davis), and he liked being addressed that way. Since we usually had a casual and somewhat boisterous mealtime, I asked everyone to be a little more reserved. I specifically requested that they refrain from passing gas or throwing food. I don't want to imply this was a common occurrence at meals, but occasionally both would happen.

P.D. called earlier that afternoon to say a scheduling conflict had come up, and asked whether it would be all right if he came alone? I said that would be fine, as Jan also had to be gone.

Just before his arrival, Jan gave the boys on meal duty some last-minute instructions, and then she headed to town. P.D. arrived, and the first item on the evening agenda was a tour of the grounds and the stable. All of us were standing in front of the barn, in a few inches of new snow, when our Saint Bernard, Oliver, walked over to see what was going on. All of a sudden Pastor Davis let out a shout and looked down at his right leg. Oliver was standing next to him, hind leg lifted, and the pastor's leg was wet from the knee down.

The boys did everything they could do to keep from laughing, but P.D. took it in stride. "That's OK. A pastor has to get used to being treated this way." I think his reaction impressed the guys. When Jan heard about this later, I think she was secretly pleased with both our St. Bernard and the pastor's reaction.

The next event on the schedule was supper, and I was hoping that would go better than the tour. One of the boys volunteered to give thanks, and we passed the food around to the left until everyone had served himself. We started to eat, and P.D. set everyone at ease as he told stories about some of his struggles as a teenager. Everyone was having a good time.

Close to the end of the meal, P.D. suddenly took an eight-inch spaghetti noodle covered with meat sauce and slapped it across the forehead of the boy sitting next to him. The room went silent as Ben wiped off the sauce and he took a few seconds to contemplate how to respond. With the overreaction you would expect from a teenager, he grabbed a handful of meat-soaked noodles from his own plate and quickly put it on the top of the pastor's head. P.D. retaliated by tossing the balance of the food from his plate in Ben's face, and

World War III erupted!

Just like a bar fight in an old Western movie, the room exploded with spaghetti and meat sauce flying everywhere. The battle ended with all of us laughing and covered with supper. P.D. exclaimed, "Wow, guys! That was great! Now let's see if we can get this place cleaned up so Mrs. Gillespie has no idea how much fun we had!" Even our Great Dane, Dino, joined in the cleanup, licking meat sauce off the floor.

It took an hour, as the red spaghetti sauce didn't easily come off the knotty pine walls. And we even had to clean some off the ceiling.

But our fun wasn't over. The last event we had planned was snowmobiling on the new Evinrude snow machines. We hiked to the vehicle shed to get the sleds out and assigned drivers. Martin, one of the highest-ranking guys, drove the front sled, with P.D. riding behind him. The other boys were on the middle four sleds, and I rode behind the driver of the last machine. A light snow was falling, and with the moon almost full, it was a beautiful evening for a leisurely ride around the two-mile Ridge Trail.

Halfway through our ride, the headlight on Martin's lead sled revealed a skunk twenty feet ahead, standing right in the middle of the narrow trail. He stopped his snowmobile, and P.D. was shocked to see him climb off and walk toward the skunk. His first words to Martin were a stern warning. "I don't think you want to do that." By then Martin had reached the skunk. He bent down, picked him up, and started walking back toward his snowmobile. P.D. lost it. He jumped off, yelling, "No, no, no!" He escaped down the trail past all six snowmobiles and passed me at the end of the line on a dead run yelling, "He's got a skunk!"

What P.D. didn't know was the skunk was our lost pet, Pepe Le Pew. He had been raised in the house from a baby, but he had been spending more time outside the house during the past couple of months. Most nights he slept with our St. Bernard in the doghouse right outside our dining room door. But Pepe had been missing for a few weeks. Martin assumed the polecat on the trail was Pepe. Luckily, it was.

We all got off our sleds and gathered around Martin and the skunk. Pepe was hugging Martin's neck, enjoying the reunion. We yelled for P.D. to join us, and he tentatively made his way back. When we told him what was going on, Elden said, "This is the craziest place I have ever visited. Let's go back and have dessert . . . if it's safe!"

Calvary Bible Church became "our church" for many years, and God would use that church to touch the hearts of many Rawhide guys. The entire congregation accepted the boys, and the youth group was large enough that it could absorb our eight to ten teenagers. The church and its various programs, led by P.D. and Associate Pastor Dave McLaughlin, provided a spiritual boost to the boys and to our whole family.

# A Lively Hearse

Our 1956 Cadillac hearse was the only large vehicle we had during our first year. Jan, our two sons, and I fit safely into the wide front seat. The eight boys loved to sprawl out on piles of cushions in the back. Before long everyone in New London, our town of five thousand, knew what was inside the hearse: a large group of boys.

We went to church in the same vehicle, only we were careful not to park in front of the church. The one time we did was when we all attended my brother's wedding. We arrived early intentionally so we could park right in front of the main entrance. After the service, several people admitted they had seen the hearse when they arrived at the church. Thinking there was a funeral, they went to the only other Lutheran church in town and found it was closed.

We had lots of fun traveling with the big hearse, and the boys kept it clean and polished. They thought it was a great ride.

One of many humorous incidents happened one Sunday as we were on our way to a restaurant after church. Jan was driving in the front with our sons, Steve and Tim. I was in the back clowning around with the guys. One of the boys, or maybe more than one, was emitting terrible-smelling gas. I rapped on the sliding glass window behind the driver section for Jan to stop and let me ride in the front. I never did figure out the reason for the glass window in a hearse, but it did a good job of keeping the constant chatter of the boys from distracting the driver.

Jan pulled over to the curb on a city street, and I opened the side door to get out. But as I tried to escape, a couple of the boys grabbed my legs to try to hold me in. With the door open, I fell out of the hearse head first with my hands on the concrete. The rest of me, from the waist down, was being held in the hearse. At that moment a police car pulled up, and the officer yelled through his speaker. "Stand up, and put your hands over your head."

The boys let me go, and I quickly stood up. One of the boys pulled the door closed. The officer came around his car asking me what was going on. I told him who we were and explained that we were coming from church with our eight teenage foster sons. "Keep your hands where I can see them," he commanded, "and come around to the back. Open the door for me."

I opened the door, and all eight boys, who had been as quiet as mice up to that point, broke out in laughter. "OK," the officer said. "You can shut the door. I can see you have your hands full, so be on your way, but do not do this again. And by the way, good luck with your load of boys."

# Bart's 1968 MVP Corvette

Over the years support for the Rawhide program has been nothing short of amazing. We went through a series of financial challenges, but time after time various individuals, companies, and foundations came through with help. This allowed us to continue to expand the number of young men we could help. It was wonderful for the boys to see how many people are willing to help others in need.

The key support team members, who led the way with their endorsement and personal support, were, of course, Bart and Cherry Starr. Their name recognition provided instant credibility for the Rawhide program, and they donated many hours of their time making public appearances and spending time at the ranch with the boys.

One of their early contributions involved Bart's 1968 red Corvette convertible that he received as part of the Super Bowl II Most Valuable Player award. Knowing Rawhide was continuing to face financial challenges, Bart and Cherry decided they would donate the Corvette to be raffled off at one dollar a ticket. Lotteries were not legal in Wisconsin then, but we had gotten special permission from our state government.

I should point out that this was a sizable donation, since National Football League players' incomes in the '60s were very modest. Most of the players, including Bart, had off-season jobs to meet their expenses.

Green Bay's Channel 11, WLUK-TV, with support of their general manager, Tom Hutchison, agreed to provide the promotion we needed to get the word out that someone could win Bart's MVP

Corvette. Interest was instant, and within a month we'd received over forty thousand tickets, raising $40,000.

Thousands of people sent their dollar, or dollars, and their raffle ticket stubs to Rawhide, the Packer office, and even to Bart's home. Cherry was responsible for collecting the stubs and the dollar bills. She stored the money in a suitcase and hid it in their basement. Every few days she went to a Green Bay bank with her suitcase filled with several thousand dollar bills. She would sit with a bank teller as he counted and put the bills into hundred-dollar bundles. Cherry said she felt like a drug dealer laundering money.

The tickets were circulated around the entire country, and some companies bought large blocks and gave one to each of their employees. The raffle helped pay all the ranch's past-due financial obligations. Ironically, a twenty-one-year-old man living within ten miles of Rawhide won the car. Over the decades since 1968, the car has changed hands several times, and all of the owners have lived within twenty miles of Rawhide. The various owners have always been delighted to bring the car to the ranch for promotional events with Bart and Cherry. They wanted to have their picture taken with the famous couple and the very special car.

# Bill and Louise Aylward

Those early days produced a number of other friends whose help to Rawhide proved to be a great benefit. William "Bill" Aylward was President and CEO of the successful Neenah Foundry. If you look at a manhole cover almost anywhere in the world, it probably has the company's name on it. He was also president of the board of a Neenah bank, and he and his wife, Louise, were major community civic leaders.

When Bart and I met with Bill, we explained the positive changes in the young men living with us and laid out the current financial deadline we were facing. The bank holding the mortgage was unexpectedly demanding the note to be paid in full. We did not know what to do.

After asking a lot of questions, Bill said he needed to consider how he could help and would get back to us.

Three days later, he called with great news. His bank would pick up Rawhide's mortgage and allow us to pay only the interest for the next two years. They would review the situation after that time to determine whether we were in a position to start paying on the principal. Another financial disaster was averted through the help and generosity of a new family on our support team.

The Aylward family, Bill's wife Louise and their sons, Bill Jr., Richard, and Andy, went on to be lifetime donors to Rawhide. After Bill Sr.'s death, Louise and her sons continued to fund various projects at the ranch, including building two beautiful youth homes and purchasing an additional forty acres of prime land for expansion. The Aylward family dedicated one of the boys homes they funded to Jan and me. At Louise and her sons' request, it was named the Gillespie Home. We knew nothing about the name until dedication day, when the sign was uncovered. We were humbled by the honor.

A few years ago, I was visiting with Louise and learned the true story of Bill's bank picking up the loan on the property. I commented that it was great for the bank to do that.

"That was not a big deal for the bank. Bill had us co-sign the loan," said Louise. When he did that I asked him what we would do if Rawhide didn't make it. He said, "'Then you'll have a very nice, twenty-seven room cottage on the Wolf River.'"

# Just Plain Chet

I met Chet Krause at a political event, and I was impressed to hear about his life. The publishing business he had started had become a world leader in literature and magazines for collectors. Little did I know that my meeting with Chet would result in finding a way to help many more boys at Rawhide.

The story of Krause Publications is the topic of several books. Chet, who calls himself "Just Plain Chet," was drafted into the U. S. Army during World War II, serving in General Patton's Third Army in Europe, where he was in the Battle of the Bulge. After returning to Iola, Wisconsin, and working as a freelance carpenter, he conceived an idea to produce a trade periodical for coin collectors like himself. He put together the first edition on his living room table and circulated it around the country. As the magazine's popularity grew, he needed help to keep up with the demand.

In the early '60s, Chet hired Cliff Mishler, a young man from Michigan who also had a passion for coin collecting. Cliff quickly rose to the role of Chet's partner and managed Krause Publications Company for forty years. The company expanded and over time published hundreds of books and periodicals for many different collectibles. Krause Publication grew to employ five hundred workers in a town with a population of thirteen hundred, and sales grew to 100 million dollars per year.

My second visit with Chet occurred when he came to Rawhide for an event attended by Tommy Thompson, the governor of Wisconsin. At the end of the event and a tour, Chet asked me a pointed question. "You have a great facility and program, but you only have one home for eight to ten foster children. Why don't you accept more boys?"

"Our cost to care for boys is more than double the fee paid by juvenile courts and county social service agencies." I told Chet. "We're having trouble funding the program even with just one house of boys."

Chet asked another question. "Do you have a five-year plan to help more boys?" I admitted we did not, and he continued. "If you develop a five-year expansion plan to triple the number of boys you can accept, I will give you a large financial gift."

At my next board meeting, I shared Chet's challenge, and the board agreed that a long-range plan was overdue. Staff and board members spent several months working on a plan that would triple the number of boy within five years. Chet was impressed with our plan, and true to his word, he followed through with a generous financial gift.

The plan worked well. In fact, we expanded to accept sixty boys within five years and developed a continuing plan to double that number in the next five.

Chet had a way of being there when a need arose. We had grown to more than forty boys and had a basketball team that competed against private high schools in the area. We were able to use the New London High School gym between five and six o'clock three mornings a week, before any school activities started. Two of our staff members and the eight to ten boys who were on the team got up long before dawn, dressed, ate something, and climbed into our old, donated van for the twenty-minute drive to the school. It was a grueling schedule, but the boys were willing to accept it because of their love for playing on a team, usually for the first time in their lives. On one dark winter morning, the van skidded on the slippery, narrow country road and rolled into the ditch on its side. No one was hurt, but the van was damaged beyond repair. Chet read about it in the paper and called to tell me to buy a van and send him the bill. Within days we had a new fifteen-passenger van for those early morning trips.

Among the numerous additional projects Chet funded, one stands out above all the others. It came as a wonderful Christmas present.

As the number of our boys increased, it became evident that we needed a gymnasium of our own. New London has an excellent school system, but the boys placed with us had a wide range of needs and learning abilities. Most were one to three years behind their grade level, and to get them caught up, they needed more individual education planning with a low teacher-to-student ratio.

The first step in our quest for a field house was to ask a local architect to donate preliminary plans for a regulation-size basket-ball court, bleachers, stage, home and visitor dressing rooms, public bathroom facilities, a fitness area, and lobby. The estimated cost was one million dollars.

I headed to Iola to meet with Chet, armed with a proposal for why we needed a field house and how it would add to our efforts with the boys. I showed him the architect's sketch of the floor plan and asked if he would be willing to lead a fund-raising team to raise the million dollars. Chet contemplated my request. "I don't like serv-ing on fund-raising committees, let alone leading them. I need some time to think about this. I'll call you within two weeks."

On the afternoon of Christmas Eve, the call came. He repeated his earlier comment about not liking fund-raising committees. He explained how when a friend asks a friend to make a contribution to a particular charity, which, in turn, opens the door for each one of his friends to follow up with a future donation request for their own favorite charity. The start of this conversation did not sound encouraging.

"If it's OK," Chet went on, "I'll just give you the million dollars."

I couldn't believe my ears. We were about to receive the money we needed to build the field house in one lump sum. All I could think to say was a silly response: "Chet, thank you, thank you! It just doesn't seem that it should be this easy."

"Well, John, you do have to send me a thank-you letter." I did.

A week later I headed to Chet's office with an artist's attractive color rendering of the field house. We had previously talked about the importance of publicly recognizing donors, so letters over the main entrance spelled out, "Chester L. Krause Field House." Chet studied the drawing for a few moments. "You know, you don't have to put my name on it." Then with a twinkle in his eye, he asked, "How large would the letters be?"

We made the letters on the field house very big.

The Iola area was blessed by Chet's generosity through his support of numerous community projects and needs. He had a love for classic cars and started the Iola Car Show which has become one of the largest such event in the nation. Our boys from Rawhide provide volunteer help getting the three-hundred-acre show grounds ready for the hundred thousand-plus visitors each year. We also set up a large tent to promote the ranch and encourage people to consider donating cars to Rawhide.

Chet was not only a major financial contributor to the ranch, but he became a business and public relations mentor to me. Chet and I spent many hours at Rawhide and in his Iola office talking about how to expand the ranch. For five decades he was a close friend and source of valuable advice.

# Jack and Ethel Keller

I first met the Kellers when they hired me to design a landscape plan for their home. Jack had recently started a business to support trucking companies in coping with the myriad of regulations required by the government. I enjoyed learning about Ethel's volunteer work and support of numerous charities. They were both passionate about helping others in need.

Early in our journey of expanding the Rawhide program, they were an obvious choice to ask for help. They responded with contributions for various projects through their Jack and Ethel Keller Foundation. Now that we had a sponsor for a field house, and it was under construction, I went to Jack and Ethel with a request for them to sponsor a major companion project. The project would add a ten-room high school facility. They agreed.

The trucking industry company Jack started, J. J. Keller & Associates, has grown to over 1,600 associates. Jack and Ethel have since passed away, but their sons, Bob and Jim, have continued to run the company, with a third-generation now at the helm. Bob & Lynne's children, Marne (CEO) and Rustin (COO), run the J.J. Keller operations. Jim and Rosanne's son Brian serves on the Foundation Board and is an advisor to the corporate operations board.

The J. J. Keller Foundation has become an anchor of strength for our area and state. Jack Keller formed the foundation in 1990 as a birthday present for his wife Ethel, and in the next twenty-three years, the foundation has created a legacy of generous support of dozens of organizations and programs that benefit the community.

As of 2017, the J. J. Keller Foundation giving has totaled more than fifty-five million dollars. Since the foundation's start giving has grown from fifty-thousand to over four million dollars annually.

# Darwin and Lois Smith

Tim Hoeksema was a senior executive in charge of the Kimberly-Clark Corporation's aviation division. In time it would grow into Midwest Airlines. As chairman of the Rawhide board of directors, Tim had, on a few occasions, unsuccessfully invited Darwin Smith, the President and CEO of Kimberly-Clark, to visit Rawhide.

Jan and I were invited to attend the wedding reception for Tim and Jan Hoeksema's daughter, and it proved to be a great opportunity to offer another invitation to Mr. Smith to come to Rawhide.

We arrived at a fancy Milwaukee hotel for the reception, and Tim greeted us as we entered the ballroom. He led us to our seats and introduced a couple we would be sitting with. They were Darwin and Lois Smith, and at their request, we ended up sitting between them. As the meal progressed, we had lively conversations getting to know the Smiths, me with Lois and Jan with Darwin.

Both Jan and Darwin have strong, assertive personalities, and I discreetly listened to their conversation, which became somewhat intense as they discussed how to raise teenagers. Jan invited Darwin to visit Rawhide and meet the boys to see how we motivate and empower them to succeed. He said he would.

"When?" she asked.

"Someday."

In a demanding tone, Jan said, "Will you visit within the next two weeks?" Darwin said he had a busy schedule, but Jan replied that she believed he could find a couple of hours within the next two weeks to visit.

Even more sternly, Darwin closed that portion of the evening's conversation with, "OK, I'll visit within the next two weeks."

When the Smiths left the table to greet friends, Jan turned to me and said, "What does Darwin do?" She had no idea about his international reputation for "turning around" one of the premier companies in the world. But if she had, it wouldn't have made any difference.

Darwin kept his word and visited Rawhide within the next two weeks. He was impressed. A $5,000 gift from the Kimberly-Clark Foundation arrived soon after the initial visit, but that was just the beginning for our newest lifetime support team member.

The next time I heard from Darwin was a phone call the first week in December. I had just finished our regular weekly meeting with all twelve of our staff. In addition to the mortgage payments, our operating expenses were running two months behind, and we were projected to end the year with a $20,000 deficit. As usual, we closed the meeting in prayer and specifically asked God to help us find a way to end the year with all the bills paid. We adjourned, and most of us were still in the conference room when our secretary, Jo, answered the phone. She came back into the room and excitedly announced that Darwin Smith was calling for me.

I quickly moved to the phone in my office and greeted our pres-tigious caller. "Good morning, Darwin." On his initial visit to Raw-hide, he had made it clear that he preferred Darwin to Mr. Smith.

"John, I'm going through our list of corporate charities and making year-end donations. Can Rawhide use $20,000?"

I was almost speechless as I told him about the just completed staff meeting. "We just prayed, asking God to help us find exactly that amount of money to end the year in the black." In my excite-ment, I went on with exclamations like, "Darwin, do you realize God had you call at exactly the right time to be a blessing to the boys' ranch? This is a miracle."

In my excitement, I was aware that Darwin was trying to say

something, but I could not slow down. After a few attempts he literally yelled, "John, if you will let me hang up now, I will send $40,000."

I quickly hung up the phone and sat in silent amazement at what had just happened. I asked Jo to round up the staff so I could share God's answer to prayer, with a prayer of thanks.

"Do you really think he will send $40,000?" one of our staff asked. I did, and that is the size of the check that came in the mail a few days later.

Darwin's support of the boys' ranch led to numerous contributions, including funding the boys home we called the Kimberly-Clark Home. When Darwin retired, the new CEO, Wayne Sanders, asked that the home be renamed the Darwin and Lois Smith Youth Home, and that became the permanent name.

# Tom Hutchison

## *Jan:*

Betty Belthazor, who worked as a housekeeper for us, was well aware of our ongoing struggle to pay the bills. One day as we were preparing supper, waiting for the school bus to deposit eight hungry guys, she said, "I'm going to have my brother come to see this place and help us."

Overhearing the conversation, John asked her, "What does your brother do?"

"He works at one of the Green Bay television stations."

"What is his job?"

"I have no idea what he does there," Betty answered. At that point John dropped the subject, not expecting much to come of the offer.

A week later I got a call from her brother, Tom Hutchison. He explained that his sister wanted him to come see what we were do-ing, and he needed directions. As I related the complicated direc-tions, he piped up. "Oh my, I think I know exactly where you are."

A few hours later, Tom arrived, and I called John to come up from the office. We sat around the dining room table with cups of coffee. John asked if he had trouble finding the ranch. With a grin Tom explained, "Our family used to lease this place. We operated a large sawmill in that open field just to the left of the driveway."

After chuckling about the remarkable coincidence, we talked about how we were helping redirect the lives of young men, and he was very interested. When John asked what he did at WLUK, a major network local television station, he shocked us by saying, "I'm the general manager. I think we might be able to help promote your work with the boys."

A few weeks later, Tom called to ask if John and I could meet with some of his staff. We excitedly drove to the Green Bay station and sat in a big conference room, waiting to hear what they had to offer. Several of the staff proceeded to share that they wanted to donate twenty hours of free airtime for an annual telethon to raise money for the ranch. It would start at nine o'clock on a Satur-day evening in March and run until five o'clock on Sunday evening. They would do all the programming and pick up all the costs. All the money to come in would go to Rawhide.

The station spent a year planning and promoting the event. They solicited area businesses and charity groups to set up fund-rais-ing projects so they could present checks during the show.

Businesses, service clubs, churches, youth groups, and others held fundraising projects and enjoyed presenting their donations on the air. Some businesses made major gifts, such as a prototype semi-tractor donated by the Oshkosh Truck Corporation, led by their president and CEO, John Mosling.

They also contracted with a different Hollywood celebrity to attend each year and picked up their fees and travel expenses. Some of the guests were Bob Eubanks of *The Newlywed Game*, Nick Barkley of *Big Valley*, actress Karen Valentine, and Harvey Korman of *The Carol Burnett Show*. In addition, Chuck Woolery, the Nashville singer who had donated our hearse, served as a co-host with Bart and Cherry on every telethon—all at his own expense. Chuck became the original host of *Wheel of Fortune* and later of *The Love Connection*.

The telethons were originally held at the WLUK-TV station, but after three years the event was moved to Rawhide. This made it much easier for the boys living at the ranch to be actively involved. They helped our staff with numerous jobs, including building the background sets, preparing the grounds for hundreds of visitors, and providing meals and snacks during the twenty-hour telethon. The boys enjoyed working next to the Hollywood celebrities, who were chosen because of their positive personalities.

In addition to raising much-needed income each year, the telethons provided widespread exposure about Rawhide to thousands of viewers. A very popular portion of the twenty hours of programming consisted of interviews with the boys about their goals and what they were learning at Rawhide. The interviews were very honest, touching, and often humorous. It was a great experience for the boys, and it helped the viewers understand the impact of the Rawhide program.

The boys were always full of surprises. When Arnie learned that Karen Valentine would be the guest at the next telethon, he said, "Somehow, I'm going to get a kiss from her." We wished him luck but did not pay any more attention to his comment. It was, however, a goal he mentioned several times in the month prior to the telethon date.

Arnie volunteered to be interviewed on the show, and he used his live interview to explain that Karen Valentine was his favorite movie star and he would pledge one month's pay if she would give him a kiss. The quick-thinking host who was interviewing Arnie challenged the viewing audience. If they wanted to see Karen give Arnie a kiss, they should call in a pledge in the next ten minutes. Several dozen new pledges came in, and Arnie got a nice, on-camera kiss on the cheek from his idol.

The boys were amazed that people would give thousands of dollars during the telethons. One day Larry asked me, "John, why do people volunteer to help us and make such generous donations?"

"They believe we are giving you guys the instruction and experience you need to lead successful lives. They want to join the Rawhide effort to help you become productive members of society so that someday you will be able to help others in need."

# The Blessings of Church Support
*John:*

Jan and I have had the blessing and support of three churches during our lifetime. Each one met strategic needs at different points in our marriage and life. We encourage everyone to find a church that can provide personal and family support, and get involved.

Earlier in this chapter we talked about the first great church we attended, Calvary Bible Church, in Neenah, Wisconsin.

The second, Celebration Church, came some years later as we got to know Reverend Arni Jacobson. We attended Celebration Church in Green Bay, which grew quickly under his leadership and biblical teaching. After several years Pastor Arni stepped down, and

Reverend Mark Gungor took his place.

Pastor Mark was blessed with a unique gift to use humor to challenge couples, and especially men, to develop loving marriage relationships. His weekend seminars, called "Laugh Your Way to a Better Marriage," grew into a worldwide ministry. Jan and I attended one of the seminars and were very impressed. We attended a couple times a year specifically to take friends, that included many of our married alumni.

The third church in our spiritual journey was Appleton Alliance Church (AAC), pastored by Dr. Dennis Episcopo. Under Pastor Dennis's leadership, the congregation quickly expanded to over five thousand adults and children who attended every Sunday. Numerous current and former Rawhide staff and several of our alumni attend AAC. It is a serving church, offering many outreach events and services, including an on-site clinic manned by volunteer professionals. Hope Clinic serves those in our community who are unable to pay for basic medical care. It is a sponsor of Refuge Church, a new ministry serving an ethnic congregation in the Appleton area. The pastor is Bee Vang, an alumnus of Rawhide Boys Ranch.

# CHAPTER 8
# USED CARS TO THE RESCUE

## *John:*

As we approached a decade of helping young men, the program was continuing to expand. More boys were being accepted. However, even with the generosity of many friends, donations had continued to fall short of expenses by about $25,000 a year for the previous four years. The bank had given us a line of credit but also an ultimatum. We had one year to at least break even or they would call in the note. Unfortunately, this was a message we had heard before.

We had tried numerous projects to produce income in addition to asking for donations. We had weekend barbeques and trail rides for the public, sold Christmas trees, built picnic tables, and even sold firewood. These efforts didn't provide the income we needed.

During this time Jan and I went to Oklahoma City for a conference. We were sitting in our hotel room watching TV when a public service commercial came on. A local sports celebrity asked the viewers to donate twelve used cars for vocational training for a city youth rehabilitation program. It struck me as a brilliant idea.

"That's the answer," I said to Jan.

"For what?"

"For our financial problems."

While she was still trying to fathom what I was talking about, I went on. "Our donors already give us five or six cars a year, and we don't even ask for them. We've sold them for about $500 each. Do you know what a car a week would be?"

"No, what is it?"

"That would be fifty times $500, for a total of $25,000. That is the amount we are short every year."

I couldn't wait to get home and ask Bart if he thought promoting car donations would be a good idea. Having a firsthand knowledge of the auto business as an owner of two Lincoln Mercury dealerships in Birmingham, Alabama, Bart immediately said, "Let's do it."

Since we were only a few months from the bank deadline, we had to find a way to buy some time. We expected it would take up to a year to reach our goal of having a car a week donated.

We met with Tom Hutchison and asked if his Green Bay TV station would donate sixty-second public service spots asking for cars to be donated to Rawhide. This was a new venture, as no organizations were asking for that type of donation in the '60s. He agreed to run two sixty-second promotion spots each day at no charge. Primarily thanks to Tom's lead, two other major network stations also agreed.

Our plan was to create two different, attention-grabbing, one-minute commercials. We involved the boys in dreaming up ideas, and they really got into it. Some of their ideas were wild, and a few were illegal, but several were very helpful.

In the first ad, I appeared on camera talking excitedly to one of our boys about how people were starting to donate cars. In the background was a nice-looking used car with the hood up and the back of a mechanic in coveralls bending over the engine.

The Rawhide boy said, "John, is that a volunteer mechanic fixing one of our donated cars?"

"Yes it is. It's Bart Starr. He knows a lot about cars, and he's agreed to help us."

Of course no one believed that it was really Bart, but it was. He came out from under the hood, his hands, face, and coveralls covered with grease. In one hand he had eight ignition wires and in the other a large pipe wrench. "John, can I break for lunch now?" he asked.

"Sorry, Bart, you have to get that car running first. We have a buyer coming to look at it this afternoon."

With his head down, Bart turned and walked back to the car as the screen displayed the phone number to call Rawhide to make a donation.

For the second ad, our maintenance staff and a few of the guys built a fake bathroom wall with a medicine cabinet above a sink. Greg, one of our portly staff with a three-day beard growth, came walking up to the cabinet in a bathrobe with a toothbrush in his mouth. He took out the brush, turned his head, and yelled, "Honey, what are we going to do with our old car now that we have the new one?"

"I don't know," a female voice yelled back.

Greg opened the cabinet, and there was Bart looking at him.

"Why don't you donate it to the Rawhide Boys Ranch?" said Bart. "You can get a tax deduction, and it helps us train young men." He handed a piece of cardboard to Greg showing the eight-hundred number to call Rawhide. "Just call this number, and we will pick up your car."

Greg slowly closed the cabinet door with a stunned look on his face and the toothbrush dangling from his mouth. He again yelled to his wife. "Honey, Bart Starr is in our medicine cabinet."

"I'd heard he'd moved," the off-camera woman yelled back.

The three TV stations started running the ads. In the first week, we doubled our original goal of obtaining a car a week, by the second month we were averaging a car a day, and by the third month we were bringing in almost three cars a day. We were excited, blessed, and overwhelmed.

When a car donation came in, we asked for the donor's name and address and then asked if the car ran. Once a donation was received, we had two of our staff leave work early and drive to where the car was located. One would drive the car home and bring it to Rawhide the next day.

The problem? About a quarter of the cars either did not run or stopped running halfway back to the ranch. As car donations became overwhelming, we put up a large Wisconsin map on the office wall with green, yellow, and red pins indicating the locations of cars. Green were cars ready to pick up. Yellow were cars that we couldn't pick up because they wouldn't start. And the red pins indicated cars that had stopped running on the way to Rawhide. They needed to be picked up and winched onto a trailer. The problem was, we had no trailer. At one point we had more than two-dozen vehicles scattered around northeastern Wisconsin that did not run and needed to be picked up.

## Dick and Audrey Pennau

With so many donated vehicles arriving at the ranch, we were desperately in need of a building both to repair the cars and hold auctions. Dick and Audrey Pennau owned a large Pepsi-Cola distribution company and had previously been involved in supporting Rawhide with their soda products. Their sons, Don and Steve, were managing divisions of the company and had also become involved in volunteer ranch projects.

I presented the Pennau family with our need for a multi-purpose vehicle building and explained how it would help to generate considerable income. They agreed to fund an eighty-by-one-hundred-foot heated structure with four large overhead doors at each end. We named it the Pennau PREP Center. This was an acronym for Preparation and Repair Education Program. It became the facility where the boys received vocational training from our professional vehicle mechanics. The building also housed the auctions of autos, trucks, boats, and campers. Within a few years, the auctions were drawing several hundred licensed vehicle dealers from five states.

## Bergstrom Automotive

Bergstrom Automotive was the largest dealership in our area, and their business was starting to grow across the state of Wisconsin. CEO John Bergstrom approached me with a fund-raising proposal. His corporation had built an impressive hotel in downtown Appleton called the Paper Valley Hotel. It was scheduled to open in a week with much fanfare, but finishing work was behind schedule. John called to ask if we were looking for a work project for the boys. "Maybe," I said. "What do you have in mind?" He asked to meet me at the hotel.

The floor in the lobby was made of twelve-inch slate tiles that could be cleaned with a power scrubber, but the quarter-inch mortar joints between each panel had to be cleaned by hand. Adding to the difficulty of finding someone to do the job, the spaces would have to be cleaned at night after the other builders had gone home. John and I estimated our eight guys could complete the job in one or two nights. "This is good work-training project for the boys," I said to John. "However, since it is a commercial project, there must be an additional benefit for Rawhide."

John agreed, and he offered a proposal: "We are planning a grand opening, and I will commit to raising ten thousand dollars for Rawhide to help with the expenses of managing the vehicle donation program."

I agreed, and two days later we reported for floor cleaning work at eight o'clock at night. John worked with us for several hours and then excused himself. He returned with sodas and pizzas for everyone. We had a midnight snack, and it was an opportunity for the boys to get to know John. After a lot of hard work and a few more short breaks, the floor was completed. Morning was breaking as the day's construction crew started to arrive.

# WATDA

For the first few years, the challenge of picking up the cars and preparing them for auction was the responsibility of our oldest son, Steve, who was also in charge of building and grounds maintenance. He soon realized he had to come up with a plan to handle the unexpected volume of donated cars, boats, and campers. The overwhelming responses to our request for cars caught us by surprise. Steve and Bart suggested we turn to the largest vehicle organization in the state, the Wisconsin Automobile and Truck Dealers Association (WATDA), for advice.

I contacted Gary Williams, the president of the organization, which is comprised of eight hundred dealerships, to explain our dilemma. Gary wanted to bring a couple of his board members to the ranch, but he was not sure they could take the time for the two-hour drive. I asked if it would help if I could find a private plane to fly them to Appleton. He said that would be a big help. Tim Hoeksema, the Rawhide board chairman, was in charge of the Kimberly-Clark fleet of aircraft, and he was soon to become the president of Midwest Airlines. He owned his own twin-engine plane and agreed to fly the WATDA officers to Rawhide.

Tim, Bart, and the ranch staff and boys hosted Gary and WATDA Board Members Ron Boldt, owner of a Ford dealership in Platteville, and Jerry Long, owner of a Chrysler dealership in Ripon. Our guests were impressed with Rawhide, the boys, and our extensive field of several hundred donated cars.

We sat at a rustic table in our modest dining room, and on the back of a paper placemat we outlined a plan for how to collect and sell the cars. Dealers would volunteer to become collection sites in their communities. Donors would bring in their cars and trucks, and the dealers would handle the title transfer paperwork. The vehicles would be stored until Rawhide could arrange to pick them up and transport them to the ranch.

Our WATDA visitors took the plan to the next board meeting of their association, and by a unanimous vote, the board agreed to partner with Rawhide. They subsequently encouraged their dealerships throughout Wisconsin to become collection sites and encouraged their customers to consider donating their older, trade-in vehicles to Rawhide.

To launch this new venture, Jan and I were invited to take our group of boys on what was called a "roll-out tour" of ten regional

WATDA meetings scheduled throughout the state. We met hundreds of vehicle dealers who were very excited about hearing details of their new partnership with Rawhide. Gary had us share information about Rawhide and the need for developing a consistent source of income. As a highlight of every meeting, some of the boys told how their lives had already changed since coming to Rawhide. The tour was the start of a wonderful relationship that exists to this day. This relationship with WATDA continues to be the heart of the financial security of Rawhide.

Within three years more than three hundred dealerships had become collection sites, responsible for collecting over five thousand cars, trucks, boats, and campers per year. Rawhide became licensed as a vehicle dealership itself but, for liability reasons, we stopped selling cars to the public. Once a month, an auction was held at Rawhide. Up to four hundred licensed car dealers attended, and some traveled a couple hundred miles. They would arrive about seven in the morning and have access to the field of several hundred cars. They were given a printout listing every vehicle, the parking lane where it was located, and a few notes about the car. The keys were in the car, so dealers could start the engines and move them forward and back a few feet. Starting at ten o'clock, the cars would run through the auction line in the order they were listed on the printout, so dealers could make notes and decide ahead of time which ones they wanted to bid on.

Jim Carlson, an area auto auctioneer, agreed to donate his time to lead the sales. Cars would come in one door and stop in front of the auction platform. When Jim yelled, "Sold!" they moved out the other end of the building. The whole process took thirty seconds per car, and we were able to sell five hundred cars and trucks in about six hours.

The auctions also provided opportunities for the boys to earn extra money and learn new skills. Some worked in the commercial kitchen to help prepare a cafeteria meal for staff, volunteers, and the four hundred or so dealers. They assisted staff in registering dealers as they arrived, distributing bidder cards and giving wristbands that allowed all-day access to the elaborate buffet and beverages. Other boys directed parking, kept the grounds neat and clean, and helped staff keep track of every sale.

Beyond the vehicle donation program, Gary Williams remained personally involved with the ranch. Every year for twenty-five years, Gary hosted all the boys for a behind-the-scenes tour of the state capitol, which included a visit to the Supreme Court judges' chambers. The boys sat in seats in the senate and the assembly and met with the Attorney General and the Governor. The day also included a visit to the University of Wisconsin and a tour through the athletic facilities, where the boys were able to run out of the tunnel and onto the football field just like the Badger players.

Gary added a supportive note: "In the three decades that I have been taking the group of up to fifty Rawhide teens on this tour, there has never been one incident of misbehavior. The guys have always shown the utmost respect and appreciation to me and everyone they meet. Legislative and university personnel have commented numerous times about how the Rawhide boys are one of the most well-mannered groups they have ever encountered."

The Auto Dealers Association of Metro Milwaukee (ADAMM) added its oar to the WATDA boat to boost the vehicle donation program. This cooperative effort helped convince even more dealers and the public of Rawhide's importance. Dealers in the big cities, where land is at a premium, deserve an extra tip-of-the-hat for providing valuable space for parking the donated cars.

One story about an ADAMM member is especially worthy of mention. Ernie Von Schledorn has several dealerships in the Milwaukee area. Ernie called me one day a few years after he had started supporting Rawhide. His right-to-the-point comment was, "John, I have one hundred low-end cars I want to donate. The only catch is that you have to get them off my lot in forty-eight hours. Can you do that?"

"Of course. Where is the lot, and where are the keys?"

Within minutes our vehicle manager was on his way to Milwaukee to find a spot where we could quickly move all the cars. He found a large, unused factory parking lot a block from the dealership and quickly got permission to use it for a month. The next morning our car carriers, and several additional staff, headed to Ernie's lot. All the cars were moved by the end of a long day. The next week our trucks hauled them to the Greater Milwaukee Auto Auction, where they were turned into thousands of dollars of income for the ranch.

# Transformation

Thanks to the WATDA Team and the vehicle sales, Rawhide was transformed from a financially struggling program to one that finally had a dependable base of support. That financial stability enabled us to improve programs and to expand the number of boys we could accept.

The vehicle donation program, with help from WATDA, has grown to net several million dollars a year in support of the ranch. In addition, WATDA members raised the funds to build a new boys home, including offices to run the vehicle program and an impressive visitor center. Income from the vehicles has provided almost one-third of Rawhide's annual income.

Support of Rawhide Boys Ranch over the first fifty years has been outstanding. Bart and Cherry Starr and the Wisconsin Automobile and Truck Dealers Association lead the team of partners. The generosity of many has changed the lives of hundreds of boys and impacted many of their families as well.

# Mack Trucks

We promised the auto dealers we would pick up the donated vehicles they had on their lots at least once a week. But as the number grew to an average of more than one hundred cars per week, this became a challenge. We had started using small, one-car trailers to pick up the cars, but we soon supplemented those with our own semi-tractor, driven by a professional driver and pulling a six-car trailer. Bart talked to Coach Lombardi, whom he knew was a personal friend of the CEO and President of Mack Trucks, Zenon C.R. Hansen. Coach Lombardi contacted Mr. Hansen, and a date was set for the Mack corporate jet to fly him from Allentown, Pennsylvania, to Appleton for a visit to the ranch. Mr. Hansen and the other Mack executives who came with him were impressed by the program and the boys. They also saw the potential to raise a sizable amount of new income with the vehicle donation program. No other charities were encouraging car donations at the time.

The result of the visit was the donation of our first Mack semi-tractor. In addition, Mack offered to provide us with a second tractor (which we knew we would need within the year) on a factory-cost basis. This was all done in cooperation with Transquip, the local Green Bay Mack dealership, and its president, Frank Otto. Roger Kriete, owner of Milwaukee Mack and a leader in WATDA, was also a key player in the effort to get Mr. Hansen and the Mack leadership on the Rawhide Team.

# Snap-on Tools

By the fourth year of the vehicle program we had five certified mechanics on our staff. They worked in our new maintenance building, but had a poor assortment of tools. I wrote a letter to the president of the Wisconsin-based Snap-on Tool Corporation, Marion Gregory. I explained our need for dependable tools for our mechanics and the young men they were training. I did not get a reply for two months and assumed we were not going to get any tools.

One day my secretary called to say someone from Snap-on was headed my way. A gentleman entered my office and said, "My name is Clarence Niemi with Snap-on Tools. I was given a letter you wrote to our president, and I have our tools catalog for you."

He dropped a half-inch-thick, full-color catalog on my desk. It showed thousands of the tools and equipment offered by Snap-on. I asked if I could show him around, and he agreed. As we toured the shop, he saw the poor assortment of donated tools our mechanics were using to work with the boys. The tools were definitely not very good, but he liked the enthusiasm the boys demonstrated as they worked on the cars.

Clarence headed back to the home office and reported to his president. "We need to support Rawhide." A few days later Clarence called me to say Snap-on would consider a tool donation to the ranch and I should have our mechanics make a list of what they would like.

Our mechanics felt like it was Christmas as they went through the catalog as they made a list of tools and equipment they would like. Our office typed up the list and totaled the retail value. It came to many thousands of dollars. As bold as I was at soliciting donations for the ranch, this was far more than I thought was appropriate to ask for. I called Clarence and said, "My mechanics have put together this wish list, but I'm uncomfortable sending it because it is pretty expensive."

"I don't remember giving you a price limit," Clarence said. "Just send me what your staff would like to have, and we will see what we can do."

We mailed off the list of several pages of tools and supplies. In a few weeks he called. "John, this is Niemi, Snap-on Tools. I got your list, and I have good news, but there's one hitch. This is more than our foundation will let us give now, but since it is December, we will send half of your requested tools this month and the other half next month." Our mechanics and the boys indeed knew this was a Christmas miracle.

Snap-on CEO Marion Gregory and his wife, Fay, planned a trip to see Rawhide, but they arrived in a very unique way. They flew their privately owned military planes to the Appleton Airport, twenty miles from the ranch. Mr. Gregory's plane was a T-34 Trainer, and Fay flew her own T-6 Trainer. They were painted bright yellow, and the tail letters were "PA" on one and "MA" on the other. After a tour of Rawhide and a meal with the boys we all headed back to the airport, where we took a picture of the boys with the Gregorys' planes in the background. Each boy got an eight-by-ten photo, which we then sent to the Snap-on office to be autographed by Marion and Fay.

Over forty years have passed since this initial gift of Snap-on tools, but it was not their last. Every year they have met our needs with tools to keep up with the growth of the vehicle program. They even provided the funds to build a second auto maintenance shop, appropriately called the Snap-on Education Center. Not surprisingly, the Rawhide alumni who have gone on to automotive careers pick Snap-on as their favorite tools.

## Miller Welders

I had met Niels Miller and his wife in 1950, when they hired me to design a landscape plan for their home on the Fox River in Appleton. We became good friends partially because they liked my site design but also because Niels and I shared a love for welding. Niels and his engineer friend, Al Mulder, had invented the world's first high-frequency AC industrial welder two decades earlier. In 1935 he incorporated the Miller Electric Manufacturing Company, and it became a leader in the industry.

When Jan and I started Rawhide, I talked to Niels about his company donating a small welder for our shop. He did much more than that. He directed his research and development team to place prototype welders of various types in our shop. He wanted our staff and boys to use the equipment and give the Miller engineers feedback on how they worked when used by novice welders. In 1971 we used the first pre-market Millermatic, MIG welder.

When Niels died in 1993, the Illinois Tool Works, a multinational company based in Chicago, purchased the company. They continue Niels's passion for providing support to Rawhide and numerous other area charities.

## Heart of America Group

A favorite place for the staff and boys to eat is a rustic restaurant in Appleton called Machine Shed. The restaurant is part of the Heart of America Group of over thirty restaurants and hotels. It is also the restaurant where Jerry Monson, our first foster son, eats breakfast frequently.

One day Mike Whalen, founder and CEO of the corporation, came to Appleton on his quarterly visit. He noticed a donation canister for Rawhide on the checkout counter, prompting him to ask, "What is Rawhide?" Jerry was at the restaurant, and he was delighted to tell Mr. Whalen about the ranch. His enthusiasm prompted Mike to ask, "Would it be possible to visit the ranch now?" Jerry quickly offered to serve as his guide.

Mike was so impressed that when he got back to his office in Moline, Illinois, he invited a group of area leaders to share his new vision to start a youth program like Rawhide. He flew Jan and me to Moline to help develop an operational plan to serve youth from their area. The next year, they purchased four hundred acres of beautiful, rolling, wooded land with various farm buildings. They proceeded to expand the facilities and partnered with social service agencies and police departments to launch their plan to work with teenagers in need of help and encouragement. Since 2001, Wildwood Hills Ranch has annually hosted several hundred boys and girls, ages eight to eighteen.

Mike Whalen also had an interest in stock car racing, so when we decided to build a drag strip race-car at Rawhide, I asked him if his Heart of America Group would be our major sponsor with a $10,000 gift. He agreed, and we were off and running—or at least ready to get a Chevy Camaro off and running.

We joined a national organization called "Beat the Heat," which partners with youth charities and local police departments. We teamed-up with our local Waupaca County Sheriff's Department. The charities build or buy the race cars, and police officers drive the cars in drag strip competition. The youth, with staff supervision, become the pit crews and enthusiastic fans, cheering as their cars go down the track.

Because of our modern shop and tools and the skill of the mechanics who worked with the boys, we were able to have our car ready for competition in the late spring. The boys did all the new suspension work, welded the safety bars in place, and topped-off their masterpiece with a creative paint scheme. The engine was sent to a speed shop and came back at just under six hundred horsepower, plenty to make a good showing at the strips it would visit throughout the Midwest.

A covered tandem auto trailer, complete with Rawhide race graphics on both sides and pulled by a matching fifteen-passenger van, produced plenty of pride for the team of eight boys, police officers, and a few staff as they traveled to the events and pulled into the race grounds. Everyone involved had plenty of fun and learned quite a bit about racing, but there was an even greater benefit. Boys who may have previously been arrested by police officers were now able to work in partnership with them on an exciting project.

# Larry Eckes

While the story of our donated cars and maintenance buildings is a heartwarming show of generosity by many people, the true impact can be seen in the profound changes the training provided for the boys. Larry Eckes is one example. After his chaotic childhood, his interest in motor vehicles would steer him onto a path that became a lifetime career.

Larry was the second oldest of nine children, and he was fourteen years old when his father left the family. His mother loaded up the entire gang and made the move from Wisconsin to Indiana to start a new life. But things only got worse. After just a few months, in early May 1966, she and the kids headed back to Wisconsin. She stopped at her father-in-law's small home and unloaded everyone. She announced to him that the children were now his responsibility, and she drove off.

Larry's grandfather immediately called the county social services department and asked for help. The next day the county picked up all the children except Larry and placed them in a foster home. Larry had just turned fifteen, and a juvenile judge ordered that he be sent to Rawhide.

He enjoyed the rural setting and the horses. He especially liked having a big bedroom that he had to share with only one other guy. This was very different from the crowded homes in which he had grown up. He also liked helping Henry, who was in charge of ranch maintenance and vehicles. At this time Rawhide had a small, donated fleet of old trucks, a tractor, and the Cadillac hearse.

Larry's dad had been a successful dirt track race car driver in a Hudson Hornet during the era when the Hudsons were the fastest cars on the road or track. Under Henry Moeller's tutelage, Larry took over most of our early auto maintenance work, ranging from checking oil levels to changing water pumps.

By 1967 Larry's parents had reunited and gathered the children, including Larry, back to their Milwaukee home. The next year he finished high school and worked with his dad, who had started a roofing business. By now his love for cars had become a passion. One day he responded to an employment ad for rebuilding auto transmissions. He was hired by AAA Transmissions and worked there for three years. Thanks to his contacts with various area auto dealerships, he was hired as a service consultant at Brendt Buick, where he worked for the next twenty years.

Halfway through these years, the Wisconsin Auto and Truck Dealers Association adopted the Rawhide vehicle donation program. Brendt Buick volunteered to be one of the donation drop-off sites, and Mr. Brendt asked Larry if he would be the dealership manager for people donating cars. He quickly agreed, and during the next decade, Larry had the privilege of checking in hundreds of donated vehicles. He proudly told each donor that he was one of the first Rawhide alumni.

Collecting and fixing up cars became a passion for Larry. In his first year working at the Brendt dealership, he purchased ten 1957 Chevy cars. All were junkers, with the cheapest one costing him twenty-five dollars and the most expensive two hundred. He fixed half of them with usable parts from the others and then sold the repaired ones at a nice profit.

Since 1970 he has owned two hundred different classic, muscle, and stock cars, all needing work. His only car at the present time is a beautiful 1969 Chevy Yenko Nova, a rare car he restored. He rebuilt the 305 Camaro engine that was in it and added a nitro kit and a 7004 R racing transmission.

Larry, like many other teenagers who have gone through the Rawhide training programs, discovered new areas of talents and interests. The boys learned to follow directions from their supervisors and to take pride in doing a good day's work. It became a new way of life that allowed them to achieve success.

*[In 2004 the law was changed to determine the value of vehicles donated to charities. It drastically reduced income to Rawhide, and many charities. For more information see the (2004 Donation Law) on our website; www.Our351Sons.com.]

# CHAPTER 9

# IF WE BUILD IT, THEY WILL COME

## *John:*

Early in our first year of operation, I developed a long-range master plan for the five-hundred-acre grounds. As part of the goal to rebuild the lives of young men, I wanted to involve them as partners with our staff as we added to the ranch facilities.

For example, if staff members and boys worked together building a rabbit coop or a major building, either one provided an opportunity to teach good workmanship, a positive work attitude, and construction skills. In the end, whatever was built would benefit the lives of everyone at Rawhide and those to come in future years.

My vision of a western frontier village was becoming a reality. We added new buildings as the program expanded and funds became available. Main Street featured a frontier hotel, dining hall, stable and livery, visitors' center, gift shop, and a railroad station. Additional boys homes were planned in wooded areas around a man-made lake.

At this writing, the development continues on the five-hundred-acre campus. Many alumni that return for a visit, some in their '60s with grandchildren in tow, point with pride to one or two buildings they worked on.

# The Frontier Hotel

I became friends with Bob Sauter and Ben Seaborne, founders of a very creative architectural design firm, Sauter-Seaborne LLC. I got to know them when my firm was hired to do site development and landscape design for some of their commercial projects. They offered to donate their time to help with the site plan and to design a general-purpose building for Rawhide. This building, which would resemble an early 1900s frontier hotel, would be one of the anchor buildings located on Main Street.

Half of the first floor would house a commercial kitchen to prepare food for the camp program, and would include a large walk-in cooler and freezer. A dining room would give us a meeting place and allow us to serve meals for service clubs, church groups, and other organizations coming for a visit. The other half would include office space needed to manage the summer and year-round programs.

The upper level would be space for a second boys home, with four large bedrooms, two bathrooms, a kitchen, and a dining/living room. In addition, the houseparents would have their own comfortable living area.

Referrals from juvenile courts and social service agencies were exceeding the eight boys Jan and I could accept, so we were excited to double the capacity of the year-round program.

The frontier hotel was to have a rustic design of open beams that would require several hundred feet of twelve-by-twelve timbers. Luckily, we found just the massive beams we needed when the seventy-year-old Menasha Corporation paper mill was taken down. Even better, they were donated. We were trusting in God to help us find individuals and businesses to donate the remaining funds, labor, and materials.

Under the supervision of the architects, Henry worked with the boys and me to provide much of the labor for construction. Technical work for electrical, plumbing, siding, and roofing was completed with donated or discounted labor from local firms.

# Generosity Equips the Hotel

John Mosling was President and CEO of the Oshkosh Truck Corporation in Oshkosh, Wisconsin. Jan and I had met him and his wife, Jane, when they donated a horse to Rawhide. His company was discontinuing an employee meal program and asked if Rawhide could use an almost-complete commercial kitchen. The timing was perfect. Construction of the new hotel building was close to completion, and the architects were in the process of designing the kitchen area. One of the architects drove to Oshkosh and measured all the like-new equipment: stainless steel tables, storage cabinets, fryers, ovens, a dishwasher system, and a large commercial mixer. The only items missing that we would still need to find were a stove, walk-in refrigeration and freezer unit, and utensils.

About this time a salesman from the South Bend Range Company showed up at my office. He had read an article about our project and asked if we needed any appliances. I said, "We need a stove."

He smiled. "We have stoves."

I called Jan and Angie Schneider, a neighbor volunteer who

was helping with food service, and asked them to meet with me and the salesman. He opened his catalogs to show them the impressive options of commercial stoves his company carried. Jan and Angie had been giving a lot of thought to the size of the stove they would need. They both said, "It should have four open gas burners and a four-foot griddle."

"That would take a special-order stove and would be very costly," the salesman explained. "The closest options would be two open burners with a four-foot griddle, or four open burners with a three-foot griddle."

I then told the salesman that we had no money. I asked if his company had any used stoves in stock they might be willing to donate. He said they didn't take in used appliances, but he would send a note to the company headquarters to see if they could help in any way.

Two months later, we were ready to install appliances, but we still had no stove. The phone rang, and the caller identified himself as Mr. Osborne, president of the South Bend Range Company. He was holding a letter that said we needed a stove with four burners and a three-foot griddle. He said that, unfortunately, the company couldn't donate a stove of that size, but they did have a stainless-steel prototype that had been on display for the past year in their show room. If we wanted it, they would ship it to the ranch. We would pay only the freight cost.

I asked what size it was. Mr. Osborne answered, "It has four open burners and a four-foot griddle."

"Oh my gosh. That is just what we wanted!"

I called our staff together to share the amazing blessing of receiving exactly the stove Jan and Angie had requested. After we closed the meeting with a short prayer thanking God for this great gift, I noticed our maintenance and equine director, Chuck Skewes, looking deep in thought.

He said, "I don't want to sound ungrateful at all, but why would God give us a stove and ask us to pay the shipping?" Chuck has an abiding faith in God's goodness, and I appreciated his comment, but I was content with the shipping costs.

Two weeks later, a truck from the Seymour Transit Company pulled into the yard with our shiny new stove. Chuck brought up our tractor with a front bucket to unload the stove while I met the driver to ask what the shipping charges would be. He found his bill of lading, scanned it up and down, and said, "Nothing due. The company paid the shipping."

When I told Chuck, he pumped his fist in the air. "I knew God would take care of the shipping for us."

# Terry and Mary Kohler

The other items needed to complete the kitchen were a walk-in cooler and freezer and a variety of stainless steel kitchen utensils. I knew just the person to contact for help.

Terry Kohler had become a good friend, and he and his wife, Mary, had become very interested in Rawhide. They owned the Vollrath Company in Sheboygan, Wisconsin, an international company manufacturing commercial kitchen appliances, utensils, and especially coolers and freezers. I asked Terry what information I would need to send him in order for his company to consider donating a walk-in freezer and refrigeration units as well as a variety of kitchen utensils.

Terry had one of his designers talk directly with our architects to get the dimensions for the freezer and cooler units, locations of floor drains, and the electrical supply that would be needed.

About a month later, Terry called to set up a time the units could
be delivered, asking me to have one staff person and two or three
boys on hand to help with unloading and set-up. He also said we
should have a refrigeration expert install the two compressor units.
Del's Refrigeration was located only a few miles away, and they were
donating time for some of our other refrigeration needs. I was sure
they would help.

On the scheduled day, a Vollrath truck pulled into the yard, and
to my surprise the driver in company coveralls was Terry himself.
We had him back up to the new kitchen, and under Terry's direction, three boys and I went to work unloading the panels one by one
and snapping them together according to the architectural plan.

I introduced the boys to Terry, but I did not mention that he
was the owner and president of the company. The guys really related to Terry, and they started doing a lot of joking back and forth.
They enjoyed learning that he was a former military fighter pilot
and owned several airplanes plus a helicopter.

About two hours into the project, we all took a soda break, and
as we were sitting around the kitchen, Bill, one of the boys, turned to
Terry and said, "What do you do at the Vollrath Company?"

"I just do pretty much what has to be done, or what people ask
me to do," he replied.

"But what is your title? Are you a driver, an installer, or something else? You must have a job title."

"Actually," Terry replied, "I'm the owner and president."

Bill paused a minute before he called Terry's bluff. "I'm serious.
What is your title at the company?"

I could tell Terry was enjoying Bill's confusion. I intervened
and explained that Terry really was the owner. He liked Rawhide
so much he wanted to deliver and set up the units in order to spend

some time getting to know some of the boys. The boys were very impressed.

Terry and Mary went on to donate hundreds of utensils and four sections of hot and cold salad bar units. Their ongoing support over the years has included underwriting the costs to produce this book about Rawhide. Without their generosity, I doubt this book would have been written.

# The Stephensons

Town and Country Electric, started by Rollie Stephenson, was a company I was hoping to add to our support team. Rollie and his wife, Sue, responded to an invitation to visit Rawhide and see the electrical help we needed to finish the frontier hotel building. Soon after their visit, the phone rang, and Rollie asked if I could use two of his employees for a week or two. He said I could have them do electrical work on the building, clean barns, or anything we needed done. Rollie went on to say that their business was slow, and rather than lay-off the men, he wanted to keep them on full pay. I was delighted. The next day the two electricians arrived, and we put them to work on the hotel electrical projects.

Early the next morning, I got another call from Rollie. He asked if we could use two more men to work for a couple of weeks, and the calls did not stop. Within three weeks we had twenty-eight electricians who worked for a month and a half!

Once the hotel wiring was finished, we had numerous other projects for this great crew. With so much expertise right at hand, we decided to put up a new building: a barn for extra horses and hay. We had the lumber cut a year earlier by bringing in a portable sawmill that harvested trees from our own woods. The boards had

been stored and stickered for drying and were just waiting for someone to make a building out of them. The barn was erected in three
weeks. One of the Town and Country foremen asked permission
from Rollie to take the needed electrical supplies from the company
warehouse. He gave the OK, and soon the barn had a state-of-the-
art electrical system.

By this time we had a completed commercial kitchen and dining room to support the summer camp, and were able to provide a
hearty meal for the twenty-eight electricians, all the foster boys, and
the ranch staff. To make the occasion even better, Tom Boettcher,
an alumnus of the Rawhide program, was an electrician with Town
and Country. He was happy to provide encouragement to the current foster boys as they ate their meals together.

# Tom and Holly Boettcher
## *Jan:*

John just explained that Tom Boettcher was one of the staff of the
electrical team donating time to help Rawhide. Tom's generosity as
an adult is a special encouragement for us, because he was one of
the boys who lived with John and me.

Tom had an ongoing conflict with his parents for a very different
reason than most of the teenagers the courts sent to. Tom worked
too hard. Besides being a good student, he worked thirty hours a
week at a grocery store as a fifteen-year-old, and he was always looking for odd jobs around his town. He began paying room and board
to his parents, but they did not like his independence. One day he
passed out at work, and they suspected he was using drugs. But tests
determined he was hypoglycemic, meaning he had too little sugar in
his blood.

Tom's mother worked full-time for the Shawano County Jail, and one of her jobs was to drive prisoners to the Winnebago Mental Health Hospital in Oshkosh for evaluation. She knew the right people to get Tom admitted without a court order, and this started his contact with the county juvenile court system. Based solely on his parents' frustration, the courts sent Tom to live with us in January 1971.

John alerted me that Tom had an interest in horses, and I showed him the stables on his first visit. Tom's positive attitude and dependable work habits were evident from his first day with us, and he soon became my assistant with the horse program. He was enrolled as a senior at New London High School.

Holly Kamba was also a senior, and she lived on a small farm two miles from Rawhide. She had a horse of her own, a mare that she loved, and we had a stallion at the ranch. She worked a deal with me to have her mare bred in exchange for her cleaning the leather on a dozen saddles. While we worked together, Holly told me her two favorite things were horses and boys, in that order. Holly was a good student, played in the band, and worked part-time during the school year and full-time every summer.

On Tom's first day in school, Holly saw him walking down the hall and said to herself, "I'm going to marry him." At that time, she knew nothing about him, not even that he was from Rawhide. They got to know each other as Holly helped me with the horses during the school year and during the summer as she helped me with the horses and as our housekeeper.

Holly's plan to marry Tom came true three months after they graduated from high school. Even though they were both very mature for their age, John and I suggested they wait at least a year or two before marrying. They married after graduation anyway, and they have proven they were more ready than we realized.

Tom accepted a job with a local electrical company and set his sights on becoming the best electrician possible. He honed his skills through the apprentice program at the Fox Valley Technical College. He moved up the employee ranks with three different companies. He became a Master Electrician and worked as a senior project supervisor for thirty years with Faith Technologies, Inc., previously known as Town and Country Electric.

Holly applied for a sales position with J.J. Keller and Associates, an international company serving the trucking industry and a major support donor to Rawhide. She advanced during her twenty years with the company to become a senior account executive, traveling around the nation to lead safety seminars for their construction and utility customers.

Holly is a Master Gardener, and in order to maintain her rating, she was required to complete thirty-six volunteer hours per year in community projects. She did much more. She was chair of the Greenville Forestry Board and served on the community gardens committee. In 2010 she was awarded the Greenville Volunteer of the Year award. Holly went on to become a senior supervisor with J.J. Keller & Associates.

For the past twenty years, Tom has been an active member of the Greenville Lions Club and has donated all the electrical work for a sixty-acre Lions mega-community park. Along with numerous shelter facilities, the park has an amphitheater that seats twelve thousand guests and a state-of-the-art stage for some of the nation's top bands. In 2011, Lions International Foundation awarded Tom the prestigious Melvin Jones Fellow award for his dedicated humanitarian services.

In retirement, they have embarked on what started out forty

years ago as Tom's hobby, making wine. Their dream to build their own winery has come true. They purchased thirteen acres of land, including a vintage barn that was ideal for their production area and a sampling and sales area. They hired an Amish family to remodel the barn and add other support buildings. In 2013, they harvested their first crop of grapes as the vines reached their third year of growth at their very popular Whistler's Knoll Vineyard in Horton-ville, Wisconsin.

In preparation for writing this book, we sat down with them to record some of their memories from their Rawhide years. In the course of talking John asked, "Tom, when did you develop an interest in making wine?"

He looked at Holly with a sheepish grin. She looked back with a smile and said, "Tell him, Tom." He looked back and said, "Well, I made my first batch of wine in my closet at Rawhide after Peter Zukas and I got a book from the high school library. We didn't want anyone to smell our experiment, so we taped a tight cover on the container. Everything was going well until it exploded after a few days. We missed the part about letting the container breathe."

## Boys Home Facilities

### *John:*

After just a few years, we realized that the good results we were achieving with the boys living with us had prompted the court and other agencies to send far more referrals than we had room for. We had to expand in order to accept more boys. The problem was that the cost of the program was almost double what the counties could pay. Therefore the expansion of the facilities had to be balanced with the funds available. The five-year plan the Rawhide Board of

Directors developed at the urging of Chet Krause helped address this funding shortage. During the first three decades, we were able to build an additional home about every four years, and with the help of growing team of donors, we raised the funds to operate them.

Our commitment to a traditional family experience was evident in the space we provided for each home. My previous building design and construction experience prepared me to develop the plans for all the boys homes except one. That home was designed by the Associated Builders and Contractors of Wisconsin, referred to as ABC. Their membership companies supplied the design and material and donated all the labor to build the ABC Home.

Each home is about ten thousand square feet. The first floor provides a large living room, a recreation area for a pool table and table games, an office, a dining room, and a complete kitchen with a food storage area.

The first floor also includes an apartment for the houseparents. Because this is their full-time home for an average of six to ten years, they need comfortable housing. In addition, we encouraged them to have their adult children and grandchildren visit often. Minor children would be living with them. This provided a great family model for the boys.

A door off the living room leads to the start of a thousand-square-foot houseparent apartment. If the door is open, the boys can knock and go in. If it's closed (and probably locked), that means the houseparents need some privacy. In addition to the living room, the apartment consists of a kitchenette and dining area, a large master bedroom with an attached bath, and two more bedrooms with a shared bath. The ample size of personal living space is a big help in attracting qualified houseparents and in keeping them for a much longer tenure than is typical for most other residential programs.

Staff turnover is always disruptive for the boys, who have had so many broken relationships. The long tenure of houseparents has been a hallmark of Rawhide's success.

The second floor contains the boys' bedrooms and private rooms for each of the three support staff members who live there and assist the houseparents. The support staff are called "resident instructors"—RIs for short. They are generally young men who recently graduated from college. Their role is building relationships with the boys, much like big brothers, as they support the houseparents. One of the three RIs per house could be a young woman. On the houseparents' days off, two RIs are on duty. When the houseparents are there, only one RI is needed. This system worked well for everyone, and they all had two days a week off, plus four weeks of vacation a year. This schedule prevents staff burnout and turn-over.

There were five boys bedrooms designed to house two boys each, and each is furnished with our unique bed arrangement from my original college dorm design. Two additional bedrooms consist of single rooms that could be used for new boys or boys going through unusual challenges. All of the rooms have private bathrooms. Each of the RIs has a large combination bedroom/sitting room with a private bath.

The homes are built on the side of a hill, so the lower level has walk-out access to the outdoors. The lower level features a large recreation room, a storage area, and a bedroom with an attached bath for visiting parents or other guests.

# ABC of Wisconsin

Associated Builders and Contractors of Wisconsin is an eight-hundred-member trade association with a strong focus on community volunteerism. I was invited to be the keynote speaker at the association's 1996 Projects of Distinction banquet. I shared the success of Rawhide, and explained that this success actually had us in a bind. We were getting referrals of more boys in need of help, but we were out of room. We needed another youth home.

Board member Tammy Altmann had been asked to research how member companies could unite to help relieve a community need. She thought building a home for the ranch might be a great state project. After the meeting, Tammy asked me for more details, and I shared the requirements for the ten-thousand-square-foot building.

Tammy didn't blink an eye. "Wow! This would be a great project."

The next step was for her to share some preliminary ideas with the state president, Jerry Stodola. He was delighted with the project and got unanimous board approval for their executive director, Steve Stone, to begin.

The project involved dozens of framers, insulators, masons, electricians, plumbers, finish carpenters, roofing and siding firms, painters, flooring and furniture suppliers, and landscapers. The ABC Team donated thousands of hours of labor and raised several thousand dollars to purchase various supplies. The beautiful building was completed in September 1999. The staff was already hired and trained, and they were ready to move in the day the building was finished.

Bart and Cherry were on hand for the grand opening to join Jan and me and all the Rawhide staff and boys in thanking the ABC Team for their stellar achievement. Boys started arriving a few weeks later, and the new home and counseling center was soon filled to capacity.

# CHAPTER 10
# HELP IS ON THE WAY

*John:*

As Rawhide expanded with additional homes, our goal was to maintain the close family environment Jan and I had established. Our challenge was to find dedicated couples who would serve as caring houseparents for each of the boys homes. We also had to find people to provide a variety of services, such as social work, academic support, and vocational training. Each member of our growing team did his or her part to help each boy have the opportunity to turn his life around.

In the early days of Rawhide, our needs were basic. We needed a secretary and help with meal preparation. In addition to our first volunteer, Henry, there were others who appeared on our doorstep at exactly the right time.

# *Jan:*

We were blessed with our next staff member, Jo Anne "Jo" Pulido, our first secretary. Jo came to the door in 1968 and asked if we needed some office help. A volunteer at the ranch, a friend of Jo's, had mentioned to her that we needed some secretarial help. We met with Jo, explaining the need but clarifying that we could only pay a small hourly wage. She accepted the job.

We kept Jo very busy with promotional mailings, daily progress records regarding the boys, thank-you letters to donors, and the constantly-ringing phone. Because she lived nearby and was a respected community member, she was a big help in sharing our mission with neighbors who were nervous about having "juvenile delinquents" moving into their neighborhood.

Jo would continue to work at Rawhide as our faithful "right hand" for thirty-five years. She became the go-to person for anything we needed to know or find. In that time our staff grew from just her and Henry to 144 employees.

We always regarded caring for our staff as an important part of Rawhide's ministry. As John and I were writing this book, we received an unsolicited message from Jo. Her letter, which follows, provides some insight into the work God has done through Rawhide to help not only the boys but also the staff who served them:

Dear John and Jan.

I'm sure looking forward to seeing the book about Rawhide when it is published, as the ranch has been such a blessing to me personally. Following are some thoughts about how working there for thirty-five years has impacted my life.

I learned to be more patient and understanding with others. It helped me develop my organizational skills that help in every part of my life. I learned to respect and submit to authority even when I didn't agree with or understand the whole concept. I learned to love and honor Angelo, my husband, especially when I don't agree with him. Best of all, because of Rawhide, I saw the need to accept Jesus as my personal Savior. Yeah!!! And the list goes on.

Please know you guys and Rawhide have helped me become the wife, mother, grandmother, and great grandmother that I am. I absolutely treasure my time at the ranch. Thank you.

Love,

Jo

The next person to come onboard was a housekeeper. John came home one day from a monthly board meeting with the exciting news that there were sufficient funds to hire someone to help with meals and housekeeping. This was a wonderful blessing, as John was gone a lot giving talks to churches and service clubs and meeting with potential donors. My days were very busy with meals, laundry (teaching the boys to do laundry was an exercise in futility), getting all the boys off to school, helping with fundraising and promotional mailings, meeting with social workers and parents, and welcoming the endless stream of visitors. We had at least one visitor a day, and it was not uncommon to have three or four cars arrive to see the youth ranch they had been reading about. Everyone was invited into the dining room, and if John was gone, I would share what we were doing. The coffee pot was always ready.

A week after I received approval to hire a housekeeper, John asked how my search was going. "John, it's under control," I said. He did not ask any more questions. A week later he asked the same question, and I gave him the same answer.

Three weeks later and a week before John had his next board meeting, he asked again, "What is happening with getting a housekeeper? I don't want to hear that it is under control." He asked if I had run an ad in the local paper, and I said no. He asked if I had called any area pastors or priests to see if they could refer someone. I said no. Very sternly, he said, "The board will want a report next week, and I need to tell them what is happening."

"I have asked God to send someone because I don't have the time to do interviews," I replied. "If I run an ad in the paper, I'll get a dozen ladies driving out here, and I will have to spend at least an hour with each one and then make reference calls. I just don't have the time to do that." I could tell he wasn't convinced that this was the right approach, but he said OK and walked away shaking his head.

Two days later, we were all eating supper when a white Volkswagen Beetle pulled into the driveway and stopped in front of our house. A lady got out, so I headed for the door to meet her.

Before I even invited her in, she said, "My name is Bernice Besch. My husband and I live about five miles away, and I have been reading the stories in the paper about Rawhide. For several years I have been in charge of food service at the Embassy Suites in Appleton. Our family is active at the First Assembly of God Church, and I appreciated reading that the boys ranch is a faith-based program." Her last comment was the biggest blessing. "I have wrestled the past month with the feeling that I should check to see whether you need a housekeeper. I would really like to be part of a program like this."

"Come in," I said. "I've been waiting for you."

I took a quick glance at John, who was sitting at the end of the dining room table with a look of amazement on his face. But it was just what I expected God to do.

Bernice worked for us for more than two years and was a wonderful blessing. Her showing-up at the door, just as Jo and Henry had done, was one more indication that God was blessing our program to help boys.

# Houseparents

## *John:*

Jan and I grew up in secure, loving homes and wanted to duplicate that environment in all of our boys homes at Rawhide. Our plan was to avoid using shift-work staff to work with the boys. We believe that the best environment for raising children includes a firm but loving mom and dad who have already successfully raised their own family. During the final interviews with potential houseparents, we insisted that they invite as many of their children, and sometimes even grandchildren, as possible to come with them to the ranch for a meal. In a couple of hours, it was easy to see whether the family was friendly and respectful by how the children interacted with their parents.

We realized that it was important for houseparents to have a lot of time to spend with the boys. This would mean that, to keep from burning out, they would need a support team to help them. We were able to develop a staffing plan to support houseparents that included a housekeeper and two or three RIs. Each house consisted of eight to ten boys at a time. With constant turnover—one boy leaves and a new one moves in—the group dynamics were changing almost every month. It was necessary to have enough staff to spend time with each boy and with the whole group. Over the thirty-five years that Jan and I were houseparents, it was our privilege to live with a total of 351 teenage foster sons. We were "Mom and Dad" while they were living with us, and five decades later, we still have close contact with many of them. And they still call us Mom and Dad.

As we added more homes for more boys, we looked for houseparents who fit certain criteria: an active couple, married at least five years, in their 40s or older, who had raised or were raising children of their own. As a faith-based program, we hired committed Christians. It did not matter what their church affiliation was, but we sought staff that were guided by their faith. We did not want to put pressure on the boys to accept Christianity, but we wanted staff to be role models of that belief and lifestyle.

Many of the boys came from homes with a parent or parents who didn't have the time or skills to do much nurturing. We wanted the houseparents at Rawhide to live with the boys as examples of how family members who love each other can work through challenges with a faith that is rooted in caring, forgiveness, and biblical values.

Each home had its own fifteen-passenger van and a car or station wagon parked right outside exclusively for staff use. The vehicles were kept clean and well maintained by the staff and boys.

Houseparents had the responsibility to manage their schedule independent of the other homes, and to be spontaneous about activities with the boys. For example, each house had a typical bedtime at ten thirty, but if the boys and staff were ending a productive and perhaps emotional discussion close to bedtime, the houseparents could ignore the rule and load up the van to head to a favorite late night eatery, like Frank's Pizza in Appleton. Those kinds of bonding experiences can be wonderful, but for them to happen, houseparents needed the authority to make spontaneous situational decisions, just like a regular mom and dad would make.

# Dave and Jeannine Rich

Dave and Jeannine moved to Rawhide with their two daughters and became the houseparents of the second house we opened. They were both excellent with the boys. Dave had been a county probation officer and summer camp counselor at Rawhide. Jeannine was a compassionate and caring housemom who built strong relationships as she bonded with the boys in their home.

Our introduction to Dave came through our summer camp program. As a probation agent, he brought some of the most difficult boys on his case load with him when he volunteered as a camp counselor one week each summer. One of the boys was Mike Lensby, introduced earlier in this book. Another one of his boys was David Seidel. Like Mike, David was a high school dropout in serious need of guidance.

David excelled during the camp week. He was the top camper out of forty boys, and this qualified him to stay for the rest of the summer as an assistant. One of his jobs was to monitor the boys from the year-round, residential program when a few of them took the three-hour GED test at a local university. We told David that we wanted him to understand what the boys were experiencing and take the test himself. Reluctantly he agreed. He was not told we had officially signed him up for the test. When we got the results back his scores qualified him to apply to a college, the same as with a high school diploma.

We encouraged David to consider college. He did, and was

accepted as a freshman at the University of Wisconsin-Oshkosh. He had gone from a high school dropout to a college freshman within two weeks. He finished his first year on the Dean's List. He transferred to California and went on to get his BA degree in Sociology. Soon after he began his professional career. He is now a Senior Investment Director with Oppenheimer & Co. in Seattle, Washington.

# Rich and Janet King

The need arose for a third set of houseparents, but we didn't have any leads. A concert was scheduled at Rawhide with a national music group, and a large crowd of adults and teens were expected to attend. Good friends of ours, Don and Sue Pennau, called to say they were bringing friends, and they hoped we could take them on a tour. "They are a neat couple," said Don, "and I think they would be great houseparents, but I won't mention this to them."

When they arrived, they introduced their friends, Rich and Janet King. Jan and I were immediately impressed. We took them through the home we were managing and introduced them to the boys. We explained what a great ministry it was to live with the boys for a year or two and then to see them succeed later in life. We mentioned that we currently needed a set of houseparents. I explained it had been a blessing to have the great staff that had become part of the ranch team and that we were asking God to send us the houseparents we would need in the next month. "It is exciting, because we believe God has already picked the couple to come to work with us, but He has not told us, and He has probably not told them, either."

On the drive home, in the backseat of the Pennaus' car, Rich turned to Janet and said, "Do you think it is us?"

"Is what us?" asked Janet.

"Could we be the couple God wants to come and work with the boys at Rawhide?"

"You have got to be kidding."

Over the next few days, the Kings talked and prayed about the Rawhide job, then said they would like to meet with us again. After our meeting, we were even more impressed; they would be excellent houseparents. After several reference calls we offered them the job. Within thirty days Rich had sold a successful insurance agency, his office building, and their home. Along with their teenage son, Brian, they made the move to Rawhide.

Rich and Janet served a total of sixteen years as houseparents for 135 different boys. Janet was a great mom, and Rich, a hunter and fisherman, was a super dad. He was also very creative. One day I saw one of the boys from the Kings' home sitting on the top rail of the corral with a scoop shovel in his hand. I asked what he was doing.

"I got into trouble, and Rich told me I would be on restriction for two days. But if I can catch the poop from every horse before it hits the ground over a one-hour period he would let me off."

As he was talking to me, he never took his eyes off the twenty horses moving around the corral feeders. Then he saw a horse hunch its back and raise its tail slightly, the clear signal it was about to produce a shovel full of what is affectionately called "horse apples." He leaped off the fence and ran, successfully catching every apple before it hit the ground.

# Tom and Jean Bair

Tom Bair was definitely a character, and his southern background endeared him to the boys. He was an avid hunter who used only an old muzzleloader. He seemed to have a catch phrase for every situation: "Haven't seen you in a coon's age;" "It's so dry the trees are whistling for the dogs;" "I feel like I was rode hard and put up wet;" "I'm as happy as a puppy with two tails." and dozens more. The boys loved his down-home wit and his practical advice and example.

Jean was a mother filled with wisdom and love. She was an excellent cook, and their home was the place to find an excuse to drop in around mealtime. You would be invited to sit down with them and their boys to share whatever was on the table.

Their daughter, Kris, worked with Jan and me for several years as one of our RI's, and did a great job. She was able to have fun with the boys, but she had the maturity and firmness to command their respect.

# Gary and Kay Thompson

Kay was Jan's cousin, and she and Gary had an extensive background in Christian ministry work when they made the move to work at Rawhide. They had two children, Tim and Tammy. Over two decades Gary held several positions other than houseparent at Rawhide, including business manager and director of family counseling. When I retired he became the executive director.

Opposite from Jan and me, Gary was the firm hand and Kay was the softie in their home. But together they formed an excellent team to mentor and care for the boys. Gary's firmness was balanced with his ability to recognize when he was being too stern.

One story in particular is very touching. Just as we expect the boys to accept and serve their discipline when they goof up, we expect staff to be open and able to apologize when they make a mistake. Most of the boys have grown up with parents and other authority figures whom they've seen lose their tempers or make other mistakes, but who have rarely apologized for their failures.

On one occasion Gary lost his temper and shouted at a boy in front of the others. After a short time, Gary realized he was out of bounds and needed to apologize. Since he had scolded the young man in front of the other boys, he knew he also had to apologize in front of all the boys.

As everyone was seated for the evening meal, Gary announced he had a public apology to make. He mentioned how unfair he had been and asked the young man if he would forgive him for his terrible response. The boy got up from his chair and ran around the table to where Gary was seated. He threw his arms around Gary, and with tears in his eyes, said, "Dad, of course I forgive you." By this time everyone around the table was wiping their eyes.

It is important that children see parents and others being willing to recognize their own limitations and apologize for their errors. Children have great respect for authority figures who are honest about their mistakes.

# George and Judy Massey

Because of a medical situation we unexpectedly found ourselves with an immediate need of houseparents for one of the boys homes. We went to our family for help. Jan's sister, Judy, and her husband George lived nearby and were experienced parents, raising a son and daughter of their own. They were excited and felt privileged to help out for a few months. George kept his job in the paper business, and Rawhide became their new home, not just for a few months, but for four years.

They were a fun-loving and nurturing couple. Their personalities were much like Jan's and mine. Judy was the strict-one and George the soft-touch. The boys were drawn to this relationship, with the challenges and blessings of a traditional family home. It was something most had never experienced.

Judy and Jan loved animals. Each had a Great Dane in their house and realized the positive influence these dogs had on the boys. Their appearance and personalities were very much alike and they shared the same affection for animals. On one occasion they decided to swap clothes to see if their dogs could tell them apart. The boys were very entertained as they watched the dogs circle and sniff to find out to whom each belonged. It was not until Judy and Jan spoke to them that they relaxed.

The Rawhide experience had a ripple effect on George and Judy's children. Their son Chad returned to the ranch after finishing college and worked for several years as a Residential Instructor in one of the boys homes, along with our son Tim. Daughter Kim has made a career as a professional fundraiser for nonprofit organizations.

After three decades, George and Judy still have close contact with and continue to provide encouragement, for many of the boys who had lived with them as part of their Rawhide family.

# Houseparent Fun

There was great camaraderie among the houseparents, and we all met weekly to talk over the blessings and challenges of each of our homes. Once a month we would go out for dinner. On a December evening as eight of us piled into one of the vans, we noticed our wives had fancy wrapped boxes, obviously Christmas gifts for us husbands.

After we had finished the meal at a nice supper club, each of our wives handed us her package and invited us to open them. What we received was a big surprise, as three months earlier the girls had driven to Green Bay to meet with a woman who had a fashion photography studio.

As each of us opened our gift, we were amazed to see glamorous shots of our wives, which were discreet but definitely on the edge of discretion for a public restaurant. A week earlier, the wives had talked about how they thought their husbands would react when we opened the pictures. Two said their husbands would show the pictures at the table. Kay said Gary would probably not show it to anyone. Jan said I would show it to all the tables within view. Their predictions were exactly what happened. My gift, unlike the beautiful single photos from the other moms, was a calendar interspersed with six glamour photos.

We housefathers were not to be outdone, and we decided to have our own glamour shots taken the next year, but we were not about to spend any money on the project. We got together and decided what each picture would be, and I set up a photo shoot at four locations around the ranch. We staged a picture to fit each man's interests, with a theme sign drawn with a jumbo marker pen on a two-by-three-foot piece of cardboard. It was early December with a foot of snow on the ground.

"Gary Golfing" was Gary Thompson, an avid golfer. In his picture he stood in a foot of snow in boxer shorts, snow boots, and no shirt. He had his red golf bag and a golf club in his hands, ready to tee off.

"Baer Hunting" was Tom Baer, an avid hunter. He carried on the theme with a coonskin cap, boxer shorts, and no shirt, standing in a snow-covered grove of pine trees with his muzzleloader rifle aimed and ready to fire.

"Car King" was Rich King, an avid car collector, lying on the snowy fender of a car giving the peace sign. He was wearing bright yellow boxers, tennis shoes, and a yellow paper crown on his head.

"John on John" was my sign, and I was sitting on an old toilet that had been discarded in the ranch dump, reading a newspaper with my shorts sort of at half-mast.

I had previously set up the signs and props at each of the four areas where we would take the pictures, and we agreed to meet in front of our house during halftime of a Sunday Packers game. Everyone was dressed appropriately, and we headed to the first site. Within a few minutes the picture was taken, and we were back in the car and racing to site number two. We finished all the pictures and were back in time for the second-half kickoff. We sent the film to a photo shop to have eight-by-ten-inch prints made. I then put them into simple frames.

In early December, a year after the girls had given us their pictures, we headed out to a nice Italian restaurant for our monthly dinner. At the end of the meal we presented our gifts to the girls and, of course, they were met with hilarious laughter as each was opened. In fact, the tables near us got into the act, passing the pictures around. Pretty much the whole restaurant crowd and the wait staff saw them in the next few minutes.

Any successful venture is built on investing time to build relationships among those working together, and it helps when they can have some fun. We had plenty of fun!

# Sometimes Knowing Less Is Better

Since we had grown to four homes, the houseparents requested that we change the policy of having only our social worker review the boys' histories before accepting them for placement. When they came to me with their request, I agreed that we would talk about it at our Wednesday morning meeting. Jan and I were joined by the other houseparents, our social worker, and Bill Kluth.

Bill had been placed with us by a Wisconsin county two years earlier. Just as with Ben, one of our first eight boys, we didn't receive the first monthly payment for Bill. His county social service agency replied that they had no record of his being placed with us. After six months of trying to work this out, we just gave up and continued working with Bill with no financial support. Over the years we have had other funding glitches, but once boys arrived, we never forced them to leave because of funding problems. They had faced enough disappointments in their lives already.

When Bill turned nineteen, he was not ready to move out on his own. We asked him to stay on as a staff assistant, and he was delighted. He had already been providing help to the houseparents, and they loved his positive attitude. In preparation for our meeting to talk about the houseparents' question, I asked Bill if I could use him as an example and share some of his history. He agreed with a grin and promised not to tell anyone the record I would read was his.

Our social worker told me that Bill's history described him as one of the most disturbed boys we had ever accepted. Since age seven he had been placed in six different foster homes, two group homes, two detention centers, and a mental hospital. Every new placement gave up on him because of terrible behavior and aggressiveness.

As the meeting reached the main topic of interest, I explained that the houseparents would like to have final approval of the boys before they were placed in their homes. I explained it was Jan's and my opinion that we could be much more objective with boys if we did not have all the details of their past. At that point I said I wanted to share the record of a boy we were "considering" accepting, and I read the first three pages of Bill's past without saying it was his background.

At the end, I asked if any of the houseparents would be willing to accept that person. In unison, the houseparents said, "Of course not!" After pausing a few seconds, I said, "You have just rejected the young man at the end of the table, Bill Kluth." He was sitting with his arms crossed and a big grin on his face. The houseparents got the point. "I guess we don't want to know the background of the boys."

# A Lifetime Invitation

The boys sent to live with us at Rawhide are told they are welcome to maintain contact with their house staff and with Rawhide after they leave. Every set of houseparents has several alumni that they are in close contact with. Of course, many of the boys are now grandparents, and their houseparents have been retired from Rawhide for many years.

It was a rare week that Jan and I didn't get a call or a visit from one of the 351 young men who lived with us. However, we would not call them young men anymore. Most of them are collecting Social Security. If I happened to answer the phone when they called, we would chat a few minutes, and then they always say, "Is Mom there?" If Jan was available, it was not unusual for the call to go on for a half hour or more.

# CATCH Homes

Some of the young men placed with us did not have a home to go back to after their stay at Rawhide, so an area couple opened the way for us to develop a series of CATCH Homes. I had a passion for using acronyms with "catchy" words. This one stands for Community Alternative Transition Children's Homes, where married couples would be licensed as foster parents and take one or two boys at a time after they left the ranch.

Don and Marion Koepke became acquainted with Rawhide when they pulled their houseboat alongside a broken-down pontoon boat from the ranch. They towed it a mile back to the ranch. During a tour, they liked what they saw and asked me if we were looking for people to mentor the boys after they leave. In a guarded response, I replied that most of the boys return to their parents. I had just learned that Don was the CEO and owner of a concrete pipe company in Appleton, but I knew nothing else about him and Marion.

A week later, we received a small check from the Koepkes and an enclosed letter that indicated they would like to be mentors for one of the boys. They requested that the boy came from Appleton, did not have a father, and was from a Lutheran background. I thought that was very specific and skeptically wondered if they had a preference for height, weight, and hair color. Our office sent a thank-you letter for the gift the next day, as was our policy, but did not mention a boy for them to mentor. I put their letter on my desk, not knowing how to respond.

After two weeks, Don told Marion that Rawhide was probably a rip-off and asked her to send a letter of frustration directly to Bart Starr. A few days later, I got a call from Bart, who read the Koepke letter to me on the phone. "John, can you follow up on this right away? It seems they want to help and are upset with our lack of response."

I said I would contact them at once. I asked our social service director if we had a boy that met the Koepkes' criteria. Amazingly, we had a fourteen-year old who was close to discharge, was from Appleton, had no father involved, and whose mother listed Lutheran as her religious association.

I called to set up a meeting with Don and Marion at their home to start an interview process for them to mentor Mike Smith. His mother was very receptive to a mentoring couple to help her with Mike. Don and Marion owned a sprawling six-bedroom, three-and-a-half bathroom home on a five-acre wooded lot with room for two or three foster boys. Their three children were grown and no longer lived at home.

Don and I became good friends, and we both had the same sense of humor. Early in our relationship, I called their home and was greeted by a new twist, a response from an automatic answering machine. The recording started, "Hello, you have reached Don and Marion's new phone recorder. When you hear the beep, just leave your name and number and we will call you back. Thank you."

I started with something like, "Hi Don, this is John, and this is my first time facing one of these answering machines. It's really neat. I'm wondering if there is a time limit or if I can talk a long time? By the way, I'm finishing a study in the Bible and it's amazing. Let me read you the first few chapters of what I studied."

I then proceeded to read every word of the first four chapters of Genesis. It probably took about twenty minutes.

I had no word back from the Koepkes that they had received my message, so I assumed their recorder didn't work, but I was not going to mention what I had done. A few weeks later they invited Jan and me to spend a Saturday afternoon on Lake Poygan in their houseboat. When we got to the middle of the lake, Don shut off the motor and asked if he could play me one of his favorite cassette tapes before we had lunch. I said that would be just fine. Don turned on the cassette player, and my message from his phone started to play. We all started to laugh, except Don. With a straight face he said, "I'm not sure what you are all laughing about. This is a really interesting story from God's Word, and I want you to listen."

We listened to all four chapters, with Don asking us not to interrupt. It was a long, boring twenty minutes, and no food or beverage was served until the end of the cassette. When it ended, he laughed and asked if I wanted to keep the cassette to play at home. He went on to say that when he got home, he saw the red light on the answering machine indicating that there were twelve messages, and mine was the first. But there was no way to fast forward to select the next message, so he had to listen to the entirety of mine in order to get to the rest. And since he ran a large corporation, he assumed at least some of the messages would be business related.

A week later Jan and I were visiting with two of the boys in front of the barn when Don pulled in the driveway and stopped right next to us. Standing with us were our two mischievous goats that the boys named Richard and John, after Rich King and myself, supposedly because we were always up to some mischief.

Don opened the door of his red Corvette and held out a certificate beautifully printed in calligraphy on parchment paper.

"So what is this?" I asked.

"I just came from the American National Bank board meeting, and I have been selected to be on their board," Don proudly replied. "What do you think of that?"

Before we could reply that we were impressed, Richard the goat took a corner of the certificate in his mouth and ripped about a quarter of the paper out of Don's hand. He proceeded to eat it. We knew we should not laugh, but it was difficult to keep a straight face during the awkward silence as Don watched the goat chomp down his prized certificate.

That meal took about thirty seconds, and as Richard finished with a burp, Don handed him the rest of the sheet. In another minute he ate that also. I do know if the bank still let him serve as a board member.

That was the start of decades of the Koepkes mentoring young men from Rawhide. Mike was the first of dozens of boys whom they mentored. Mike and Don hit it off from the start. In later years, Mike told me he thinks part of the attraction was that, in a lot of ways, he and Don were the same age emotionally. In truth, Don and Marion had fun with the boys and were excellent mentors who were full of wisdom.

Don taught Mike to play the guitar, and he soon became part of a start-up band. That led to forming a band that provided most of the money Mike needed to work his way through college. He earned a degree in education. He went on to teach and get involved in politics, serving over a decade as an alderman on the Appleton City Council. Mike married Babs, and the Koepkes assisted at their wedding.

The experience with the Koepkes prompted us to recruit two-dozen more CATCH couples to become foster parents. They would take one or two Rawhide boys who could not return to their families but still needed help until they turned eighteen, and in some cases beyond that age.

# Social Service Staff

One of the things Jan and I learned from visiting residential youth programs around the nation was that young staff members were usually hired to work shifts in the homes, but they were supervised by social workers who didn't live with the youth. The houseparent staff were not seen as parents but just shift workers who had very little authority. The youth could manipulate the social workers to override decisions of the houseparents and the other living unit staff. We did not want that to happen at Rawhide. The state of Wisconsin and each county have requirements for youth programs to have social workers on their staff with college degrees. We set up a special balance that involved a master-degreed social worker who reviewed the activity and progress of each boy, but houseparents were given the authority to run their home as a traditional family, where parents called the shots.

Realizing that people have different meanings for some words, we made a change in our literature. Social service agencies commonly refer to a boy's "treatment plan." But when most youth hear the word "treatment," they think it means they have a mental problem and use this label to provide an excuse for not trying to change. We substituted the word "training" as a term that was more appropriate. We asked the boys not to say they are in treatment, but in training.

Each social worker would support two homes, and as the number of homes grew, we had several social workers who reported to a director of social services. The houseparents reported to the boys home supervisor, who was not part of the social services team.

If a conflict arose between the social worker and houseparents, they could take their concern to both the social work supervisor and the houseparent supervisor. If the two supervisors could not agree how to resolve the issue, it was referred to me as the Executive Director. In the thirty-five years Jan and I managed Rawhide, I was advised of concerns at times, but I never had to get involved in resolving the issues.

Our first social worker was Ron Petrick, a fun guy who loved to play the part of a country bumpkin. On first meetings, he kept the boys guessing whether he had all his marbles. He had a square bowling ball and numerous other silly items in his office, and he acted like he used all of them when he met the boys. About ten minutes into their meeting, they always figured out Ron was pulling their leg. His demeanor had a way of breaking the ice and helped many of the boys decide Rawhide might be a fun place to live. He had the responsibility of determining whether a boy referred to us was appropriate for our program. We ended up accepting almost every boy referred to us by a placing agency.

We learned that a boy's juvenile record was not a good indicator of how he would respond to the family environment at Rawhide. Social workers are very dedicated, but they are required to write a lot of reports. It is easy for a boy in the juvenile court system to amass a large file describing him in ways that would make anyone nervous to have him visit for dinner. But Jan and I never wanted to know about a boy's records.

Our social workers reviewed those histories and rejected a few boys who posed a likely threat to others. We told each boy we accepted that we did not want him to recount his tales of offenses to us or the other boys. After a while their successes at the ranch in academics, sports, and new, positive relationships gave them something to build their self-esteem and provide more positive topics of conversation.

We did review a boy's family background and his relationship with his mother and father. That alerted us to how he might respond to us or the other houseparents. Many boys had no involvement with their fathers, and a good number had never met them. We also needed to know if and why they were on medications. We found that most of the boys could be phased off their medications, with a physician's approval, as they settled into the busy and secure life at the ranch.

# Rodovan "Bob" Stojanovich

Our social service personnel were excellent at supporting the house-parents and providing professional support and encouragement to the boys. The goal of the staff was for each boy to realize that, despite his past, he had great potential for the future. In one case the confidential reports about a boy's potential changed the course of his life in one afternoon.

Rodovan "Bob" Stojanovich grew up in a Wisconsin family, the second oldest of ten children, with a stern, abusive father. When he was twelve, his older sister ran away from home to escape the conflict. Bob decided he would do the same thing. Over the next three years his life continued to spiral downward as he missed more and more school and started to use drugs. He was living on the streets, sleeping in vacant buildings, open cars, or any place he could find a little shelter during the cold days and nights.

At age fifteen, he was arrested for joyriding with a friend in a stolen car. The judge, who had seen him several times before, was about to have him locked up, but at the last minute, he decided Bob should be evaluated by a psychologist. The evaluation reported that Bob was very intelligent but reclusive and defiant when faced with authority. The report encouraged the court to consider a rehabilitation program. The judge subsequently directed placement at Rawhide.

Bob's first impression of Rawhide was the panorama of horses eating in the corral, boats in the channel by the Wolf River, and rustic, western-style buildings lining the frontier street. The scene reminded him of Disneyland.

He met his houseparents, Terry and his wife Pat Cowan. They went over some basic information, showed Bob his room, and allowed him to get settled. He related right away to Pat, but Terry reminded him of his dad, so their relationship took some time. Bob would not speak unless spoken to, and his answers were as brief as possible. He had grown up in a home where his father did not allow talking during meals, so the constant interaction by boys and staff while eating was strange to him. He refused to talk at meals, somewhat out of past habit, but somewhat out of stubborn defiance.

Bob loved to eat and would fill his plate as the food was passed around the table. But if he wanted seconds, and he always did, he would point to a dish he wanted, saying nothing. Pat instructed the boys not to pass food to Bob unless he asked for it like everyone else, saying, "Please pass the potatoes," followed with, "Thank you." He refused to cooperate, and he made sure he took extra food when the dishes went by the first time. Various boys asked him why he would not say please. "No one can make me say please," he said. They let him know they thought he was being stupid. His attitude changed once he realized that his conduct was conflicting with his love of food.

As his comfort level with Pat grew, he asked to help with meals. She was delighted with his help. As Bob's first Thanksgiving with us approached, he asked if he could prepare the whole meal. With only minimal guidance, he did just that: turkey with stuffing, mashed potatoes made "from scratch," cranberry sauce, squash with marshmallows, coleslaw, and two pumpkin pies. There was no end of praise from his houseparents and from all the guys, who thoroughly enjoyed the meal.

A few months into his placement, we noticed a dramatic change in Bob's attitude. He started interacting with staff and with other boys. Bob excelled in job training projects like yard work, building construction, and cleaning and feeding the horses. At the end of each day, the staff supervisor on the project would rate every boy in the four areas of performance, with the possibility of a high score of twenty. Bob thrived on the praise he received from his houseparents at the end of each day as a result of his good scores. We didn't know the reason for his dramatic change in attitude until many years later, when Jan and I were interviewing him for this book.

Bob shared with us that the day after Christmas in 1975, he was the only boy in the house. Terry and Pat had to run to town and told Bob he would be on his own for a couple of hours. He walked down to the office to find it open, but all the staff were gone. He went into the social worker's office and found a key for the file cabinet. He opened it and pulled out his folder. Next he made a copy of everything in his file and then carefully put the originals back as he found them.

That afternoon he sat down on his bed and proceeded to read every note and every report. He was especially surprised to find a five-page psychological report along with IQ test scores. He remembered taking the long tests but had no idea what they were for.

Every note in his file from the social worker, teachers, houseparents, and job training staff reported that Bob was very intelligent, likeable, who wanted to please people, but was afraid of being rejected. Notes by the staff indicated that he could have a bright future if he would open up to accept help from others. But the biggest surprise was the test that showed he had an IQ of 141, along with a glowing report on his potential from the doctor doing the evaluation. His score placed him in the genius category. That was the day he realized he was valued. Everyone was pulling for him. They were not out to get him.

Bob spent a year with us at Rawhide before moving back with his family in the Milwaukee area to finish his senior year of high school. After graduating, he decided to take a year to hitchhike around the nation. He traveled to eighteen states and found work for a few weeks at a time when he would get low on money. In Amarillo, Texas, he held two different jobs. First he worked on an interstate highway crew, and after that he was part of an independent company changing guardrails along the freeway. Both his bosses praised him as their best employee.

Next was Lubbock, Texas, where he took a job at a Whataburger fast food restaurant and at the same time worked on a landscape crew. Both complimented him by calling him their best employee.

In Washington, DC, he went to work on a masonry construction crew. Again he was told he was their best employee.

After completing his year-long trek, Bob was accepted as a student at Marquette University in Milwaukee. At the same time, he enrolled in a manager's training program for the Big Boy fast food chain. After completing the training program, he was assigned as a shift manager at one of the area Big Boy restaurants—and all this time he was getting top grades in college.

He had read about the Mensa Society for people with high IQs and decided to send in an application. His supporting enclosures consisted of the psychological report with the accompanying 141 IQ test reports he had taken from his Rawhide file. A few weeks later, he got an acceptance letter, and he has been a member for forty-five years.

The summer before his junior year in college, he traveled to Nairobi, Kenya, to attend the wedding of his best friend's sister. While in Nairobi, he purchased two suitcases full of handmade bracelets, earrings, and necklaces. Upon returning to Milwaukee, he spent several days hawking them along the Lake Michigan beach. He sold them all—at a very large profit.

Thinking bigger, he contacted the Milwaukee Grand Avenue Mall and rented a kiosk in the mall lobby for ninety days. Taking his initial sales profits and some money he had saved, he headed back to Nairobi. This time he purchased $10,000 worth of jewelry, handbags, and native clothing he thought Milwaukee shoppers would purchase. Within three months his investment produced tenfold profits. He renewed his kiosk lease for six months this time and headed back to Nairobi.

His profits allowed him to rent an entire store on Milwaukee's east side. He named it Hieroglyplus, and it became the new home for his growing import business. His trips to East Africa involved numerous other cities, and his product line expanded to hundreds of items.

Over the years Rawhide has grown to working with about two hundred different young men each year, but it has not lost the personal touch of developing close relationships that often last a lifetime. We use the same personal approach as we meet with hundreds of families every year in our community counseling centers. The success with redirecting young men's lives is due to a combination of impressive facilities, a practical and positive program, a team of confident and caring people, and even a variety of four legged friends.

# CHAPTER 11

# THIS PLACE IS A ZOO

## *Jan:*

John and I grew up in families that loved animals, and we both inherited an appreciation for any creature of the animal kingdom. My parents required that the dogs and cats live outside or in the barn. I had a parakeet in the house, and John's parents let him have a dog and even a cat that slept on his bed at night.

When our own sons, Steve and Tim, were young, we knew the value of children having pets. Our first home was a rented farmhouse, and we were finally able to have all the animals we wanted in the house. We had dogs, cats, rabbits, and even a pet crow. Some lived in the house at night and went outside during the day. We also had two horses, and our boys had two ponies. The horses stayed in the barn, but John said if I could have figured out a way, they would have moved into the house with us.

Soon after we moved to Rawhide, we got Dino, the first of

several wonderful Great Danes. He was a friend to all the boys. He slept at the top of the stairs leading from the dining room to our private living space. Every night Dino slept on his own fuzzy blanket on the landing after making his visit to each bedroom to kiss us all good night.

## *John:*

On one particular evening I noticed Dino's blanket on the floor next to Jan's side of our bed. I asked why the dog's blanket was not in the hall. She told me that Dino wanted to sleep next to her. I replied that he had not talked to me, and I was not at all in favor of that decision.

Was I being insensitive toward the poor dog? You might appreciate my position more if you knew about Dino's unpleasant habit of passing some of the most obnoxious gas you've ever experienced.

A stare-down between Jan and me followed, and then I made the big mistake of laying down an ultimatum: "Well, it's the dog or me. Whom do you want sleeping in our bedroom?"

"I want both of you in here."

I exclaimed that was not an option.

"I can't believe you're putting yourself on the same level as a dog!" Jan replied.

Steve and Tim each had a second bed in their rooms, and I picked up my pillow and went into Steve's room, stating I had decided to spend the night with him. I got up in the morning, assuming that by the second night Dino's bed would be back on the landing. Evening came, and the bed was still next to Jan's side of the bed.

"Where is the dog sleeping tonight?" I asked her.

"Where he slept last night. Where are you sleeping tonight?"

On night number two I stayed in Tim's room, and he was also

happy to have me use his extra bed. That started a nightly ritual. Every night, when our boys were getting ready for bed, they would ask, "Dad, where are you sleeping tonight?" They loved having me in their rooms and had no idea this was a major battle for a man's position of dominance in his castle.

This went on for a full two weeks—fourteen long nights of sleeping alone. Finally, I had had enough. Time to give in and admit the dog was going to be sleeping on the floor in our bedroom. But I didn't realize that was no longer an option. By now the dog had moved onto our king-size bed, and his floor blanket was nowhere to be found.

I got ready for bed on day fifteen and without a word climbed into my side of the bed, only to find our 150-pound Great Dane between us! I said nothing, and Jan said nothing, but we both knew who had just won a major victory. The most humiliating part of that first night was that every time I moved and bumped Dino with my foot, he gave a soft grumble, making it clear he was not happy that I had moved into his new bed.

## *Jan:*

Many of the boys at Rawhide had never had a pet of their own. Animals of all types gave them a way to give and receive love. As the ranch expanded, one of the questions prospective houseparents usually asked was if their dog would be welcome. Our reply was that the dog was not only welcome but essential. We wanted every house to have a pet that could interact with the boys. Even a cat or two was OK.

We only had one state inspector question the animals having free run of the house, including access to the kitchen. We explained that these were therapy pets that played a key role in the guys' emotional adjustment. That response was met with the full agreement of the inspector.

Henry and other neighbors would bring orphaned animals to us when the animals' mothers had been killed on the road. The first were two baby foxes that the boys named Winnie and Pooh. They grew up sleeping in a bed inside an unused fireplace, an arrangement that was necessary to allow their strong scent to be vented up the chimney. They were soon running all over the house, playing with Dino and the two cats. During the day they would go outside, but they would come back when they saw the school bus drop off the boys. They would come in to get their supper and spend the night in the house. We never tried to keep them from running off, but after two years they were coming back to the house every few days, until one day they both stopped showing up. We would like to believe they both found foxy ladies who put them to work ending their bachelor days.

Someone brought us a baby skunk that was only a week old. He was squinting through barely opened eyes. He already had a strong odor but was too young to spray. It would have been a big challenge to successfully bottle-feed such a fragile young animal. Luckily, we had a house cat named Cleopatra nursing a litter of kittens about the same age. I said to John, "Let's give him to Cleo and see if she will nurse him."

We put the baby skunk in the box with Cleo and her four kittens. The mother cat sniffed and turned her head away and sneezed. She sniffed and sneezed again. But after a few sneezes she licked his face, then started to give him a complete bath. And within minutes the newly adopted skunk was convinced he was a black kitten with a long white stripe. He started nursing next to his four multicolored kitten friends. It was a beautiful story of a foster mother taking in a youngster and giving him a chance to have a better life.

The "Five Musketeers" became the hit of the house, delighting guests and neighbors who dropped in. Pepe Le Pew, the skunk, his three foster kitten sisters, and one foster brother were soon spending their days chasing each other around the house, nursing on Cleo and sleeping all in a pile.

At a month old, Pepe was old enough for our veterinarian to remove his scent glands. We knew it was about time to have his operation, but we waited one day longer than we should have. John was the first baseman on the local Howie's Bar softball team and was late leaving for a game. He ran up the stairs to our bedroom landing, where Pepe was sound asleep on the floor in the palm of John's softball glove. He grabbed the glove, scaring Pepe, who instantly gave a little squirt of terrible scent. John put the glove in the trunk, and as he drove to the game the whole car stunk. He had to leave the glove in the grass between innings, and even then everyone could smell it. After a couple of innings, he took it to the woods and threw it away, borrowing a glove from someone on the other team for the rest of the game.

We eventually gave Pepe's kitten kin away, but Pepe remained a favorite of the boys. He would sleep in their rooms, or sometimes outside in the doghouse with his best friend, Oliver, our 180-pound Saint Bernard.

# Unusual Pets

Henry was going home from work one day when he came across a mother raccoon that had been killed by a car. Her baby was hiding in the grass at the side of the road. He quickly put on his gloves, caught the baby, and brought it back to our house. We were not excited about raising a raccoon, but one of our foster boys, Peter Zukas, pleaded with us to let him raise it.

Peter named her Lisa, and he did a good job of caring for her. He kept her fed, cleaned her cage, and spent a lot of time helping her get comfortable with people. Like other pets before her, Lisa had the run of the house, but she couldn't be left alone at night. Lisa had to sleep in her cage because she was a very naughty girl.

One evening, John and I were going out with all the boys for supper and then to a high school play. We would be gone for five hours, so Peter asked if he could put Lisa in the guest bathroom with her water dish and pan of kitty litter. It was an old-fashioned half bath with an antique sink and an old hand pump hooked up, so when you pulled a handle in front of the cabinet, the water came on.

We took the rug and magazines out to make the room as raccoon proof as we could, and left for town. When we got back about ten o'clock that night, Peter went to get Lisa to put her in her cage. He let out a yell for us to come look at what she had done!

Somehow she had turned on the water, luckily only lukewarm, and was lying on her back in the sink with water slowly flowing from the old hand pump onto her stomach, then onto the floor. She had unrolled the entire toilet paper roll and had scratched almost all the kitty litter out of the tray, carefully mixing it into the floor full of wet toilet paper. The toilet seat was left up and, by the evidence of kitty litter in the toilet, it seems she had been swimming in there during the evening. We all had a good laugh, but that was the last time Lisa spent any unsupervised time outside her cage.

Another unusual pet a neighbor gave us was a day-old orphaned pig that the boys named Bertha. Within a few weeks, she loved being handled and enjoyed sitting on laps like a ten-pound baby. As she grew bigger, she became a friend of all the horses and would spend her days with them in the corral. She joined the horses when they came in at night, and went into her own stall. But lap sitting became a problem as she grew larger. There is no way to safely snuggle with a five-hundred-pound pig. We had to make the difficult decision to send her away.

# A Horse and a Boy

In my many years helping my father with his horse business, I had become a quick judge of a horse's personality and temperament. In the first few days after a new boy moved into our home, I also tried to get a handle on his temperament. I was often able to match a boy who had an interest in horses to a horse with a similar personality. That produced a near miracle with a boy named Dennis Green.

Dennis was thirteen when he was brought to us by a social worker from Milwaukee County. He had a rough childhood as the second youngest of eight brothers and sisters with a very abusive father. The social services department moved several of the children into foster homes, and at the age of three, he was one of them. Dennis grew up an angry child, and he lashed out at everyone. Over the next few years, he moved through eight different foster and receiving homes.

When he was ten, the only home Dennis liked had a pony. His foster parents let him make a bridle out of binder twine and ride by himself in a fenced area. Yet even that didn't last, and he was placed with us at Rawhide.

Dennis recalls his first impression when being driven into the ranch. He thought he had arrived at the Ponderosa, from the TV show *Bonanza*. He expected Little Joe to come walking out of the barn. He was excited to see several horses lift their heads from the corral feeder to glance at his arrival.

I asked Henry to repair a junior saddle that had been donated some months earlier. It needed new stirrups and a girth strap. I decided to match Dennis with Frisco, who was a small pinto horse that was barely broken and stood thirteen hands, about fifty-two inches. He was small, just like Dennis, who weighed a hundred pounds, but both were very naughty.

After a few weeks of getting to know Dennis and watching him help around the barn, I was sure my idea to match them was a good plan. After feeding Frisco one Saturday morning, I had Dennis follow me to the front of Frisco's stall, where Frisco was eating his oats, and I explained my plan. "Dennis, Frisco has had a tough life. He was living outside in a muddy barnyard with no place to get out of the weather. He doesn't trust people, and he has only been ridden a few times. I want you to be his friend and teach him to trust you. No one else can ride him while you are living with us. Will you do this for Frisco?"

Dennis stared at Frisco for a few seconds, and then with some emotion said, "Yes, I will be his friend. He looks just like Little Joe's horse." And he did resemble the black and white pinto from the TV show.

That began a wonderful journey for both a boy and a horse. As the school bus pulled in each day, bringing our ten boys home, the guys all piled into the dining room and sat around for a few minutes eating the snack that was always set out—all of them except Dennis. He grabbed a carrot or an apple and headed straight to the barn to give his horse a hug and a treat. Then he came back to the house for his snack.

After only a few months, Dennis had Frisco riding calmly inside the corral. Soon after that they were ready to go on trail rides around the ranch. By the time Dennis had stayed with us for six months, we trusted him enough to saddle Frisco and go for a ride on his own. He would always check with John or me when he was going and tell us when he would be back. He would spend time every day with his horse, going for a short ride almost every day. With over five hundred acres and three miles of forest trails, it was a safe and beautiful place to ride. Dennis loved spending time with Frisco, and if we had let him, I think he would have moved a cot into the barn and slept there.

Dennis spent five years with us. The day after he graduated from high school, he left for San Diego for Marine boot camp. He went on to infantry school and was trained as a machine gunner before he shipped out for his first duty station in Vietnam. He was later assigned for guard duty at the US Embassy in Phnom Penh. Dennis was a dedicated Marine and reached the rank of corporal after his first two years in service.

He returned to the United States to be discharged, to face the antiwar climate consuming the country. After arriving back in California, he and several other Marines in uniform were walking through the Los Angeles airport when they were met with jeers and cursing. Someone spit in Dennis's face and called him a baby killer instead of giving him the thanks he deserved for serving his country.

After returning to live in Kaukauna, Wisconsin, he volunteered to serve in the VFW Patriot Guard unit. Their mission was to attend military funerals of servicemen and women, some of whom had lost their lives on active duty. In the first seven years, his guard team attended over one hundred memorial services throughout northeastern Wisconsin, earning him special recognition. On November 11, 2011, as part of Veterans Day services, Dennis was presented with a painting of himself done by another Patriot Honor Guard member and famous artist, Navy veteran Laura Taylor. It is one of Dennis's most prized possessions.

In the years after returning from the service, Dennis would visit Rawhide almost monthly to give Frisco a hug. If the horses were in the field, all he had to do was yell Frisco's name, and his good friend would come running for the carrot or apple that he knew would be waiting—and for the hug that would follow. They were a matched pair and helped each other grow up.

# Free Spirits

## *Jan:*

David Claus had a different personality than Dennis. He was cocky with a sense of humor, and he definitely did not like authority. This combination got him in a lot of trouble and ultimately resulted in his being sent to Rawhide.

David had been born to a fifteen-year-old Irish girl in Ireland. Abortion was an option for her, but she decided to have the baby and put him up for adoption. At five months of age, he was adopted by Bob and Gayle Claus, of West Bend, Wisconsin. His adoptive parents jokingly told us David never walked. One day he started running and never stopped. With his daredevil attitude and red Irish hair blowing in the wind, he was never one to turn down a dare. One day he rode his bicycle down the local ski jump. That was the end of the bicycle and almost the end of David.

One day in junior high school, the principal sent a letter home to Bob and Gayle saying something had to be done with their son, and it would have to be done somewhere other than at a West Bend school. The letter said that out of 2,200 students in the junior and senior high school, David was the most disruptive of them all.

During a test that David knew he would fail because he was just putting down funny answers to amuse himself, he noticed one of the test papers hanging over the edge of the desk of the student next to him. He took out his Bic lighter and set the paper on fire. The other student also thought it was funny, so he just let it burn, leaving it for the teacher to put out. That was the last straw for the teacher and the principal.

He went before the local juvenile judge, who was like an uncle to David. The judge and his wife were best friends of his parents. With tears in his eyes, the judge made David a ward of the state and recommended placement at Rawhide.

David arrived with a young probation agent who had just graduated from college. At age fifteen, David had a head of bushy red hair and a full red beard that made him look like he was at least twenty years old. John stuck out his hand to David, thinking he was the social worker. After a few seconds of embarrassment, everyone figured out who was who. David told me later that he could barely keep from laughing out loud at the mix-up. The thought crossed his mind that maybe he could leave the probation agent at Rawhide and take his car and go home.

For the first two weeks David was with us, he didn't go to school because we were waiting for his transcripts to be forwarded to our local high school. One of his chores was to clean the barn every morning, which took a couple of hours. He didn't like being at Rawhide, but he did like horses, so he figured the barn duty was OK. I would help him feed the horses. Then he would clean the stalls.

He kept asking me about a gray horse named Smokey, who was a character very much like David. Smokey would stay in the corral for an hour every morning until the hay was gone. Then he would walk over to the chest-high fence and, while standing still, rock back and forth a few times before lifting his front feet and jumping over the fence. He would then spend the rest of the day eating the grass that actually was greener on the other side of the fence. He would roam around the ranch eating or napping all day until he heard the other horses being let back into the barn for their evening feeding. At that point, he would jump back into the corral and join the other horses to get his grain and hay. Smokey was a free spirit and very self-confident. He didn't like being told what to do and liked to make his own rules. I could see David and Smokey relating to each other very well.

A few weeks later, I told David that Smokey was going to be his horse while he was with us. David got tears in his eyes as he heard the news, and during the next three years they became inseparable.

As soon as Smokey was loose for the day, no one could call him in, including me. If we planned to ride him during the day, we had to feed him in his stall in the morning and leave him there. But after a few months, David could call him—even if he was out of sight—and we would see him trotting back to his pal for his predictable handful of oats.

When David turned eighteen, he moved to North Fond du Lac, WI and struggled for a few years to settle down. He kept in touch with us, asking for advice from time to time.

David went on to develop his own public relations business and had a weekly radio show. During the Packer football season, he had a weekly postgame radio program with different players as guests. He also worked with some auto racing clients, including NASCAR, in various promotions.

At age twenty-seven, David was out one evening with some friends and saw a beautiful woman across the room. Never the least bit shy, he walked over and introduced himself. David and Gloria have been married for over thirty years, have two children, and live in North Fond du Lac.

We would get together a few times a year, and the conversation turned at some point to "Smokey," his best animal friend ever. He would occasionally ask if we had any pictures of Smokey, and surprisingly we could never find any. But when we went through thousands of photos and color slides in preparation for writing this book, we found a great picture of his beloved horse. We made an enlargement and put it in a frame, and John scheduled a lunch date with David. He presented the picture, and both of them teared up as they fondly remembered David's special friend

David called to say he was going to write and record a song to thank John and me and Rawhide. His song, "I'm a Rawhide Guy," is amazing. (You can listen to it on our website: Our351Sons.com.)

# Pets Can Pull a Family Together

Dogs, cats, fish, birds, and hamsters, and, once in a while, even a skunk, can really help children learn about love and responsibility. Every child can benefit from having a pet, but it's important for parents to see that choice as a partnership and a family project.

One of the sad realities of family pets is that they have a short life span, and children inevitably have to face a painful loss. Some parents avoid pets to spare their children that pain. But loss is something all of us need to learn how to handle. Experiencing the pain of loss helps us develop the confidence needed to weather the tough storms of life.

Children don't realize how much effort goes into taking care of a pet, but pets offer a great opportunity to learn responsibility and experience unconditional love from them. They give mom and dad an opportunity to train a child to follow through with responsibilities. The benefits of pets can far outweigh the effort they require.

# SOME OF THE RAWHIDE BUILDINGS

Darwin & Lois Smith Youth Home

Bill & Louise Aylward
Youth Home

Frontier Hotel & Cafe

Chester L. Krause Fieldhouse,
Jack & Ethel Keller High School

WATDA Youth Home, Vehicle
Donation Offices & Visitor Center

Kay & Gary
Thompson Center

Mike & Cindy Sheldon, Kathleen Searl,
Equestrian Training Facility

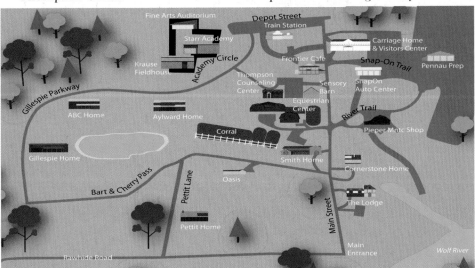

# RAWHIDE BOYS RANCH MAIN CAMPUS MAP

# 1 - JERRY'S OVERNIGHT STAY

Steve, Jan & Tim

Jerry Monson, age 1

John & Jan's wedding

God provides a house

# 2 - LEARNING
## TO SERVE OTHERS

Jan leading the trail ride

TOMORROW ONLY

WISCONSIN
"TEENS ON PARADE"

50 TEEN-AGERS —— "300" MILES ON HORSEBACK
(Milwaukee to Rhinelander)

FOND DU LAC FAIRGROUNDS

JUNE 14, TOMORROW
AFTERNOON and EVENING

★ Wells Fargo Stagecoach Rides          ( .50)
★ 3 To 7 P.M. Buffalo-Burger Lunch      ($1.00)
★ 7 To 9 P.M. Western Sing-A-Long
   Youth Rally                          (FREE)
"Bring the Family — Bar-B-Que Chicken for Mom"

BY: WISCONSIN YOUTH FOR CHRIST & FORT WILDERNESS CAMP
Challenging Teens to be Mentally, Physically, and Spiritually Fit,
In An Age of Space

John in the Army

Trail ride flyer

Fifty teenagers start a 14-day, 300-mile trail ride on horseback

# 3 - RAWHIDE BOYS RANCH IS BORN

...ackers at "Rescue" luncheon. Boyd Dowler, ...rry Kramer, John, Bart & "Fuzzy" Thurston

John Gillespie visiting

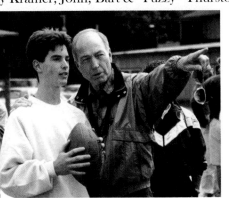

Bart Starr coaching

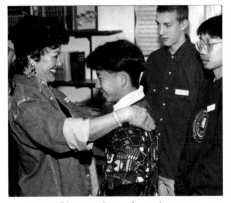

Cherry Starr hugging

# 4 - EXPECTATIONS AND MEMORIES

Home from school

Summer fun

Trimming the tree

A new friend

Doing dishes

Henry Moeller & Bart

Highway clean-up

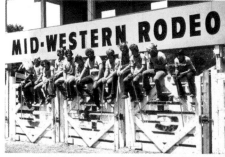

Haulin' hay

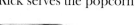

Rick serves the popcorn

Laying sod

Rodeo grounds clean-up

Farrier, Marty Forman at work

Lawn mowing team

# 6 - PLAY WITH A PURPOSE

Jan teaches riding

Biking

Ranch houseboat

Ranch pontoon boat

Loading the hearse for a ski outing

On the slopes at White Cap Mountain

Home game at the Krause Fieldhouse

Rawhide Basketball Team

Dick, Bill Jr., Andy & Louise Aylward, Bart & John dedicating the Aylward Auditorium

Mike Lensby, Wm. Aylward & Joh

Bart & Cherry Starr,
Ethel & Jack Keller, the Gillespies

Jim Keller, Bart, Jan, John & Bob Kel

Chet Krause & Niece Patti Dickhut
at start of the Krause Fieldhouse

The Starrs, Chet Krause, the Gillespies

John with Darwin & Lois Smith

Bart , Gov. Tommy Thompson & John

Bart & Cherry in the Corvette

Bart's MVP Corvette donated to Rawhide

Tom Hutchison, General
Manager, WLUK-TV & Bart

Chuck Woolery & Elkin Thomas
perform at the Rawhide Telethon

Chuck driving the Ranch Semi-Tractor

Hearse donated by Chuck & Elkin

Rawhide tent at the Iola Car Show

John & Chet at the Iola Car Show

# 8 - USED CARS TO THE RESCUE

Highway billboard for car donations

Just a few of the donated cars

The Starrs, Gary & LuAnn Williams,
the Gillespies

Paul Michiels, Auctioneer Jim Carlson,
John & Bart

Snap-on Vehicle Repair Shop

Pennau Family Auction Building

Ranch guys with the Rawhide race car

Cherry in donated
Mack Semi-Tractor

# 9 - IF WE BUILD IT, THEY WILL COME

Back: Laurie & Rick Schinke, Patti,
Rollie & Sue Stephenson, Paul & Carol Gehl
Front: John, Clyde Stephenson & Jerry

Bart and the motor home
donated by Oshkosh Corporation

Mike, Bart, John & Tom Boettcher

Bart & Rollie Stephenson

t & Bob Stephenson, ABC board member

Guys with Kohler & Vollrath Salad Bar

Jo Pulido, 35 years as
John's executive assistant

Janet & Rich King

Kay & Gary Thompson

Kim, Judy, "Farrah", Chad & George Massey

The Starrs, Bob & the Gillespies

Marion & Don Koepke
at Mike & Babs Smith's wedding

Bart & Helen Wilson with
her famous Monster Cookies

# 11 - THIS PLACE IS A ZOO

Dennis Green at age 13 & Frisco

Dennis giving Jan a kiss

John, Dave & pictures of Smokey

Dave Claus at age 15

Moses napping on Cherry

Janet King & a day-old lamb.
Rich & Janet were houseparents
& raised "Bucky" in the home

Jimmy the donkey wants
Dave Rich's picnic lunch.

A naughty goat resting on a car

Rawhide guys ready for fire training

All-terrain fire pumper donated by Pierce
a division of Oshkosh Corperation

2,000-gallon fire tanker donated by
the Don Koepke Company

Ranch guys fighting a structure fire

Christmas tree sale drew thousands

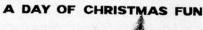

Four teams hauled families to the trees

Roger & Sue Devenport with Laura
& A.J. Hawk, Green Bay Packer, hosting
a hunting trip for a disabled youth

Roger & Chuck on a
fishing trip for disabled veterans

Bart & Cherry, John & Jan

A Starr Academy high school class

Woodworking

Miller welding equipment

Snap-on Tools

About Face Color Guard

About Face squad with leaders
Jeff & Brenda Stump

ongressman Tom Petri, About
ce Dir. Ed O'Brien & a cadet

Pastor Bee Vang, his wife,
Amanda & sons
Silas, Isaiah & Abram

Habitat for Humanity
home build

Tornado clean up

# 14 - TOUGH LOVE WITH A HEART

Peter Zukas with the ball

Peter with a presentation to
Wis. Gov. Tommy Thompson

Jim Lysaght, ranch foreman, training the guys

Jim and his wife Paula

## 15 - FROM HEARTACHE
TO HOPE

Al Phillips and his wife Mary

**Press-Star**

Mark Romies (right) leads
the boys rebuilding the home

The Lodge home is rebuilt

Rob Strauss after
youth home fire

Christmas Eve stable fire

Mural of the lost horses

Bart & Cherry at Bret Starr
Memorial Fitness Center

# 16 - FAMOUS FRIENDS

Dale Evans, Roy Rogers & Mike Lensby

Col. Jim Irwin. Apollo 15

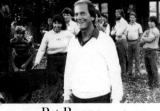

Pat Boone

hael Sajbel & Shawn Morrison

Reggie White having fun

Roy on the Rawhide
Bucking Barrel

The 65-member Rawhide Youth Choir preforming with
Frank Sinatra Jr., Monica Mancini & the Henry Mancini Orchestra

# ACKNOWLEDGMENTS

John, Jan with daughter-in-law,
Shannon & our son Tim

Our son Steve and his mom Jan at
our 50th wedding anniversary

Bart & Cherry Starr with Jan & John

John & Dal Wood editing the book

Terry Kohler funded writing costs
to allow this book to be completed

Jerry's new home

**Amazing**

Sommerville Flag
Kolosso Toyota
Absolute Asphalt
Senator Roger Roth
Northeast Asphalt
Hallman Lindsey Paint
Hoffman Planning & Const.
Decorative Curb & Concrete
D&D Excavating/Landscape

**Veteran's Home Build Volunteer Team**

City Disposal
Ric Huss Excavating
Keller, Inc. Builders
Vander Loop Construction
MCC Concrete Division
Welch Builders
Harris Construction
Watters Plumbing
Faith Technologies
KSG Gutters
Price Home Services
Wisconsin Building Supply

A-1 Cartage
Giordana Home Builders
Modern Heating
H.J. Martin Flooring
Lee Harke Plastering
Leo Van de Yacht Wells
Hoheisel Painting
Arn's Cabinets
Signarama Appleton
A & B Tree Service
Bay Therm Insulation
Able Distributing

**Unbelievable**

Romenesko Crane
Goodwill Industries NCW
Northtown Lighting Center
Outagamie Housing Authority
Fox Valley Veterans Council
Machine Shed Restaurant
Brenda B Interior Design
Van Vreede's Appliances
Gabriel Furniture
Werner Electric
Roger Williams - Sheet Rock
Rawhide About Face Team

For Info: John Gillespie • 920-427-9000

Forty-five builders donated a home for Jerry Monson, a disabled Vietnam war veteran

# CHAPTER 12
# GROWING BY SERVING OTHERS

## *John:*

Ryan was a new placement who had been dropped off an hour earlier by his probation agent. I was going over some of the details a new boy needed to know about living at Rawhide when the phone rang. This was a special "red" phone that only rang when the Rawhide Fire Department had to spring into action.

The Wisconsin Forestry Department, area fire departments, or individuals used it to call us in fire emergencies. I answered the phone. It was the dispatcher at the Waupaca County state fire ranger's office asking for the Rawhide fire truck and crew to respond to a marsh fire twenty miles from the ranch. I wrote down the address, and Jan immediately put out an intercom call to the other staff and boys to report for a fire run.

I asked Ryan to follow me as I explained to him that Rawhide operates a professional fire department, and he would be going on his first fire run. As we hurried to the garage, where our pumper truck was parked, I told Ryan he would be riding in the cab with me, and I would explain more on our trip to the fire. I found him some boots and a hard hat. By now six other staff and a dozen boys had arrived in two vans, ready to follow me.

Ryan and I were joined in the cab by one of the higher-ranking boys, and we started out on the thirty-minute trip to the fire. During the drive I gave Ryan an explanation of safety procedures. I said the forest ranger in charge would give us our role at the fire once we arrived. Regardless of that role, it was important for Ryan to stay in the truck cab unless I told him he could get out. And once he was out of the truck, he was to remain within five feet of me at all times.

The marsh fire was easy to access, and no buildings or wooded areas were in immediate danger. The ground was dry and safe for our ten-wheel, off-road truck to approach the fire from the burned-over side. Our fire truck was a two-and-a-half-ton army truck provided to us by the state and retrofitted into a modern firefighting vehicle by Pierce Manufacturing Company, now a division of Oshkosh Truck, the largest builder of fire trucks in the country. One of the volunteers who served on the Rawhide Fire Department was Ron Becker, a neighbor and a foreman at the Pierce Company. The CEO of Pierce, Doug Ogilvie, gave Ron permission to do a major rebuild on our truck as long as employees volunteered their time after work hours.

The truck had a five-hundred-gallon water tank and a separate pump engine so we could drive and spray water at the same time. It was well-equipped with several hundred feet of inch-and-a-half soft hose for structure fires, plus two short sections of hard line with nozzles on top of the truck bed, where two men could safely sit and attack a ground fire. In addition, we carried a dozen water backpacks, commonly called Indian Fire Pumps, and a variety of shovels, rakes, brooms, picks, and other hand tools.

When we arrived at the fire scene, we stopped for the guys to remove the water packs and hand tools in preparation for following our truck along the fire line. We had practiced this procedure many times in drills, and in less than two minutes everyone was ready to attack the fire. Other than the state forest ranger's three-quarter-ton pickup with a small water supply, we were the first large unit to arrive.

Dick Walkush, the forest ranger at the scene, directed us to attack the fire on the left flank, since it was headed for a nearby wooded area. I had one of our staff get on the top with one of the nozzles and take Ryan with him to man the other nozzle.

We always approached a fire from the upwind side and drove in the burned-over area. It was very safe. I drove along the fire line at the speed of a fast walk with the two lines on top of our truck putting out the fire as we went.

The other boys and staff, carrying the backpacks or shovels and brooms, followed behind the truck, making sure every spark was out. Smoldering wood pieces were wet down and covered with dirt.

Shortly after we began our attack on the fire, another truck arrived that could also drive and pump. They were directed to work down the right flank. Along with men from that department, some of our staff and boys worked behind the new truck doing mop-up.

An hour after we arrived, Ranger Walkush declared that the fire was out, and we headed back to the ranch, proud of the job everyone had done.

Rawhide is located in Caledonia Township, in Waupaca County. The township had no fire department. Excellent fire departments from New London and Dale served our township, but their arrival time could be up to twenty minutes after receiving a call. We saw a need to provide help with grass or forest fires until another fire department arrived and to offer cleanup support on building fires. Over the years, our cleanup help would save taxpayers thousands of dollars, as our department would stay at the scene many hours after the other fire departments were released. We remained on site to protect other structures while the fire smoldered out.

Professional interest for the idea of a boys ranch fire department had attracted a lot of support. Cal Phillips, the Oshkosh Fire Chief, offered to come to the ranch two mornings a month and teach a course in firefighting to our staff and boys and even some neighborhood volunteers. Dick Walkush also volunteered to come to Rawhide one Saturday a month to lead a class in forest firefighting.

The Appleton fire department donated an older pumper truck they had just taken out of service. Concrete Pipe Corporation and its president, Don Koepke, donated a two-thousand-gallon semi water tanker. We already had a semi-tractor, donated by the Mack Corporation, that could pull the tanker trailer. And we had the impressive ten-wheel drive, all-terrain pumper unit.

Safety was always a primary concern. At a fire every boy was assigned to work with a staff person and had to be with the staff at all times. They could not climb ladders or enter buildings even if there was no danger of fire at the time. All the boys and staff took a basic first aid and CPR course. The boys understood that a fire call was not the time to be disobedient or have an attitude problem. In twenty years, with more than two hundred responses to grass fires, house and barn fires, and even a few vehicle fires, we never experienced a single incident of disobedience or injury to any of the boys.

People sometimes ask why we would risk the liability of an activity as dangerous as firefighting. We believe that everyone has a

God-given desire to make a positive impact in the world and to make a difference in the lives of others. In the opportunities we created for young men, we looked for practical ways our staff and boys could serve others. There were some risks. Riding horses, skiing down steep hills, fishing in a river with a strong current, cutting and splitting firewood, and fighting fires all have risks. But boys need the chance to participate in risky ventures, in the company of adult mentors, to help them become strong men themselves. In our overly cautious society, it seems that we've surrendered too many opportunities for boys to become confident as they engage at an appropriate level of risk.

Imagine Ryan's experience in his first few hours at Rawhide. Here he was, just having been sent by his juvenile court to live at this place for a year, wondering what was going to happen to him. Would his peers accept him? What would the staff be like? And I'm sure there were numerous other anxious questions.

An hour after arriving at Rawhide, he was riding on the top of a huge fire truck, putting out a blazing marsh fire. He enjoyed the compliments from the other guys and staff plus other fire department volunteers.

By the time our crew arrived back at Rawhide, many of Ryan's questions were answered. He had faced and overcome a man-sized challenge. He had done well and felt accepted by his peers and appreciated and valued by our staff. And why not? He had just performed an adult job in an emergency situation serving others. In just a few hours, Ryan experienced how it felt to enjoy being a person of value. That's why we had a fire department. Every firefighting experience helped the Rawhide boys build confidence.

A large annual rodeo that is held over the Fourth of July weekend in Manawa, Wisconsin draws thousands of fans. Saturday featured a rodeo parade, and we were always one of the entrants with our big pumper truck. A dozen or more of the higher-ranking guys would ride on top of the truck dressed in their tan Rawhide fire department shirts, matching khaki pants, and yellow hard hats. They looked sharp and waved with pride as the people along the way clapped in appreciation.

The parade ended at the rodeo grounds on the edge of town, and we drove to our premier parking place right next to the bucking chutes. This was in the restricted section, to which only the rodeo contestants had access. We were able sit on the top of the truck and have a ringside view of all the events. At intermission, our job was to spray down the arena to control dust.

Just before intermission one year, we heard the PA announcer tell us to respond across the road to a grass fire. As thousands of spectators watched, we turned on the siren and red lights. With the guys and staff on top of the truck, we carefully made our way through the crowd and across the road to a roaring grass fire that was headed toward a barn. We stopped the truck, and our trained crew flew into action. One staff member and one boy stayed on the truck, manning the top hoses. The rest unloaded and quickly put on backpacks, and I started driving down the fire line, leading the way on the side headed for the barn. The grass was only a couple feet tall, making the fire easy to put out. Within five minutes we had the fire under control.

We had stopped the fire fifty feet from the barn and were in mop-up mode when two trucks from the Manawa Fire Department arrived. Their chief, John Pope, had glowing praise for the boys and invited all of us to their fire station so he could fill our truck with water and share sodas with the boys.

After the truck was topped off with water and the boys were topped off with soda, we returned to the rodeo grounds amid a standing ovation from the crowd. For a dozen teenagers who might have been locked in a juvenile detention facility only a few months earlier and who might have been told they were never going to amount to anything, this was pretty heady stuff. They knew they had amounted to something that day.

# Christmas Trees

We were always searching for ways to serve the community, provide meaningful training for the boys, and generate income. Raising funds was an ongoing challenge. It was with that in mind that, in one of our staff meetings, someone said, "Let's sell Christmas trees."

It sounded like a project that met all of our goals, but there were no suitable trees growing at the ranch, so we decided to build a Christmas tree field. A company that manufactured pike poles for power companies had donated thousands of imperfect two-inch by twenty-foot wooden poles that were lying in a huge pile, waiting for us to figure out a way to use them. We decided they would be the supports for our new Christmas tree field.

We cut the poles into five-foot lengths, and before the ground froze, we drove two thousand of them two feet deep into the sandy soil across a ten-acre field. We then contracted with a Christmas tree farm in northern Wisconsin to buy enough trees to tie one to every stake.

In early November we took our enclosed semi-trailer, a tree baler we borrowed, a dozen boys, and several staff, and headed one hundred miles north. We were able to stay at a large summer home that belonged to a family that supported Rawhide. It was located a mile from the tree plantation where we had to cut, bail, and load the two thousand trees we would haul back. The next step was for two-boy teams to hold and tie a tree to each stake with binder twine.

Starting in mid-November, three local network TV stations started to run attractive sixty-second promotional ads. They featured Bart Starr and a family headed for the tree field on a wagon pulled by a team of horses and then cutting down their tree. Santa Claus was on the wagon, along with Oliver, our Saint Bernard, with an empty brandy keg hanging around his neck.

A printing company donated a quarter million two-color restaurant placemats picturing the tree field, the team and wagon, Oliver, and Bart Starr. The placemats were an invitation for families to visit the ranch the first three weekends in December. The Wisconsin Restaurant Association endorsed the project, and Wisconsin J.C. chapters distributed free placemats to hundreds of restaurants throughout Northeast Wisconsin.

We had no idea how many customers would show up, since we were ten miles from a small town and twenty miles from a metropolitan area. Since we promoted the event as a family adventure, it seemed we would draw the biggest crowds on the weekends.

The staff and boys assembled at five o'clock that first Saturday morning to get ready for our eight o'clock opening. The horses had to be fed, the boys on the customer parking crew had to set out lane markers, fresh donuts had to be prepared, cider and hot chocolate had to be heated, and Oliver had to be brushed. Santa, played by one of the older boys, had to get into his suit, and the horses needed to be harnessed to pull the wagons from the visitor area to the nearby tree field. The ranch had two teams of Belgian draft horses, and we were able to borrow two more teams from Henry.

Cars started arriving an hour before the advertised start time, and we were almost ready for them. The drinks were hot, and the sugared donuts were fresh out of the fryer, so the early arrivals did not mind waiting for the teams to be hooked up while their children hugged Oliver and visited with Santa.

We had a big bonfire at the entrance to the tree field to warm guests while we baled their trees prior to loading them onto the wagons for the ride back to the parking area. Most people brought their own saws, but we had a supply of extras. Families would browse through the field, pick out their special tree, and saw it down. Actually, they sawed off both the tree and our stake, but they were sure they were cutting down a tree that had been growing there.

By eight o'clock the first morning, a steady stream of cars was already filing through our main entrance, and by ten o'clock we realized we had a major problem. There was a traffic jam of historic proportions on the narrow, two-lane town road. Drivers had driven down both sides, preventing impatient families from turning around and leaving. We had to call the county sheriff's office and ask for help.

By the time the officers arrived, the roadblock stretched two miles from the ranch. The officers shut off the road at an intersection ahead of the jam and turned everyone around. It took about two hours before everyone was able to get into the ranch or turn around and go home.

That night we got creative and developed a new parking plan that allowed us to get cars parked much faster. We attracted another huge crowd the next day, but this time a traffic jam was averted.

We ran our tree sale three weekends in December. We sold all but about a hundred trees and almost covered our costs. The project provided an opportunity for hundreds of people getting to see Rawhide and meet the boys.

When the last weekend of the sale was over, our staff and boys were exhausted. The boys had school every day, and they'd put in fourteen-hour workdays on Saturday and Sunday, but they found great value in the satisfaction they experienced in helping others and enjoyed the attention and praise of our visitors.

# Dude Ranch Activities

The Christmas tree sale was very demanding on both staff and boys, and because it lost money every year, we decided to drop it after five seasons. The next venture was dude ranch activities we offered on weekends through the summer.

We provided three strings of twelve riding horses each, plus guide horses that would take a dozen people on a two-mile ride through our forest trails. We had a two-foot-high by 140-foot-long walkway where the riders could easily climb on and off. The next dozen people were already in position, waiting to get on. One of the higher-ranking boys led each string, and one of our staff rode the last horse in case of problems. The ride took forty-five minutes, and each string could be unloaded, loaded, and back on the trail in ten minutes.

One of the ranch teams pulled an old-fashioned covered wagon for thirty-minute rides, with one of the boys driving and a staff person supervising. Another boy we called the "wagon master" would help people on and off the steps at the back of the wagon. This was always a higher-ranking boy who liked talking with the visitors.

Shane Besler was a wagon master and an excellent tour guide, and explained the Rawhide program during the ride. Sometimes I would climb on the wagon if I wanted to spend time with some of the guests. Usually the boys were a little nervous if Jan or I were one of their passengers, but not Shane. As I reached for the handrail next to the rear loading step, he greeted me. "Well, good afternoon, sir. Are you having a good time today? Please move forward, and find a seat. We will be starting our tour as soon as we are loaded." Within five minutes up to thirty adults and children were loaded, and the team of horses was given the signal to go.

Shane immediately launched into the welcome speech he would repeat more than a dozen times during his tour on the wagon that day. "Welcome to the Rawhide Boys Ranch. Today we will be traveling on a small portion of our several miles of forest trails, and I will point out various buildings we will pass and explain how they are used to train the boys. About fifty boys live here at any given time. They come from all parts of Wisconsin, and a few from outside the state. As we continue, please feel free to ask me any questions you have."

On virtually every trip the first question was, "Where are all the boys today?" We had instructed the boys that they did not have to say they were Rawhide boys, but they all did. They took pride in what they were doing and the fact that visitors saw them as employees.

"Well," Shane would reply, "I'm one of the guys that was lucky enough to be sent to live at Rawhide. All of the other teenagers working here today are also residents of the ranch. We are all considered part of the staff."

The guests asked a steady stream of questions during the ride. If the wagon master couldn't answer the question, he would call on a staff person to help him with the answer.

For the younger children, we had two rings of four ponies each. The boys also ran these, with a staff member supervising.

Another crew of staff and boys prepared and served three hundred to four hundred meals of barbequed chicken, beans, baked potatoes with toppings, and coleslaw. There was coffee and "sarsaparilla" (root beer) to drink.

# Firewood for Needy Families

The ranch has an almost unlimited supply of downed trees that can be turned into firewood. Throughout the year, staff cut logs into sixteen-inch lengths, and the boys would run them through a power splitter and pile the wood into four-by-eight-foot face cords. They put together dozens of face cords every year.

Through the Waupaca County Social Service Agency, we would get the names of needy families who heated their homes with wood. We would call and ask if they could use some free fire wood, and then set up a time for a staff member and a few of the boys to deliver and stack the wood. On occasion, I would make the delivery, driving the pickup truck with two boys. One Saturday morning Alan, Dennis, and I loaded almost a face cord of wood for delivery to a New London family.

We arrived at a small home at the edge of town and were greeted by an elderly gentleman who invited us in. We met his wife, who was in a wheelchair. We will call the couple Jim and Jane. We all introduced ourselves, and Jane said, "I've made some hot chocolate and cookies. Would you like some?"

I said, "Let's unload the wood first, and then we would love a snack. Where do you want it stored?"

"If it is not too much trouble, we would like it in the entry room by the back door," Jim said.

Carrying the wood from the truck and stacking it neatly in the entry room took about half an hour. Now it was time for the snack. We sat around the table, and Jim and Jane shared how hard the past few years had been and how grateful they were for the wood. "Last winter we couldn't afford enough wood and had to let the fire in the stove go out after supper time," Jim said. "It was usually fifty degrees when we got up in the morning."

Some of the boys had lived in homes without enough heat, and it was very touching for them to be able to help a family facing that challenge. "Well, this winter, you can burn as much wood as you want," I said. "When you get down to about a week's supply, you call us. We will bring another load."

When it was time to go, all of us gave Jim and Jane a big hug. Jane was wiping her eyes, as were all of us. When we got in the truck, we were all silent for a few minutes. Then Dennis said, "When we have to deliver another load of wood to Jim and Jane, I want to go along." Alan quickly added, "Me too."

# Friday Fish Fry

Wisconsin is noted for Friday night fish frys. They are served in thousands of taverns and restaurants. A program developed under the creative leadership of John Solberg, Rawhide's Executive Director, has become a very popular event. All the boys take a culinary course, and part of their training is preparing and serving a fish fry the third Friday evening of each month from April through October. Guests can order deep-fried perch, shrimp, haddock, or broasted chicken and help themselves from an extensive salad bar. In addition to helping prepare the food, the Rawhide boys gain practical experience serving as table waiters.

The rustic dining room in the Frontier Café seats 150 guests with extra outside seating in good weather. About 600 people are served on each occasion. A country band entertains throughout the evening, and guests can take a twenty-minute tour-bus ride around the Rawhide campus and visit the extensive Bart and Cherry Starr Museum. This event has become so popular that some guests drive an hour or more to attend. Prices are modest. The Green Bay Packers Foundation and other donor friends provide financial support for the fish fry.

# One Boy's Passion to Serve Others

Roger Devenport's teen years were filled with fun at the expense of others. Here is a summary he wrote of his life before coming to Rawhide:

## *Roger:*

My life was totally out of control in spite of my parents doing everything they could to try to straighten me out.

At age fifteen, several of my friends and I were in northern Wisconsin on a school canoeing trip. On the first evening, a couple of my classmates said they had broken into a radio shop and showed me some neat stereo equipment they had stolen. They asked if I wanted to come with them the next day and steal some more stuff. I agreed. The police were waiting and nabbed the three of us before we could get in. We were all expelled from school.

My parents tried to find a school that would work for me, but the school was not the problem. My attitude was the problem. They sent me to the Wilson Center in Minnesota. I had only been there a short time when some other students and I went to a county highway equipment parking area and broke the windows out of several trucks. We got caught, and I was moved to a juvenile program in Minnesota. We went out one night and broke into the county dog pound and let about fifty dogs loose. They were happy, but I was not when I got caught.

It was my birthday, and I was back in a public school. One of the teachers said she was asked to bring me to the principal's office. I assumed it had something to do with turning seventeen, but it wasn't the type of birthday surprise I expected. Two police officers were waiting for me and said I was under arrest for suspicion of providing drugs. They handcuffed me, read me my rights, and then walked me through the crowded high school hall to their police car.

Within days, a juvenile judge committed me to Wales, a Wisconsin juvenile correction facility that is a high-security prison, with locked cells and a double fence of razor wire. This was to be my home for almost six months, and I hated every day I was there. But one day I got an unexpected visit from John Gillespie, the Director of a place called Rawhide Boys Ranch, and my life was about to change.

## *John:*

We received a probation agent's request to transfer Roger from the state correctional facility to Rawhide if we would accept him. I drove the hundred miles to interview Roger, and he seemed like an appropriate placement. We set a date for him to visit the ranch to see if it was the type of place where he would make an effort to apply himself.

On his visit he was impressed with the wilderness setting of the ranch. He had enjoyed some memorable hunting and camping trips with his dad, and he liked horses. Roger also said, "One of the most impressive things during my visit was Jan's cooking. I had been eating institutional food for almost half a year, and I could tell she was a great cook. And we could eat as much as we wanted!"

"A guy that I had gotten to know at the correctional facility, who had tried to shoot his sister, had been transferred out," Roger continued. "I had no idea where he went. To my amazement, when I sat down at the dining room table at Rawhide, he was sitting next to me, being treated just like everyone else. That convinced me that

I would be accepted at this place and have a chance to make some major changes in my life."

Several months after Roger came to live with us, we took all of the boys roller skating in Appleton. He met a girl that evening, and she gave him her phone number, but she was understandably disappointed when she found out he couldn't call her for a date. Boys were not allowed to date until they reached the Wrangler rank, and even then any dating happened only with Jan or me chaperoning.

One very cold, snowy evening, Roger and his roommate decided they would walk the nine miles to Readfield, hitchhike the remaining twelve miles to Appleton, and try to meet up with the girl. Realizing we would be looking for them along the roads, they headed straight into a mile-wide wooded swamp, trudging through a foot of snow. We followed their tracks on snowmobiles into the woods but had to turn back because of the heavy brush.

We posted staff members in four cars at road locations on the other side of the swamp, hoping the boys would not get lost and die from exposure. It was about five degrees above zero. The boys did make it through the swamp and emerged within fifty feet of where Jan and I were waiting. They were exhausted and freezing from their three-hour walk, and it was easy to persuade them to jump into the warm car. We drove directly to the Waupaca County Jail, where they were put into cells for the night to decide whether they wanted to return to Rawhide. I visited them the next afternoon at the jail, and both were glad to see me and when asked said they wanted to return to the ranch.

Roger loved horseback riding. One night he and a roommate saddled two horses and rode them nine miles to New London, got some beer, and rode back. The next morning, Jan was concerned when she saw two horses with dried sweat in their hair. She thought they might be sick and took their temperature, but both were normal. Later that day, we got a call from someone in New London, wondering if it was our horses they'd seen being ridden through town sometime after midnight. Mystery solved. The boys admitted to their escapade and were assigned blocks to move.

After a year, the disobedience continued, and Roger and his houseparents reached an impasse. We started planning for his to return back to his county.

At this time, our son Tim was beginning his junior year at New London High School. Because of the growth of Rawhide, Jan and I were in the process of phasing ourselves out as houseparents. Partly because of their mutual love for horses, Roger and Tim had become good friends. Tim came to us with an unprecedented request. "I know we don't transfer guys between homes, but I have a feeling Roger would do well if he could stay with us."

We were not sure this was a good idea, but we had our social services director put Roger's departure on hold for a few weeks. Roger and Betty Devenport, Roger's parents, were very much in favor of our giving him another chance at Rawhide. They were concerned that he was not ready to move home. With all the Rawhide staff in agreement, we explained the plan to Roger. He was willing to try.

Tim and Roger participated in several horse shows around the state, and they both did very well. Roger's attitude dramatically changed, and he stayed another year at Rawhide with no more block-hauling discipline.

After graduating from high school, Roger went back to West Bend, Wisconsin. He moved into a small apartment, and his parents helped him with the rent. He got a job and was doing well when a new opportunity came into his life. He was out one evening and saw a beautiful girl across the room. He introduced himself and learned that her name was Sue and that she was eighteen. He asked if he could call her. She gave him her phone number, and a friendship quickly developed.

With encouragement from Sue, Roger got his real estate license and did quite well in sales. He and Sue were married a few years later and bought a rundown hunting ranch in northern Wisconsin, which they named Three Lakes Preserve. They subsequently built it into a nationally acclaimed whitetail deer hunting destination, drawing hunters from around the country.

One day Roger and Sue were asked if they would allow a twelve-year-old boy to come to the preserve and shoot a deer. The boy had terminal cancer and only six months to live. They quickly agreed, and that experience changed the focus of their lives. When Roger saw the excitement the young man displayed when he shot a six-point buck, he was determined to offer this opportunity to others who were disabled or terminally ill. They remodeled the hunting lodge to make it wheelchair compatible.

Shortly after deciding to accept more hunters with physical challenges, Roger traveled to Utah to set up a hunt for disabled youth. At the hunting lodge, he met Camron Tribolet. Roger saw him walking with a cane and asked if he had hurt his leg.

"Well, sort of," Camron replied. "I have no legs." Camron's life had hung in the balance after being shot in a carjacking attempt. Both legs were amputated above the knees due to infection, and he had to be resuscitated thirteen times during the emergency surgery. It was six months and numerous surgeries later before he returned home.

Camron's experience gave him a passion for helping others. He had hosted close to one hundred hunting and fishing trips for the disabled. He and Roger developed an instant bond and decided to work together to help others with serious disabilities.

Roger contacted me for help setting up a nonprofit organization, and I was more than happy to assist. The Way Outfitters was established as a federally approved charitable organization dedicated to providing hunting and fishing trips for youth and veterans with disabilities or other serious health challenges. Their stories were later told in a thirteen-week, half-hour TV series on the Outdoor Channel.

# Shawn Morrison

While we were gathering material from interviews and letters from former Rawhide boys to consider for this book, we received a letter that was so striking we decided to let Shawn tell his story in his own words.

## *Shawn:*

My parents were divorced when I was two years old. I remember spending one of my first Christmas days sitting in the back of a police car while my parents were outside arguing over who would have to take me. They got it worked out, but they told me I could not take any of my toys with me to my new home. I didn't understand this, and it made me feel bad.

In third grade a girl in gym class beat me up. I suppose I did something to cause this, but I don't remember what it was. All I remember is the humiliation of her pounding me. I found her gym locker, took her clothes, and tried to flush them down the toilet with a stick. Some went down; others got stuck in the toilet. I got suspended from school for a few days.

In sixth grade I discovered beer, and some of my friends figured out ways we could get it, usually by stealing. Alcohol became a passion that was to become a serious problem for me. I was very antisocial. I started to skip school a lot. My relationship with my dad was nonexistent, and my relationship with my mom was getting worse. I continued to hang out with a bad crowd.

My freshman year ended with me being kicked out of school for basically not showing up. I am sure I was failing every class. The only thing I liked about school was art class. I learned I had some artistic ability and would create and draw cartoon characters. I think this was a way for me to retreat into a comic-book world.

I carried a gun and had a portable police radio I'd stolen from a police car. In my high school years (not that I went to school much) I was drinking to the point of blacking out on at least a weekly basis. I ended up being placed in a psychiatric hospital for a month. After discharge from the crazy house, I was placed in a group home. I barely talked to anyone and just kept to myself. I was depressed and angry, and I wore nothing but black clothing.

I was arrested with the handgun and police radio, and that was the start of some jail time. They put me in a secure receiving home, but it was not very secure. I ran away several times. They gave up on me, and I was put in a holding program with locked doors. It seemed the next step for me would be one of the two state youth correctional prisons. One day as I was waiting to see where I would be locked up, I was told there were a couple of policemen to see me. But they were not policemen. They were Terry Egan, the director of social services at Rawhide, and George Massey, one of the housefathers who, to this day, is a father to me and one of my best friends.

They said they wanted to show me a short video about Rawhide Boys Ranch to see if it looked like a place I would be willing to go. The video showed a beautiful, peaceful place with guys riding horses, fishing in a river, caring for animals, and working on cars. It looked like a resort to me. "Heck yes," I said. "Sign me up."

A few days later the judge approved my move to Rawhide. I was excited. I didn't even ask how long I would be there. Forever was fine with me! I figured this would be an easy gig, but little did I know what was in store. And my stay was almost forever. Well, actually, four years.

## *Jan:*

John and I had taken our house of boys on a weeklong trip to the South Dakota Badlands. Shawn had been at the ranch for only a few weeks before we left, and we decided he would go with us. At this early stage, he was not ready to give up the right to make his own decisions. But that would change by the time the trip was over.

We camped overnight near one of the cities along the route, and the next day we went to a big water park. It was going to be in the low 90s, and we told everyone to dress in a swimsuit and a t-shirt. Shawn came out of the tent in black jeans and a black long-sleeved shirt. I asked if he had brought his swimming suit with him. He said he didn't swim and was dressed just fine. So he spent a long hot day sitting in a chair while everyone else had a great time in the water.

A few days later, as we were heading back to Wisconsin, we pulled into a gas station for fuel and a "pit stop." John told everyone to go to the bathroom, as we would not be stopping for another two hours. Shawn stayed in the van, and when I encouraged him to go to the bathroom, he said he did not have to go. I emphasized that it would be two hours before he could go again. He ignored me. Shawn didn't know that John and I always followed through on anything we told the boys we would do. If you make idle threats, it doesn't take long for teenagers to discount or challenge anything you tell them.

After half an hour back on the road, Shawn announced from the back of the van that he had to go to the bathroom. John said we would be stopping in about an hour and a half, and he would have to hold it. In a few minutes he reported he could not hold it much longer, so I told him to find an empty pop can and go in that. Somehow he did it. Then he said, "Can I pitch this out the window?" John told him, "of course not." He had to hold the can until we got to the next stop. He held his warm pop can for an hour and a half. That was a turning point for Shawn, and we saw a positive change in his attitude from that time on.

After his discharge from Rawhide, Shawn and a good friend, Shawn Kostrzewa, decided to get summer jobs in the resort area of Door County, Wisconsin. He worked the early morning shift, assisting the baker at the Wagon Trail restaurant. As the summer drew to a close, he started to look for winter employment. He enjoyed spending time with elderly people and decided to try working at a nursing home. He envisioned sitting in a sunroom visiting, playing checkers or cards and helping residents with meals. He was eighteen, but still a few months away from getting his driver's license due to some driving infractions, so our son Tim drove him around to visit nursing homes.

He applied for employment as a Certified Nursing Assistant, back when training was done on the job with weekly technical school training. Assistants could be hired with no formal training. He was hired at Brewster Village, a county short-term rehabilitation and long-term nursing facility in Appleton. His first day on the job was nothing like he expected. Ruth, the nurse he was assisting, introduced herself and said, "Shawn, here are some rubber gloves and a roll of towels. You need to clean up Bill in room four."

"Do you mean clean him up for supper?"

With a grin she said, "Oh no. Bill has a bowel problem and has messed his clothes and bed. You clean him up as best you can, and I will come in and help change the bedding."

Despite this shaky start, he loved all the patients, and they loved him. There was a lot of hard work, but he did have plenty of time to visit and play checkers. He also helped with Lady, a golden retriever owned by another nursing assistant, Jane Douville. Lady was a service dog and was loved by the patients. She wore a service dog jacket and a knapsack. She knew most of the long-term patients by their first names, and when Jane or Shawn put a newspaper in her knapsack and said, "Take it to Mary." Lady would trot right to Mary's room and wait for her to take the newspaper. Then, without any command, she'd return to the nurse's station to wait for her next task.

The supervisor of the psychiatric unit was Sara Bohlman. She was beautiful and very personable, and Shawn was smitten with her. Almost every day he faked that his unit was out of something thing as an excuse to ask Sara for help.

One day Shawn and Sara were visiting during a break, and she asked him what it was like living at Rawhide Boys Ranch. He asked if she would like to see it, and Sara said yes. They went out to dinner and then took the thirty-minute trip to Rawhide. Sara was impressed with the tour, and with Shawn. They have been married for twelve years.

Shawn stepped down from working at the nursing home due to some health challenges and began working in movie production. Michael Sajbel, is a successful Hollywood movie director who had worked four summers at Rawhide while he was getting his college degree, he became aware of Shawn's artistic talents and hired him to sketch scenes for production shoots. That led to reading scripts and finally to serving on the production crew for some of Michael's films. Shawn has even appeared in some of the films as a bit actor.

But he enjoyed the years he worked in nursing home care and it made an impact on refining his compassion for others in need. We encourage parents to find a service project they can get involved in as a family. It might be working a few hours a month at a local food pantry, serving meals in a free meal program, ringing a bell for the Salvation Army at Christmas time or, like Shawn, volunteering at a nursing home. It can be anything that can be done as a family that will help others.

Visiting an elderly person who does not have a family is an excellent project for parents and children of any age. Most nursing homes even allow family dogs to be part of the visitation team. Many elderly residents love to have visitors, and they particularly like to interact with children and pets. Luckily, altruism works in both directions. Your children will feel they have brought joy to someone's life, and that is one of the best feelings of all

# CHAPTER 13

# LEARNING CAN BE FUN

## *John:*

Our local school system provides an excellent choice of educational opportunities. Our two sons graduated from New London High School, and they were proud to be "Bulldogs."

In the early years of Rawhide, all of our foster boys attended junior or senior high school in New London. But the boys that were placed with us often had not applied themselves in school and many were a year or more behind. We quickly learned that we had to provide more learning opportunities for them.

The academic levels of the Rawhide boys varied widely. One sixteen-year-old would have enough credits to be a junior, but another might have only the credits of an eighth-grader. Since we would have the boys for only one or two years, it was difficult to fit them into appropriate classes and schedules.

We started with on-campus tutoring at Rawhide for boys

approaching seventeen years old who had little chance of earning a high school diploma while they were with us. We knew it was very unlikely that they would go back to school when they turned eighteen. We assigned a staff person to mentor and tutor them in a suitable study setting, and we achieved excellent success in helping boys earn their GED certificates.

Within a few years, we made the transition to educating all the boys at Rawhide. The academic progress the boys made by attending school at the ranch was encouraging. With classes running through the summer, educational field trips, and special projects, many boys could gain two years of public school credit in twelve months.

With the addition of the Krause Field House, we were able to involve more boys on our basketball and track teams, which competed against other private schools. For some of the boys, it was their first opportunity to compete on an athletic team, and they loved it.

The school was officially named the Starr Academy, after Bart and Cherry Starr. In ten years it grew to over a dozen teachers. Once we gained official state certification by the Wisconsin Department of Education, New London High School started to send some of their "at-risk" students to Rawhide for their education.

Our teachers all had master's degrees in special education as well as teaching experience with at-risk students. Each student had an individual education plan based on his current academic level. One sixteen-year-old might be working on fifth-grade math and another at a twelfth-grade level. The goal was twofold: first, to make learning fun; and second, for students to succeed every day in class.

Instructors were encouraged to relate class instruction to real-life situations. A math class might use purchasing a new Corvette to learn how much interest would have to be paid during a particular loan period.

We also developed a motivational system for students with negative attitudes about school. If a boy refused to study or be attentive, the teacher would take him aside and privately ask what the problem was. The policy throughout the ranch was to always praise in public and correct in private, so correction was always done out of sight of the other students. Sometimes, a boy would break down and share that his mother had called the night before to say she and his father were getting a divorce, or that a family member was seriously ill. The teacher would then contact one of the houseparents to help the boy with his concerns.

Depending on the student's response, he might be asked if he could turn his attitude around or if he wanted to go back to his ranch home for the day. When a new boy was offered this option, he always opted to leave class, but he only did it once.

A staff person from the boys ranch was asked to come to the school to talk about the student's attitude. The student and staff person would meet privately with the teacher in the teacher's office.

If the boy said he did not want to stay in class, one of the house staff and the boy would walk back to the home. Here is a typical conversation, this one with Bill, one of the boys in the Aylward Home, and Sara, one of the three RI's:

"Bill, I'm really sorry that you were not willing to stay in class today and change your attitude," said Sara. "But I know your housemother will be glad to see you, as she has several things she wanted to do around the house and was not sure she could get them done by herself."

"What kinds of things?"

"I don't really know, but she will be glad to tell you."

When they arrived back at the home, the housemom, Janet, had been alerted by the teacher that Bill would be arriving shortly, and she had located the standard list kept on hand for precisely such occasions.

"Bill, I understand you didn't want to study today," Janet said. "Do you want to talk about what the problem was?"

"Not really. I just don't like school."

"Well, I'm disappointed, but I'm actually glad to have some help. We need to vacuum the first-floor carpet, and then we will wash the insides of all the windows. Sara will show you how to use the vacuum and how to clean the windows so there are no streaks. She will be checking on you, and I will be in the kitchen getting lunch ready."

The volume of work was arranged to take all the boy's time until supper. If a boy refused to work, he had to stay in his room with the door open, knowing that his access to privileges would be on hold while his discipline continued.

At the end of supper, the housedad, Rich, announced, "Bill decided he did not want to study today and has done a good job helping Sara and Janet with housework. One of his house chores is doing the supper dishes. I will be giving him a little help, showing him where things go. Janet and Sara will be leaving with everyone else right after the meal to go to the mall in Appleton. Our house party fund will give each of you two dollars to spend in the arcade. If you want to spend more, you'll have to use your own money."

Bill spent a long evening alone with one staff member and missed out on the fun. It was always amazing how an evening in town, a night on the houseboat, riding the horses, skiing, or any other exciting event automatically happened on the very day a boy refused to stay in school. The next time Bill or any one of the other boys was struggling in class and given the option of going back to the home, he almost always agreed to stay in class.

# Vocational Training

Starr Academy offers a variety of vocational classes. Over the years several well-equipped shops and half a dozen certified instructors have been able to provide excellent training for the boys. Companies such as Miller Electric and Snap-on Tools donated the shops' equipment.

If a boy planned to return to public school after leaving Rawhide, he would be scheduled to attend academic classes full time. But that included a ten-week survey of vocational training in five areas:

- Building maintenance and repair
- Automotive servicing and repair
- Food service preparation and serving
- Office functions and marketing
- Grounds and animal care

He would spend two weeks in each area, and every two-week vocational training segment was followed by two weeks in academic classes at Starr Academy.

The reason for switching back and forth after two weeks was to provide needed breaks. Most of our students had not done well in public school. They may not have applied themselves for years and been simply moved through the grades. After two weeks of intensive classes at Starr Academy, they reached a state of academic exhaustion and were ready for a break. Likewise, most had never put in a six-to-eight-hour workday, and after two weeks of vocational training, they were glad to switch back to school. After a few months of this schedule they would reach a point of being able to work full-time or attend public school.

The students at Rawhide are exposed to a variety of experiences in the trades such as auto repair, welding, carpentry, electrical, plumbing, masonry, grounds upkeep, food service, computer, and office functions, just to name a few. Those who have an aptitude and interest in a particular area are encouraged to consider technical school training. Fox Valley Technical College (FVTC), located twenty miles from the ranch, is an excellent school, and numerous students have attended and received certificates and associate degrees. Many of our students have the opportunity to participate in military-type training at the ranch, without weapons of course. Several have gone into the Army, Navy, or Marine Corps after graduating, and all have done well.

Two of the Rawhide alumni attended FVTC: Tom Boettcher and Peter Zukas. Both took courses as electrical apprentices, became Master Electricians, and went on to lifetime careers as electrical supervisors.

# About Face!

When we expanded to two homes of ten boys each, our oldest son, Steve, directed the facility and grounds care. Soon he needed more help. We were looking for someone with on-the-job experience working with teenagers. Steve told me about Ed O'Brian and suggested I meet with him. I interviewed Ed and was impressed. He was a supervisor at a large lumber outlet store and was responsible for training new employees, many of whom were in their teens. He was very qualified to be our maintenance director and work with the boys. He had developed the ability to get along with others while growing up in a family of ten brothers and five sisters. Ed liked the fact that we taught by example, with staff working shoulder-to-shoulder with the boys, and that we were a faith-based program.

In the '70s and '80s, several military-type youth boot camps were developed around the country. I knew that my own military training helped mold my character and work ethic. Jan and I visited a few places to see if this was a program we might want to try at Rawhide. I liked most of what I saw, but I totally disagreed with one aspect: the humiliation leveled at boys as young as twelve years old. In regular basic training, a military drill sergeant screams at an eighteen-year-old recruit to build respect for authority, but it is not productive for a staff person to verbally humiliate a twelve-year-old, even if the boy has a delinquency record.

I challenged Ed to develop a program with a military approach but without the humiliating harassment. He accepted the challenge and set up a one-hundred-day program we named "About Face." Boys were referred to this program through the courts and social service agencies. They lived together with houseparents as in our other homes. They were all provided matching, attractive work and dress military uniforms. They could advance through a special ranking system and change their uniform insignias from private to PFC to corporal.

The challenging program was scheduled for exactly one hundred days, but if a boy showed poor performance or attitude on any given day, that day was added back on to his time needed to complete the course. Initially, all of the boys were determined to make every day count so they could leave as soon as possible. But after a month or so their goal changed. They still wanted every day to count, but now their motivation was to move up in rank and enjoy the experience of achieving success.

Each squad of ten boys kept up their academic studies, but the character development occurred while they were spending three to four days a week working together on community projects. The squad had a four-wheel-drive, half-ton Suburban and a fifteen-passenger van. They had a matching dark-blue covered trailer loaded with construction tools, generators, and portable lighting, plus sleeping and cooking gear. They were mobile and self-contained, able to stay overnight on a project if necessary.

The About Face teams had no shortage of projects. Natural disasters were a top priority, and both squads could leave on an hour's notice for tornado, flood, or fire cleanup. As many as twenty teens and six to eight staff members would work several days at disaster sites. They also worked in community and state parks, at nursing homes, and with other nonprofit organizations like Habitat for Humanity, where they helped build homes.

The boys were told there could be news media covering any event, and they may be interviewed. At disaster sites, the boys might meet local officials, mayors, and even, on occasion, the Governor. They understood they must be on their best behavior, as they were representing a proud tradition at Rawhide. If they had a negative attitude, they were told to meet privately with their supervisor to talk it out.

Most correctional youth programs have policies that the students are not to be photographed or interviewed. We had just the opposite approach. During the placement process, we asked parents for approval for their sons to be photographed and interviewed in a positive way. We explained how proud the boys are when recognized for their hard work, and parents always gave their unconditional approval. Over the years numerous boys saw themselves on the evening news or pictured in a local paper, giving them a sense of pride they had never felt before.

Students who reached the proper rank could apply to serve on the About Face Color Guard. They marched in numerous parades and posted the colors at many events throughout Wisconsin. They looked and felt sharp in their impressive dress uniforms. After a while requests for the guard to appear even came from other states.

# Vacation Planning

I remember fondly the one or two annual vacations my parents took my brother, Dennis, and me on as we were growing up. We enjoyed the excitement of planning for the event weeks ahead. But that was not the story we heard from most of the boys sent to live with us at Rawhide.

I decided to teach an eight-hour course, spread over four sessions, on vacation planning. This sounds like some of the college courses we have all heard about, like underwater basket-weaving, but this was a very practical class. It was another example of instruction that we provided that would have lifetime benefits.

At the start of session one, I asked how many had gone on at least a four-day vacation with their families. Almost every boy raised his hand. My second question was, "Do you remember the vacation being fun?" Seldom were any hands raised.

I asked them to share why the vacation was not fun. The answers ranged from such depressing incidents as, "We drove twenty hours, and Dad got mad if he had to stop for us to go to the bathroom;" "My mom and her boyfriend got into a fight and did not speak to each other for two days;" "Dad got drunk, and Mom drove us home two days early." They needed to learn that vacations should be fun.

At the time Jack Olson was the Wisconsin Lieutenant Governor and a close friend of Bart Starr. Jack owned the Olson Boat Lines in the Wisconsin Dells, a famous year-round vacation destination. He offered our staff members and boys free access to more than two-dozen major rides and events. They could go for a ride in the World War II military "Ducks" that travel over land and water, spend a day at one of the country's largest water parks, enjoy several go-kart tracks, and go for a cruise on the Wisconsin River.

The Wisconsin Dells Visitor and Convention Bureau publish an impressive, full-color book every year. It lists hundreds of events, rides, campgrounds, motels, and restaurants in the area. I gave one of these to every student.

Next I gave them a sheet of paper with the details of their project. It said they had a wife and three children. One was a boy age fourteen, and the other two were girls ages six and eight. They had to plan a vacation of five days and four nights at the Dells. The project sheet said they had $1,000 to spend. If they ate in restaurants, they could figure on three dollars per person for breakfast, six dollars for lunch, and eight dollars for supper. If they planned to prepare their meals at a campsite, they could figure half that amount. Campgrounds, motels, and all the activities listed their prices in the book.

We had a question-and-answer time, and by then we had used up the first two-hour class period. They were to come back to the second class with a day-to-day list and timeline showing where they would stay, their meal costs, and the events they would do every day.

The results were predictable. When each student read his four-day vacation list of what he would be doing, every choice revolved around him. They would stay in a hotel, eat in restaurants of their choice and participate in the events that were interesting to them. Events for the six-and-eight-year-old girls were not represented. After they had all finished reading their vacation plans, we opened the class up to comments. Little by little, they started to see that the plans did not serve the whole family. Plus, they used most of their money on hotel accommodations and eating out, with little left for activities.

Before I dismissed the second session, I gave them my classic statement about vacations: "Vacations are not for fathers; they are for fathers to make sure everyone else has a good time." Then I told them to rework their plans.

The revised plans they brought to the third class were much better. Most planned to camp out, or at least stay in an economy motel. They would do at least some of their own cooking, and they had scheduled at least one event a day that each of the other family members would enjoy. And they were able to do it within their budget.

During the last class, everyone collaborated on planning an actual trip to the Dells. This time they did not have young sisters or daughters they had to account for, so the events could all be for guys. They usually included attending every go-kart track available plus numerous other high-energy rides.

Soon after the completion of the class, the actual trip to the Dells took place. We would arrive and set up our tents for our four-day vacation. We prepared all our meals at the campsite, so our costs were modest. Each of the boys was assigned responsibilities such as taking pictures, keeping a daily journal, preparing meals, cleaning up after meals, or keeping track of the budget. After the trip each boy had a class project in which he put together a journal and pictorial record of the vacation. We know from visits with numerous alumni that they use their knowledge from this class and the trip when they plan vacations for their own families.

# Florida Trips

In the '70s we provided an exciting, annual, two-week trip to Disney World. We planned the trip three months in advance, and we told the boys they had to earn it with good behavior. In the ten years we ran the trips, I only remember that three boys out of dozens had to stay home because of their attitude.

We took the trip during the New London High School spring break, usually around Easter. The boys' teachers understood that this was an educational trip, so they were given another week off, but they had to present a journal of the trip upon returning back to school.

The boys would volunteer for at least two of these areas of responsibility.

- Working with staff to develop a budget and record daily expenses
- Taking pictures every day
- Journaling the events of each day
- Packing and unpacking the tents, camping gear, food, and cooking supplies
- Helping with meals and clean-up (Everyone helped with this on a schedule.)
- Studying the history of the Civil War battle of Lookout Mountain, Tennessee

We would travel with a motor home Jan and I owned, plus a fifteen-passenger ranch van that pulled a covered twin-axle storage trailer. The trailer carried suitcases, tents, camping gear, bedrolls, and lots of food. It had a full-size refrigerator and freezer that we plugged in at a campsite. We were able to carry food for the entire trip, only stopping at a few McDonalds on the way down and back. Gas was under fifty cents a gallon, and ten days in Disney's Fort Wilderness Campground cost us under a thousand dollars.

As the boys boarded the school bus for the last day before the trip, they had their personal gear all packed. They got home at four, had lunch, and climbed into the van or motor home an hour later for the fifteen-hour trip to Chattanooga, Tennessee. Jan and I, plus our two RIs, were ready for the all-night drive. By about eight the next morning, we were eight hundred miles from the Wisconsin winter, with temperatures usually at sixty degrees or warmer. We had reservations at a campground, and we set up camp for the next twenty-four hours.

After breakfast the next day, we all got in the van and headed up the steep, winding road to the top of Lookout Mountain. It is a beautiful view from the top, looking out over four states, and the boys already knew about the famous battle where Confederate General Braxton Bragg was soundly defeated by the Union forces. They were also able to ride the world's steepest railway, the Incline. It is a mile in length from the base of the mountain to the top, and it reaches seventy-two degrees in grade at some places.

The next day we would break camp and travel the final five hundred miles to Disney World. Our motor home had a large bed in the rear with a big picture window. Four or five boys would pile on the bed and hold up funny communication cards to cars pulling in behind us, since we were usually traveling slower than most traffic. The cards said things like, "Send Money," "You're Cute," "Please Push Us," and other jokes. On one occasion in Georgia, cars were passing us and laying on the horn, shaking their fists, or giving us the one-finger wave. I asked Jan to go to the back and see what was going on. She found the boys had taken a magic marker written a new card that said, "The North Won." Jan quickly tore that card up and delivered a short lesson about why you do not talk about who won the Civil War when you're visiting the South.

The ten days at the campground were great, and the visits to the theme parks were exciting. But the most productive time of the whole trip was sitting around the campfire in the evening. This was a time of bonding, laughing, and counseling with the boys. They all said someday they would bring their families on a trip like this one. It was certainly different than the unfortunate trips they had taken with their families.

# EAA Young Eagles Program

Rawhide is half an hour drive to the Experimental Aircraft Association (EAA) grounds at the Oshkosh airfield. It has a large aircraft museum, and we planned a visit during their fly-in event every year.

Those boys with an interest in flying went on a plane ride with my brother, Dennis Gillespie, a pilot and owner of a Cessna 172 Skyhawk. He has taken more than 1,200 boys and girls for an hour-long flight as part of the EAA Young Eagles program. He would spend an hour prior to takeoff explaining the principles of flight. During the ride, each of the three student passengers was able to take control for ten minutes and experience the thrill of flying.

Some years ago, Dennis took a thirteen-year-old and his mother for their first airplane ride. The flight impressed the boy, and as a young adult, he took flying lessons and went on to get his instructor's certificate. He would go on to teach flying to others at a local flight service.

Jody Gawthrop, a sixteen-year-old girl from Illinois, became the two-millionth Young Eagle to take to the air. She had the extra honor of receiving her preflight check and flight from famous actor and flyer, Harrison Ford, at the July 2016 EAA World Air Show. They flew over the show grounds, on which about ten thousand airplanes from around the country and the world were parked.

# Rawhide Training Pays Off

Another class at Rawhide involved creating a resume, finding job openings, and learning how to look and act during an interview. We initially made some calls to open doors for our ranch graduates for job interviews. Some employers were very willing to hire alumni out of respect for Rawhide, but many of the boys who accepted those first jobs didn't value them as much as if they had worked hard to get them on their own. Some worked a few weeks and quit.

We changed the policy and told boys they had to find their first job by themselves. If they held the job for a year, were successful, and wanted to move up, then we would make some contacts on their behalf. That system worked much better, as the guys that had held a job for a year had usually already found opportunities to move up the employment ladder on their own. The success rate for graduates finding steady employment after Rawhide was high. All of the boys who went into the military also did very well. They reported back to us that their basic training and service time was "no problem." because of the structure and demands placed on them at Rawhide.

# Dan Zimprich

Dan definitely learned how to make work fun. Like all the boys, his life did not start out in a promising direction. His first ride in a police car came when he was in second grade, and a pattern of delinquency continued for many years. After Dan's placements in a couple of other correction homes, his juvenile judge decided to try Rawhide.

Dan had asthma, and cleaning barns caused him to sneeze, but he loved animals, including horses, and he could ride without a problem as long as he stayed out of the barn. He enjoyed cooking and housekeeping, so Jan counted it as a treat to have his help around the kitchen and to have him supervise the other guys on the Saturday morning housekeeping duties.

We soon discovered that Dan was also interested in cars and office work. He was a natural for learning office practices, and he worked as a secretarial assistant to Barb Smoll, who handled all the records for the vehicle program. It was a demanding job with an ever-increasing volume of donated cars, trucks, boats, and campers coming in every month. Dan's attention to detail and dependability would serve him well in the years to come.

After leaving Rawhide, he showed that his Dells trip was a positive influence, as his first jobs were both in the Dells. The first was full-time at one of the water parks, and the second was as a waiter at a Dells pizza restaurant. His next employment was at the Madison IHOP, where he quickly moved up the ladder to restaurant manager.

One evening after serving the Wisconsin traditional Friday Fish Fry to a large IHOP crowd, most of the staff had already been dismissed, and Dan was finishing cleanup when another customer came in the front door. The customer apologized, not realizing the restaurant was closed, but Dan said it was not a problem and he would be glad to serve him something simple. Dan turned on one of the cleaned grills to make him a hot sandwich and sat down with the customer and a cup of coffee. Going the extra mile for that customer led to a whole new career for Dan.

The unexpected customer explained that he had rented a store in the East Towne Mall to market his line of wildlife prints, and he was looking for someone good with customers to work for him part time. Dan had Wednesdays and Thursdays off and said he would be available on those days. Working seven days a week was not new to Dan, as this was common during the Dells summer vacation months.

Within a few months, Dan bought the wildlife collection inventory, took over the store, and jumped into this new opportunity with both feet. Dan's dad chipped in to help him buy the Deck the Walls franchise. Included in the large inventory of framed pictures were two hundred autographed prints of Brett Farve, the Green Bay Packers quarterback. This was a huge, unexpected benefit that brought in Packer fans. Dan and his business partner, his wife Ciara, decided to specialize in marketing sports memorabilia.

They renamed the store "On 2 the Field," and they now carry thousands of sports memorabilia items featuring players from the Packers, Milwaukee Bucks, Wisconsin Badgers, Chicago Bulls and Bears, and Minnesota Vikings. They have become good friends with numerous Packers and have had them at their store for signing parties. The stars whose memorabilia they market start with Super Bowl I and II players Jerry Kramer and Fuzzy Thurston and go on to more current players like Jordy Nelson, James Jones, Aaron Rogers, and Clay Matthews.

They attend all the Packer games and invite customers and sports celebrities to tailgate with them at what they call their "H2 party." Their H2 Hummer is customized inside and out in green and gold and sports a forty-two-inch HD television screen.

Dan and Ciara have grown their business into a very profitable enterprise. Dan credits his time at Rawhide with teaching him how to make work fun.

# Bee Vang

I made plans to have coffee with Bee Vang, an alumnus of the

Rawhide About Face program, at the Copper Rock restaurant in Appleton. Bee had excelled at Rawhide, gone on to college, and become a pastor. I was looking forward to learning more from him about his amazing story.

## *Bee Vang:*

My mother and dad divorced before I was born. When I was two years old, Mother came to America as a refugee from Thailand. She came over with four of my brothers and sisters, who ranged from three to fifteen years old, and me. We were sponsored by a Lutheran church and came to live in Eau Claire, Wisconsin. We attended the Lutheran church for a few years, and at about five years old I went to a children's program at an Evangelical Free Church. I didn't understand much of it at the time, but I heard about Jesus at both churches.

I had been aware of racial discrimination since arriving in the United States, but I was seven years of age when an older boy called me a racial name and spit in my face. The racial comments and bullying continued from other students. Up until I became a teenager, I was in numerous fights, almost all of which were racially motivated, and I also found myself in various trouble with the police.

Through all of my years of frustration, I kept wishing I had a dad. I even remember on a few occasions asking God, whom I really did not know anything about, if he would help me find a dad. Little did I know that I would get several very soon.

In September of 2000, I went before the judge again, and this time he had seen enough of me. He directed that I be sent to a place called Rawhide Boys Ranch. I didn't know at the time that this would be a wonderful blessing from God.

I arrived for the hundred-day About Face program and moved in with the About Face houseparents, Jeff and Brenda Stump. Jeff was the first to show me what a dad was like. He loved me just like one of his kids. He was the first man to ever hug me. He was the first man to tell me he loved me.

## *John:*

The About Face program runs one hundred demanding days. If a student gets any demerits, that day does not count and is added on. It is rare for anyone to go through with no demerit days, but Bee's days were perfect, and he was one of the few to graduate on schedule.

It was now time for Bee to leave Rawhide, and we had room for him with Dave and Barb Lehman, a great Christian couple who were one of our CATCH home families. "Dave became like another Dad," Bee said, "and Barb, just like Brenda, was a wonderful Mom."

He still had three years of high school left, and with the help of scholarship money from the Bret Starr-Rawhide Memorial Fund, Bee attended Valley Christian Academy, a private high school in Oshkosh. He was a good student and played on the football team. At the time, Dan Birr was an administrator and the football coach at the school. Shortly thereafter, Dan went on to be the superintendent of Starr Academy, Rawhide's high school.

When Bee was a high school junior John Solberg, the Rawhide Executive Director, asked him to accompany him on presentations about Rawhide to service clubs and churches. Bee became the hit of the programs.

He also started to research colleges about this time. With the help of Craig Smoll, his caseworker at Rawhide, he visited Moody Bible Institute in Chicago and toured the campus. Bee liked what he saw. Backed by several impressive support letters, he was accepted.

At this point Bee told me, "Now it was time to pray about how I was going to come up with the thousands of dollars to attend college. But I was just going to concentrate on asking God for the funds for the first year. I applied for a scholarship to the school. They have what is called the "Presidential Scholarship program." There were five hundred incoming freshmen, and five students would be selected for that scholarship. I was one of the five. That covered more than half the fees, and once again the Bret Starr Rawhide Foundation blessed me with help for the rest. In addition, I qualified for a Lutheran Social Services grant for students who have been in foster care. They also provided a new computer and some living expenses. I only had to raise fifteen hundred dollars the first year. Scholarship funds from Rawhide and others covered a large portion of my expenses the next two years."

During his three years at Moody Bible Institute, Bee worked with other students in one of Chicago's toughest neighborhoods, the Carbrini Green Projects. He also mentored a Little Brother from that area, a boy without a father, like Bee.

In 2008, with only one semester left to get his degree in Bible studies, Bee was offered a position that had just opened up as the junior high youth director for the two-thousand-member Christ the Rock Church in Menasha, Wisconsin. It was a difficult decision, but it was what he had been preparing for. After praying and consulting with others, he accepted the position and served in that job for six years.

Bee and his wife Amanda, a pastor's daughter, felt God leading them to start a ministry for the hundreds of Hmong and other ethnic peoples in the Appleton community. They learned that the Christian and Missionary Alliance denomination was looking for someone to head up a missions program. After several meetings, Bee was hired as the pastor for this new venture. In September 2015, Bee and his family opened the Refuge Church in Appleton.

The C & MA church association has about 2,500 churches in the U.S. and 12,000 worldwide. The 5,000 member Appleton Alliance Church is a supporting congregation for the Refuge Church.

Bee concluded, "We are honored and humbled that God would choose us to take on such a task. Starting a new church is hard, and when you invest in the lives of people from different socioeconomic and ethnic backgrounds, you have to totally rely on the Holy Spirit to lead and love you through it so you can do the same."

# CHAPTER 14
# TOUGH LOVE WITH A HEART

## *John:*

Most of the boys sent to Rawhide by social service agencies and juvenile courts had serious delinquency records. Also many had great
leadership skills, but they were using those skills in the wrong way. Our
approach was "Tough love, but always fair." We handed out lots of
praise, but our standards had to be met. Because the boys were with
us for only a short time and they had deeply engrained destructive be-
haviors, we didn't have time to go easy on them. Doing so would have
encouraged them to manipulate and take advantage of us.

Tough love at Rawhide meant that misbehavior led to losing
privileges. For serious offenses boys would face appropriate discipline. Because there were so many fun activities going on, like weekend ski outings or a day of tubing on the river, the risk of missing
out on the fun was often all that was needed to encourage positive
change.

Offenses such as stealing, drug use, and running away some-times earned the discipline of hauling cement blocks. We created a penalty that was physically demanding yet gave a boy a clear goal and allowed him to work off his discipline faster if he wanted to. As was referred to in an earlier chapter, each home had a pile of one hundred cement blocks weighing twenty pounds each. The blocks were easily visible from the home, as was a stake in the ground three hundred feet away from the pile—the length of a football field. This stake was also visible from the home. A boy on discipline would move the pile from its original location to the other location. He could then move it back, and that counted for two piles moved.

The number of times the pile must be moved was dependent upon the seriousness of the offense. A small lie might be one or two piles. A serious problem could incur up to twenty piles.

We laid out guidelines so a boy would not hurt himself. He had to wear a long-sleeve shirt and use leather gloves. He could haul two blocks at a time, but not move more than one pile a day for the first three days. Then he could move two piles a day but was only required to move one. After six days he could carry four blocks at a time if he wanted to. He could do this by putting two blocks on top of each other, then putting his arms through the center holes and grabbing the lower block.

Supervising the boy was simple because there was no way to cheat. He would get permission to go outside to move blocks, and a staff member would look out the window to see where the pile was. When the pile was moved, he would come in and staff would take a look to check that the blocks had all been moved to the new location. If a boy refused to move blocks, one pile was added for each day he refused. We never had a boy go more than three days before accept-ing his discipline.

Moving blocks proved to be a great deterrent to breaking the rules, and at the same time, the boys felt pride in accomplishing the block discipline. After moving half a dozen piles over a few days, boys would show us the muscles in their arms and shoulders. As Jan and I visit with alumni who are now in their 50s and 60s, some brag about the number of piles of blocks they had to move before they finished the program.

Hauling blocks is no longer one of the disciplines at Rawhide. It is too demanding for our protective society, but it proved to be very effective at the time.

# Looking for the Facts

We had a very successful way of getting the facts about possible disobedience. It worked well even if we only had a suspicion that something was going on. It might just be a rumor, like someone had brought back drugs from a home visit.

Jan and I would meet with all the boys in the living room and explain that we were aware of some things going on and wanted to talk with each boy privately. At that point we had all the boys sit so they could not make eye contact with each other. Jan would remain in the living room to make sure the guys did not communicate.

I would start with one of the newest boys and meet with him in our home office. I would have the boy sit facing me, intentionally letting him glance at a full page of notes on the first page of my note pad. The notes were just sentences that said nothing, but he assumed I had already obtained information about the problem.

Next I gave a short speech explaining the importance of honesty and that if guys were honest with us, any necessary discipline was always reduced. I then looked at him and said, "Tell me your part in what is going on."

A newer boy might not have been involved at all, but he usually knew a little about what was going on. He might say something like, "I'm not involved, and I refused to even attend the meeting the guys had last night after hours." I wrote down every comment and used them when I questioned the next boy.

The same process took place with boy number two, but my importance-of-honesty speech ended with, "We are aware of last night's late meeting, and we would like to hear your version of why you're involved in this." More notes followed. By the time we got to the final boy, I would have compiled four to six pages of details. Sometimes a totally different problem surfaced from what we had suspected based on the original rumors.

After completion of the individual visits, Jan and I would privately confer on the proper response and specific discipline for each boy. We presented our decisions to the whole group, usually a couple of hours after the start of the individual interrogations.

We rarely decided on group punishment, but sometimes we would respond with group forgiveness. Depending on the seriousness of the problem and how the guys cooperated, Jan and I might conclude the debriefing with total forgiveness and maybe even take everyone out for pizza. After the boys' long evening sitting in the living room and wondering what was going to happen, forgiveness was a very welcome conclusion.

## Creative Discipline

The houseparents sometimes assigned creative disciplines appropriate for the offense. One day I saw a boy walking across the grounds carrying a saddle on his shoulder. When I asked what he was doing, he said, "I left the horse I was riding yesterday in the paddock all night with his saddle on. My housedad said I have to keep this saddle within three feet of me for twenty-four hours. I had to sleep with it in my bed last night."

# Boys Missing

The phone rang at three o'clock one morning. A voice on the other end said, "This is the Outagamie County Sheriff's Office. I'm looking for John Gillespie."

"That would be me."

"We have four of your boys who were picked up trying to outrun one of our squad cars," the officer said.

I learned that they had taken a fifteen-year-old, six-cylinder Rambler that had been in our shop for a tune-up. When they took it, one of the spark plugs had been removed for a compression test. They were speeding when a patrol car behind them put on its red lights. They tried to outrun the patrol car with a car running on only five cylinders. It sounded like a steam engine with the compression hissing out of the missing spark plug hole. The side street they careened down turned out to be a dead end. It was fortunate that their recklessness ended safely with their arrest. They were booked at the county jail, and the officer wanted to know what we wanted done with them.

This occurred in the early '70s, before there were clear regulations on how long you could hold someone in jail without a court order. From conversations with numerous boys, we knew one night in jail was not a deterrent. The boys thought it was cool, a badge of honor. A boy's first time in jail needed to be long enough that he didn't want to return ever again.

He gave me their names. The first two had been placed with us recently, but Jim Lysaght and Peter Zukas had been with us several months and were both leaders, though not always in a positive way. I asked the officer to hold the boys overnight, and said I would stop in the morning to discuss a plan. I asked if he had room to put them in separate cells where they could not see each other. I didn't care if they could talk to each other. He said they had plenty of space to separate them.

The next morning, I met with the jail supervisor and explained the plan. We wanted them all to sit for a full week, and then I would come in and get the boy who had been with us less than a month. After seven days, I came to the jail and asked them to get the first boy but not to say who had come for him or even that he would be leaving.

The first boy was taken from his cell and brought to the intake area, where I questioned him on his involvement in the runaway. At the end of my questions, I asked if he wanted to come back to Rawhide. He definitely wanted to come back. I explained that he would be on disciplinary restriction, and I took him back to the ranch with me.

The other three boys had no idea where their partner in crime had gone or who picked him up. The officers at the jail told them they were not sure what happened.

Seven days later, I repeated the same process, secretly picking up boy number two. Jim and Peter still remained. Now very concerned, they started writing Jan and me letters every other day. They were begging to come back and pledging they would never do anything wrong again.

Letting them sit that long may seem harsh, and it was tough on them. There are good reasons our courts no longer allow teenagers to be held in jail without a court order, but that doesn't mean we shouldn't encourage our judges to be tough on juvenile crimes. An extended stay in jail can be a life-changing experience, and in this case it helped all four of the boys.

The two new boys did just fine in their next year with us. And when Jim and Peter finally returned to the ranch, they became positive leaders. Both shared with the other boys that their long stay in jail made them resolve to never land there again.

# Peter Zukas

At the end of his third week in jail I picked up Peter Zukas. He was so relieved he hugged me, and Peter was not the hugging type.

He had a delinquency record starting in his preteen years. His father was a tough and demanding state patrol officer. In Peter's memory, his dad was a police officer first and a father second. Following are notes Peter wrote about his childhood:

## *Peter:*

I had run away because my father was angry about something, and that usually meant he would find some reason to beat me. His beatings went on until I cried. By age thirteen I would not cry even during a five-minute beating, and I guess that took the fun out of it for him, as then he stopped beating me. He would just have me locked up in jail.

I was hitchhiking into Green Bay when a police officer stopped to question me. He knew my father and called him to see what to do with me. He told the officer to take me to the county jail and said he would call them. My father knew all the jail personnel, and he got a hold of the person in charge and told them to teach me a lesson and put me in jail. So at age eleven I spent my first full weekend in jail.

By age twelve I was into burglary, shoplifting, and drugs. Some of my teenage friends were into drugs and recruited me to make drug deliveries for whomever they were working for. I would carry up to a thousand hits of LSD in a grocery bag. I never got caught.

By age thirteen my drug dealing had gotten me connected with at least five street gangs in the Green Bay area. I always carried a switchblade knife and sometimes a gun.

At age fourteen my father moved our family to Tomah, a town in central Wisconsin. I was in ninth grade and quickly became the main junior and senior high drug supplier, bringing drugs from my Green Bay sources. I hung-out with the worst four kids in school. I was arrested for distributing drugs and was waiting for the court to determine whether I would be sent to a secure juvenile correction facility. But at this point, I think God took my future in his hands. Little did I know when two couples who were definitely not in my social group invited me to go with them to a concert, that my life was about to change. I assumed it was a rock concert.

## *John:*

We met Peter in an unusual way. Jan and I took our sons and foster sons to a gymnasium in Oshkosh, where several hundred youth were gathered to hear Nicky Cruz, a national youth speaker who had been a gang leader in New York. The boys were enamored with the story of Nicky's life, and at the end of his talk he stuck around to talk with the students.

Upon reaching the front of the line, we introduced ourselves as coming from the Rawhide Boys Ranch, and Nicky shook hands with each of the boys. We stood to the side as others came forward to meet Nicky, but after a few minutes we heard him call out, "Hey, Rawhide!" We turned around to see him waving us back. He pushed a teenager dressed all in black toward us. "Here, this is Peter, and he needs a friend." Nicky turned back to meeting others, letting us awkwardly stand facing this obviously angry young man.

I broke the awkwardness by telling him who we were, that we were going to stop for pizza, and that he was very welcome to come along. Peter's blunt response was, "I'm here with my gang, and they would not be interested." At that point two well-groomed teenage girls and a guy standing behind Peter said, "We brought Peter with us, and we would all like to go with you for pizza. We are from a church youth group."

Peter and his unlikely "gang" followed us to Shakey's Pizza, where Jan and I purposely sat across the table from this self-proclaimed gang leader. We tried to make conversation and talked some about Rawhide Boys Ranch, but he showed no interest. He was trying to project a tough-guy image. When the pizzas were delivered, Peter calmly pulled out his four-inch switchblade, snapped it open, and carefully cut the pizza that was already very well cut.

Several months later, we got a call from the Brown County Juvenile Court in Green Bay, asking if we had an opening. We didn't, but we were going to have one in less than a month. When I asked the boy's name, I was told, "His name is Peter Zukas, and we need an immediate placement."

I explained that we had already met Peter and would accept him right away. We would double up somehow to make room for this young man. We were quite sure he would fit in at our house.

Peter did fit in as soon as he realized he couldn't intimidate us or our guys. He knew from our previous evening together that we cared about him. But he still had a combative nature. That would soon be put to good use on the football field.

On one of Bart and Cherry Starrs' early summer visits to Rawhide, Peter spent some time talking privately with Bart. After their visit, Bart asked me if it would be all right to take Peter to his week-long football camp at the University of Wisconsin campus at Stevens Point. When they were talking, Bart learned that Peter had never played organized football but wished he had. Bart explained that he would be leading a camp for high school athletes and would be glad to pick Peter up and drop him off for the Monday-through-Friday sessions. Picking up Peter meant adding another twenty miles to the ninety-mile trip from Green Bay to Stevens Point twice a day. We were awed by Bart's generous offer and absolutely in favor of Peter attending the camp. Peter accepted Bart's invitation.

Peter was a quick learner at the camp, and no one suspected that playing football was new to him. He became the center of attention, since the other high school athletes saw him arriving every day with Bart and climbing back into his car to go home. Everyone assumed this was one of Bart and Cherry's sons, and Peter did nothing to alter that assumption. When he was asked what it was like to live with a famous father, Peter just said, "It's great." After all, his father was a state patrolman, and his response was sort of true.

One of the biggest impressions Bart made on Peter did not take place on the football field. On one of the trips home, they stopped at a Dairy Queen, and Bart ordered two malts. Before the malts were done mixing, one of the teenagers working behind the counter said, "Are you Bart Starr?" When Bart said yes, the server asked if he could have his autograph on his Dairy Queen cap. Bart graciously obliged, and that created an instant line of staff and customers asking for autographs. They all wanted to meet Bart Starr and get his autograph.

The signing went on for over half an hour, with Bart taking the time to ask questions of every person he met. Peter could not believe someone as famous as Bart Starr would take that much time with people he did not know. He said Bart never did get to drink his malt, and when the autograph signing ended, they got into the car for the return trip to Rawhide.

High school football practice started two weeks before Peter's senior year began at New London High School, and he loved it. A few days after the team began practicing in full pads, he came home and announced, "This is great. It's the first time in my life I can knock someone down and get praised for it." And knocking opposing players down became a regular Friday night occurrence for Peter, who was the starting middle linebacker.

A few months into the school year, Peter told us after supper about a suggestion he had made to one of his teachers regarding what he thought would be a good policy change for the school. The teacher agreed and said he should present his idea to the student council. "What's a student council?" he asked us.

We explained that a few students were elected from each class to serve as leaders, with an opportunity to impact school policies and activities. A teacher advisor would take appropriate ideas to the principal. Peter said he'd look for a student on the council to present his idea. He found a council member, only to be told it was a dumb idea. When he complained to me, I suggested he run for the student council at the next election. A month later, Peter announced that he had been elected. We congratulated him on winning a position on the student council. He replied, "Oh no! I found out the class president has the most say. You're looking at the senior class president."

As we already knew, Peter was a good communicator, and he did a great job as class president. He honed his leadership skills and wrote articles for the school newspaper.

After leaving Rawhide at age eighteen, Peter enlisted in the U. S. Marine Corps, where he was able to continue to develop his newfound skills. He demonstrated leadership in boot camp by graduating second out of one hundred Marines. He was assigned the First Squad Leader position and received his first meritorious promotion. He went on to graduate from the Defense Information School of photojournalism in Indianapolis. His primary duties were as photographer, journalist, and later editor for a newspaper serving three east coast Marine bases. Peter supervised five reporters from each of the three bases. He received an honorable mention for a feature story in *Stars and Stripes*, a national military magazine. He and his team printed and distributed five thousand copies of a twenty-plus-page paper every week.

Peter received four meritorious promotions and was discharged as a sergeant after three years of service. When I asked him what the key was to becoming a successful military journalist, he said, "I always made sure the generals looked good in the weekly newspaper."

# Jim Lysaght

After his four full weeks in jail, I picked up Jim Lysaght. He was the third oldest of eight children and had become a ward of the state at age ten. His mother was in a variety of ongoing legal troubles and spent a lot of time in jail. Jim's father would not take any of the children, so they were all sent to different foster homes. Jim had been placed in four foster homes before coming to Rawhide. During times when he was able to go home, the environment he experienced was anything but stable. His mother moved a couple times a year, which meant Jim and his siblings were constantly changing schools with little academic success along the way. He grew up angry at life, feeling like he had no family.

The four weeks in jail did wonders. Jim meant everything he said in the pleading letters he sent me from jail. If he were allowed to come back to Rawhide, he would never break the rules again. That is what happened. He became a good leader with the other guys and became a member of the ranch maintenance crew. After turning eighteen, Jim went into the Army and became an Airborne Ranger. He was stationed in Italy and the Philippines, making dozens of jumps.

Several months after his discharge, he showed up at Rawhide asking if we could use his help. We had an opening, and he served several years as our grounds maintenance director.

A great fringe benefit for Jim was meeting Paula, who was working at Rawhide in housekeeping and helping Jan in the horse program. She had grown up on a nearby family farm, and she was a hard worker. They were married a few years later and lived on the grounds in a caretaker's cabin.

Jim went on to work as a high-rise steelworker with the Milwaukee Local 1343 Union, and helped erect several downtown Milwaukee office buildings. This was before the OSHA rules for safety lines, and as Jim relates, he got a nice view of the Lake Michigan shoreline while standing thirty stories in the air on twelve-inch-wide steel beams, without any tether lines.

# An Unusual Collection

Discipline for the boys was based on what we thought would best produce an attitude change. Sometimes the penalty even for running away might be very lenient. One summer day just after supper, one of the boys told us that Kurt and Francis, two fourteen-year-olds, had run away. Jan and I jumped in a car and drove up and down the town road looking for them. But after a few miles, we found nothing. Heavy woods bordered both sides of the road, and they could easily hide from sight when they heard a car coming.

We returned to the lodge and helped the other boys finish the dishes before relaxing with a cup of coffee at the dining room table. We couldn't do anything but wait for word from the boys or the police. To our surprise, an hour after they had left, Kurt walked into the house and sat down at the table right next to Jan and me, out of breath. "I'm never gonna run away with Francis again. He's stupid." I asked what he meant.

"He made me carry his suitcase for over a mile, and I couldn't do it anymore. I asked him what he had in it, because it was heavy and would clunk once in a while. Francis said, 'Well, I have a pair of underwear, and then I have my railroad spike collection.' At that point I threw his suitcase in the ditch, and about thirty railroad spikes fell out. I left him and walked home."

It was difficult not to laugh as Kurt shared his story with total disgust. Only a few minutes later, guess who came in the dining room door, dragging his suitcase? Of course it was Francis, also looking exhausted.

As we talked with both of the boys, it became apparent this was not a very successful runaway experience. Both seemed sincerely sorry they had left, and we decided on a minimal punishment. They were put on a week of restriction, meaning no fun activities for seven days. After three days we forgave the rest of their restriction because of their good attitude. During the next two years, they both became very promising young men, and they never ran away again.

# Moving In and Out

## *Al Phillips:*

I was sent to Rawhide because I had severe anger issues. A lot of it came from my father using me as a punching bag when I was about eight years old. In our home I was never taught how to communicate without anger or violence.

I was constantly in fights in school. When anyone would confront me about anything, I would strike out. As a teenager I got into a fight with two guys at a roller rink and beat them up pretty badly. I put them in the trunk of their car and tossed the keys in a field in back of the rink. Their brother called the police, and they came to my house and arrested me. Shortly after that the social services department asked the court for permission to send me someplace where I could get help. Lucky for me, they decided Rawhide would be that place.

## *John:*

Al fit in quite well in our home, but he had a hefty chip on his shoulder. He did not take direction without bristling. This was an area we were constantly working on, and we thought we were making some progress until he ran away.

One snowy winter day, Al got upset about something at Rawhide and decided to go back to Green Bay, his hometown forty-five miles away. When we discovered he was gone, we drove down the road, but he had ducked into the woods and was nowhere to be found. A staff member, Paul Michiels, lived in a farmhouse a mile away. Paul was just returning to the ranch on a snowmobile when he saw Al trudging along the road, through the snow. He pulled up to Al and asked if he was cold. He was freezing, dressed only in light clothes and tennis shoes. He climbed onto the snowmobile with Paul, and they returned to the farmhouse, where a fire was roaring in the wood stove. Al downed a cup of hot chocolate that Lyn, Paul's wife made for him, and got thawed out enough to talk. Paul asked him, "Al, do you want me to take you back to Rawhide, or do you want to continue walking the two miles to the county road to see if you can get a ride?"

"Please take me back to Rawhide," Al said.

When Paul brought Al back, Jan and I sat down with Al. He had been telling us for a few weeks that he did not want to be at Rawhide, and we had also been thinking it might be time to return him to his county social services agency. We said we would talk again the next day, and if he wanted we could start the process to see what options his county might have for him. "If you stay," I told Al, "your discipline for running away will be to move ten piles of blocks." Oh yes, the guys on discipline had to move the blocks in the winter too. But first they had to shovel a three-hundred-foot trail through the snow.

Al decided he wanted to leave. His social worker worked out a plan for him to live with his mother, and we packed him up and drove him home.

In early spring we got a call from Al, asking if he could come back. He was no longer under supervision of the county authorities, but things were not working out at home. We talked to his mother, and she was all in favor his of returning to Rawhide.

When Al arrived, Jan, our social worker, and I asked him why he wanted to come back. He convinced us that there was a definite change in his attitude. When I told him we would let him come back with one condition, he said, "Great. What's the condition?"

"You still have ten piles of blocks to move before you will be off discipline." He agreed, and impressed us with further behavior that showed he truly was a changed young man.

During his second time with us, he attended one of Bart's summer football camps. Shortly after that he returned a second time to live with his mother and enrolled in his local high school to finish his senior year. He went out for the football team and became an outstanding defensive linebacker. Bart's football camps were very successful in developing Rawhide guys into linebackers.

Mary, another student at the high school, knew Al as a hoodlum before he went to Rawhide. But she really liked him after he came back. They dated and were ultimately married. In time they moved to Des Moines, Iowa, a hub for the company Al worked for as a professional truck driver. When we interviewed the two of them for this book, I was surprised to learn that Al had played seven years with a semipro football team called the Blue Knights. He also was a member of the practice squad for the Barnstormers, an Iowa team that has produced several pro players, including Kurt Warner, the quarterback who led the St. Louis Rams to a Super Bowl victory.

Always a big Packer fan, Al was asked to share the stage at a dinner prior to the game on Thanksgiving Day 2015. It was called a "Chalk Talk", and it was sponsored by Rawhide at the Resch Center in Green Bay. Twelve hundred people paid ninety dollars apiece to hear talks by Bart Starr Jr., Cherry Starr, and Brett Favre. They got another treat as Al gave an excellent ten-minute talk about his life and how Rawhide had helped him become a good husband and father. He got a standing ovation.

Al called recently to ask how the book was coming along. I said we had just finished the chapter about him. He said, "John, be sure to say that the thing Mary and I are most blessed with is God's love and patience, especially with me. We have been married thirty-one years, and we have three girls and eight grandchildren. We have our faith and family, and everything else in life is just stuff."

# CHAPTER 15

# FROM HEARTACHE TO HOPE

## *John:*

At three o'clock in the morning on October 4, 1984, the intercom rang in our bedroom. I picked it up, but before I could say anything, Rob Strauss, the housefather in the boys Lodge home shouted, "John, the Lodge is on fire, and it's bad! I have all the boys out." I quickly turned to Jan and asked her to call the New London Fire Department and then notify the other boys homes. I threw on some clothes and ran for the fire truck in the equipment shed.

Before I could see the Lodge, which was hidden behind other buildings, I could see the red glow of a major fire. I positioned the truck about fifty feet from the kitchen, which was already engulfed in flames. The heat from the fire had melted the glass from one of the windows. It took less than a minute after stopping the truck until we had pressure on a pre-connected inch-and-a-half-inch hose line. You have to fight a building fire from the inside. you can't just spray water in through a window. Initially, it looked like a hopeless task. But most of the fire was on the surface of the varnished, knotty pine kitchen walls and wood ceiling. After pushing inside the kitchen door, I was able to hose down all the visible flames within a couple of minutes.

My son Tim, who was assisting me with the hose line, yelled that the fire had broken out in the room above the kitchen. We backed out and saw a red glow behind the second-story bedroom window. A staff member and two boys got a ladder off the truck and extended it about three feet above the bottom of the window. That way, when they dropped the ladder against the house it would break the glass. I headed up the ladder with Tim behind me, realizing it was going to be a challenge to contain the fire for twenty minutes until the New London fire trucks arrived. The fact that the fire had traveled up the wall to the second floor was not a good sign.

Our truck carried only five hundred gallons of water, so it would be important to conserve as much as possible. In keeping with our training, I sprayed when I saw flames, and then shut off the nozzle. The truck could pump five hundred gallons a minute at full capacity with multiple hose lines out. With one line and intermittent spraying, I estimated we had used half of our water after about ten minutes. We had to conserve the rest until the New London trucks arrived.

In a minute or two the visible flames were extinguished, but people were shouting that the fire had flared up in the kitchen again.

We headed back down to put the kitchen fire out and then up the ladder a second time to extinguish more flames on the second-floor. As the first New London pumper came around the corner of the Lodge, we ran out of water. A second pumper truck and a bulk water tanker quickly followed. We were able to step back and let the New London firefighters take over.

"The smoke alarms woke my wife and me, and we escaped out

the front door," Rob said.

One of our RIs and the nine boys who lived on the second floor couldn't exit through either of the inside stairways because of the smoke and heat. They used a fire exit onto a porch roof and then climbed down a fire escape ladder to the ground. Rob had assembled everyone at the large tree outside the lodge, the designated emergency gathering point, just as they had practiced in fire drills. Everyone was accounted for except Mandy, the home's Yellow Labrador Retriever. Sadly, the dog did not make it out.

It is always difficult when facing any tragedy to understand why God allows bad things to happen. And it is easy to lose hope and forget that God may have blessings in store for us in the future. The insurance company adjuster determined that the fire was caused by a refrigerator motor. The structural damage was so severe that he considered the Lodge a total loss. We knew it would take longer to repair the damage than to tear the building down and start over, but we also knew that rebuilding would be a great training experience for the boys.

The insurance agent said his company would give us a total loss settlement. But if we decided to repair the building they would pay what it cost. They approved a pay rate of twenty dollars an hour for staff members working on the home, and the boys would get two dollars an hour. These wages were about double what our staff members and boys were getting at the time.

Our maintenance staff didn't have the time or experience to undertake such a large project. We hired a local two-man construction team consisting of Mark Romeis, a Master Carpenter, and Bob Schaffer, an electrician and plumber. They both welcomed the chance to teach the boys the variety of construction skills needed for the restoration.

It took a year-and-a-half to finish the work, but the end result was wonderful. Rawhide's very first boys home now had an upgraded electrical system, from two hundred to four hundred amps and a new hot water heating system with five separate control zones.

When the lodge was about a month from being completed, I started to wish we could keep Mark and Bob on our staff, as we had plans to erect another boys home. I sat down with both of them. "I would love to have you guys stay on as full-time staff, but we would not be able to pay you at the rate the insurance company has been paying."

"Make us an offer," said Bob.

"We could pay $12 an hour plus some benefits."

Mark didn't hesitate. "We'll stay."

It has been thirty years since the completion of the rebuilt lodge. Bob has since passed away. Mark continued to work twenty-five years as our foreman on the construction of additional homes and many other projects. He recently retired, but his legacy is on display in every structure at Rawhide. Several of the boys have gone on to work in construction, and dozens more know how to tighten a doorknob or install a light switch because of his patient mentoring.

# Favorite Horses Lost

## *Jan:*

At midnight on Christmas Eve 1999, a staff member was returning to the ranch when he saw smoke rolling out of the cracks in the hay loft of the stable. He jumped out of his car and ran to get the horses out. He could see flames in the feed room, and the smoke was so thick he could not take a breath. He held his breath and ran to the end of the aisle, opened the sliding door, and stuck his head outside to grab a deep breath of air. Then, holding his breath, he dashed back into the smoke and opened one of the seven box stalls. He peered through the smoke that was stinging his eyes and grabbed the halter of an anxious horse, leading him out of the barn. He grabbed another lung-full of air and headed back inside. He was able to rescue two more horses before the flames were so hot it was impossible to enter. He ran to the nearest phone and called the New London Fire Department. Then he called John and me. By now the whole barn was in flames.

The four horses that remained trapped in the barn did not make a sound. The intense smoke had overcome them before the flames had reached them. There were no other buildings in danger, so there was nothing we could save with our own fire equipment. By the time the New London Fire Department arrived, the barn had collapsed, and all they could do was douse the smoldering hay that had been in the loft. The fire investigator later informed us it had been started by a heating cable wrapped around a water pipe.

John and Henry, with lots of help from the boys, had built the barn with lumber from a neighbor's barn. It was dismantled and then rebuilt at the ranch.

Everyone loved Katie, Babe, Flaxey, and Tuffy, and they were special to many of the boys. There were tears in our eyes as we all gathered the next morning, on Christmas Day, to stare at the still-smoking rubble that had, a day earlier, been home to our lost horses. One of the Rawhide boys, Phil, was on a home visit over Christmas when he learned about the fire. On his return he wrote an essay for the Rawhide school newspaper about his feelings over the loss.

## *Phil (one of the Rawhide Boys):*

At first I couldn't believe this had happened. Katie was my favorite horse, and she had died. As we drove into the ranch the day after Christmas, there was still smoke coming from what had been the barn, and it smelled terrible even with the van windows closed. I can't even imagine how horrifying it must have been for my four horse friends. All they wanted was a clean bed, an extra handful of grain, and an occasional hug . . . just like us guys need.

I loved being able to care for those horses, whether it was cleaning the stalls or just dropping into the barn to say hello after school. Sometimes I would get a couple of apples and cut them up to divide equally among the four horses. Though they may not be here physically, they will always live in my memory and in my heart.

## John:

A relationship with a children's program in Russia resulted in a special memorial for Katie, Babe, Flaxey, and Tuffy. Dan Leach, one of our academic instructors, had made a connection with leaders of the Yukhta Special School, located in the Amur region of Siberia, close to the border with China. They work with about 130 children in trouble with the law who were placed there by authorities.

Dan recruited Gary Thompson, a housefather at Rawhide, to accompany him on our first trip to the school. Teams of three or four Rawhide staff members would travel to Russia so they could share teaching techniques and values that have made Rawhide successful. Teams of three teachers and an interpreter from the school have made visits to Rawhide.

Through these visits our staff met Maya Valeyeva, renowned writer and artist. She is an accomplished author of children's books and writes about the relationship between children and animals. She is especially known for the murals she paints for parks and nature preserves in her country. Maya had agreed to travel to Rawhide to see the ranch and live with Gary and Kay, and do a painting for us. As it turned out, Maya arrived at the ranch with the group from Russia two days after the barn fire.

It did not take Maya long to choose the subject for a large mural she offered to paint. It would be the four horses lost in the fire. She asked Jan if we had photos of the horses, and of course we had several snapshots of each. We set up a studio in an area of the maintenance shop where she could go to work on a six-by-fifteen-foot canvas. She spent her first few days sketching the outline of the horses and then starting to add color. Boys would drop in each day, and they were amazed to see her progress. After almost four weeks, the masterpiece was complete. She had captured exactly the facial expressions of each horse as they raced through a pasture together into the sunset.

Maya titled her work *Memories of Freedom*. Over those weeks the experience of watching the four horses come back to life on canvas helped the boys deal with their loss. We moved the finished mural to a prominent space on a wall in the dining area of the Frontier Hotel, where the boys and hundreds of visitors see it every year. A plaque tells the story of the fire and of God's timing. For a ranch reeling with pain and loss, Maya had arrived at just the right time.

With the help of several generous donors, the old barn has been replaced with a new equestrian center. Major gifts by Kathleen Searl and by Mike and Cindy Sheldon funded an extensive complex that includes a stable, an indoor riding arena, and a two-story training center named in honor of longtime employees Gary and Kay Thompson. As was true with rebuilding the Lodge, the ranch staff and boys handled most of the construction as a training project. Through the experience, the boys learned practical skills and developed the self-confidence that comes from a big job done well.

# Bret Starr

Bret Starr, Bart and Cherry's youngest son, was born in the mid '60s, the same time Rawhide was founded. In his younger years, he visited the boys ranch many times with his parents. He loved animals. As a four-year-old he partnered with our son Tim, who was the same age, to catch pan fish in the Wolf River. To the boys, catching a four-inch bluegill was like catching a trophy bass.

Bret was very popular in school, and as a teenager he became involved in music and formed a band with some friends. His love for animals grew over the years, especially for unusual pets.

Jan was very nervous that she might meet one of his less huggable four-legged friends on a visit to the Starrs' Green Bay home. During one visit, as Jan and Cherry went into the living room, Cherry said, "Let me check under the couch before you sit down. Bret's pet rat was running around the living room this morning. He really loves people, but Bart gets upset when he climbs into bed with us early in the morning." Jan is an animal lover, except when it comes to mice and rats. Luckily, Bret's rat did not show up on that visit.

On a hot summer day in mid-July 1988, Jan and I had taken the day off to relax on the beautiful Chain of Lakes in Waupaca, Wisconsin. We had enjoyed a meal on the lakeside deck of Clear Water Harbor and were unwinding on a small, rented pontoon boat when a special news report came over the radio. We could not believe what we were hearing. Bret Starr had passed away and had been found by his father. Bret was only twenty-four years old. We were shocked, and prayed for strength for Bart, Cherry and Bart Jr.

The following excerpt is from a news story by Bob Oates, a Los

Angeles staff writer, published a few days after Bret's death.

# *Bob Oates:*

Bret Starr had plenty of reasons to go on living. Bright and sensitive, he was also young and good-natured. He loved music and animals. And he was the son of former National Football League quarterback and coach, Bart Starr of Green Bay, Wisconsin, a sportsman widely esteemed for high principles, exemplary behavior, and plain decency.

Nevertheless, Bret lived only twenty-four years. Plagued by a drug problem that had gripped him in his teens; he died a lonely cocaine-related death at his home in Florida, where he was found dead on July 7.

"It's frightening," Bob Long, a former teammate and business associate of Bart Starr said. "It shows you how insidious cocaine is."

Connie Grunwaldt stated "Parents who tragically lose a child to drugs can either bury themselves in grief or try to reach out to others. Bart and his wife Cherry have made a decision to reach out, to fight.

They loved Bret so much, and they were such caring parents. They never abandoned Bret, and they don't want to abandon him now—though this is hard on Bart because he's such a private person."

Starr, forfeiting his privacy, delivered the eulogy at Bret's memorial service in Green Bay.

In a recent interview, Bart said he doesn't minimize the problem that they and others face in seeking to convince a seemingly reluctant public to forsake drugs.

"I hate cocaine," he said. "I hate the cocaine evil. I'm angry that it's doing all this damage, but I question whether the country is angry enough to lick it . . . We desperately need better information."

# Bret Starr-Rawhide Foundation
## *John:*

Bart is of the old school and has never been comfortable with charging for his autograph. But autographs have become big business for athletes, so he and Cherry came up with a plan that would provide help for others without compromising their beliefs.

They proposed setting up an account called the "Bret Starr-Rawhide Foundation" that would receive all the money Bart would get for signing autographs. The interest earned would be used by Rawhide to help alumni, who in many cases were much like Bret: in their early twenties and struggling to make the right choices. The foundation would help Rawhide alumni with counseling, scholarship support, medical costs, and other needs important to their success.

Since the Starrs set up the foundation in 1988, the fund has grown to over a million dollars and is providing thousands of dollars in interest income each year to help Rawhide alumni. Bart and Cherry's character is esteemed by all who know them. In many ways their legacy is felt throughout the Packers organization, where integrity is expected of those who are part of the Green and Gold. Their character was on display in their response to the tragic loss of their son. They shared their grief openly. They faced the pain and turned the tragedy into an opportunity to help others. No one could do more. And with the depth of their love for others, they could do no less.

The two major fires at Rawhide, and especially the death of Bret, were difficult challenges to face. But out of the tragedies came blessings of hope for the future.

# CHAPTER 16

# FAMOUS FRIENDS

*John:*

As the reputation of the Rawhide Boys Ranch spread throughout Wisconsin, and beyond, it enabled the boys to experience new and exciting opportunities. They were able to meet famous people and in some cases get to know them quite well.

In February 1999, I got a phone call from David Wannamaker, a friend who was a vocal director and event promoter. David launched into an excited explanation of an event he had planned for mid-April at the beautiful Weidner Center For The Arts, in Green Bay. He had booked singers Frank Sinatra Jr. and Monica Mancini along with the Henry Mancini Orchestra. I was impressed but not surprised, since David planned events like this all around the country. However, his next comment caught me off guard. "John, I want to do this as a fund-raiser for Rawhide. It would be really great if we could somehow work a few boys into the evening. Do you have any boys who are good singers?"

"David, this is amazing," I replied. "We have sixty-five boys who love to sing. They would be a sure hit in the show."

I was stretching the truth just a little bit. When they went on trail rides with Jan, the boys would sing campfire songs with gusto. But none were trained singers.

David then started to ask some questions I couldn't dodge. "Have they had professional training?"

"Not yet," I answered, "but we have someone who is going to set up voice lessons for all of them."

"Who is going to teach them?"

"You are, David!"

Now it was my turn to get excited. "David, the guys would love this. They are all outgoing young men who love to be the center of attention. We can have them perform two or three songs at the end of the concert. Tell you what: I'll have them all in tuxedos."

"Do you have sixty-five tuxedos?"

"No, but I can get them donated."

We chatted enthusiastically for a few more minutes, and David was on board to host the debut performance of the Rawhide Boys Choir.

I shared the plan with the boys the next morning, and they were thrilled. When I explained they would all wear tuxedos one of the boys asked, "What's a tuxedo?" We knew this was going to be an interesting challenge.

We scheduled rehearsals two nights a week for ninety minutes each. David was able to persuade two music teachers from Appleton East High School, along with several senior music students, to volunteer their time to work with the boys.

The first few sessions were amazing. That is, amazingly terrible.

But the boys loved it, and they were having a blast. As the practices moved forward, little-by-little, they learned their vocal parts. A few weeks into the rehearsals, Jan agreed that they sounded considerably better.

Jan contacted some tux rental stores in order to round up sixty-five tuxedos. Their support was wonderful, and by her third call, we had them all donated. Two weeks before the concert, the house-parents took their boys to the rental stores to be fitted.

The day before the concert, Monica Mancini and her mother came to visit Rawhide. A group of higher-ranking boys guided their short tour, which was followed by lunch with all of the boys. Monica was a delight and chatted nonstop with everyone. The boys were very taken with her, and she and her mother were impressed with them.

Sunday, April 11 arrived, the big day. By midafternoon sixty-five boys and chaperones were loaded into a caravan of vans to make the trip to Green Bay. When we arrived, everyone headed to the lower level into the dressing area. A dozen Rawhide staff members were ready to help the guys into their tuxedos, knowing this would be the first experience for all of them. The boys posed for numerous pictures and videos, and an hour passed quickly before everyone was dressed. The boys stood in front of the mirrors, admiring how handsome they looked.

We set out the soda and sub sandwiches we had brought along, and everyone had a bite to eat before heading upstairs to enjoy the concert from backstage. As they peeked into the auditorium, they were amazed to see more than one thousand people, all dressed in their finest attire, in their seats half-an-hour before program time.

The show began. The Henry Mancini Orchestra was superb. Monica and Frank Sinatra Jr. were great performers. Just before intermission, David called Jan and me out to greet the crowd, and we thanked them for supporting Rawhide.

When the second half of the program was nearing its close, David walked to the microphone in the center of the stage. He announced that the show would close with a special treat. "I am proud to introduce the first appearance of the sixty-five-voice Rawhide Youth Choir!"

The boys filed in from both sides of the stage, looking every bit like professionals. David raised his arms and pointed at the orchestra to start the first of three patriotic songs, and as his hands lowered, the singers all boldly hit the opening note. The audience knew there were two more songs to follow, but they gave the boys extended applause at the end of the opening number.

In the last two numbers the boys added some harmony. After the third song, the audience jumped to their feet in a longstanding ovation. At this point we realized we had not talked about how to bow in unison. A couple of the boys started to bow. This was followed by more and more boys bowing, everyone at different times. As they kept bowing, it looked like sixty-five of the little plastic woodpecker toys sitting on the edge of a water glass. The more the boys kept bowing, the louder the crowd applauded. After a few minutes David went to the front of the stage, thanked the boys and the audience, and said the boys would be waiting in the lobby to visit with the guests.

Guests spent more than an hour chatting with Frank, Monica, and the Rawhide singers. The boys were the center of attention. Several guests asked various boys to sign their programs, and that caught on. Soon the boys were offering to sign everyone's program. By the time the crowed had thinned, all the boys had signed dozens of programs.

We put together a video of the program and gave a copy to each boy. Many of the boys' parents attended the concert as Rawhide's guests, but for those who could not, the boys were able to take the video home to share with their families. It was a remarkable evening for our boys. Every one of them came away knowing they had been the stars of a very special musical evening.

# Meeting Celebrities

When we started Rawhide, we would watch the newspapers for area events celebrities would be attending and inquire about the possibility of introducing our boys to them. Even better, we would try to get the celebrity to visit the ranch. Occasionally we would volunteer to help at special events, which sometimes led to meeting the celebrities.

One year the Appleton International Airport had a large air show planned for the summer, and the Navy Blue Angels precision aerobatic team was slated to perform. I contacted the air show coordinator and asked if he could use a few dozen boys and some staff to help with preshow setup in exchange for the boys being able to shake the hands of the Blue Angel pilots. He jumped at the chance for some free help, and we were assigned the three-day job of putting up a mile of temporary security fencing.

On the day of the show, we were asked to use our fire truck to lead some of the planes to safely taxi through the crowd. After each trip, we parked next to the Blue Angels' planes. The boys got the pilots' autographs and spent considerable time talking with them.

Roy Rogers and Dale Evans were scheduled to appear at a local county fair, and with the help of a phone call from Bart Starr, we convinced them to fly in a day early and visit Rawhide. The boys sat around a circle on hay bales as Roy and Dale sang their theme song, "Happy Trails."

Pat Boone was doing a charity event in the area and agreed to spend a couple hours with the boys at the ranch, in his white buck shoes, of course.

Author Paul Thomsen and his wife, Julie, were close friends of ours. Paul had written a book titled *Flight of the Falcon* about astronaut Colonel Jim Erwin, who flew on the Apollo 15 mission to the moon. Paul invited Colonel Erwin to spend a day with the boys at Rawhide, and he very graciously accepted.

Frank Abagnale, whose life of crime was portrayed in the movie *Catch Me If You Can*, also visited Rawhide. He did a great job of sharing his story without glamorizing his deceptions. He helped the boys see the pain he had caused his parents and others through his crimes.

Michael Sajbel worked at Rawhide four summers while getting his undergraduate degree in film studies at the University of Wisconsin-Oshkosh. He went on to be a Hollywood movie director with several successful movies to his credit. Early in his career, his company handled the stunt shots for the *Dukes of Hazard* TV show. Michael would visit Rawhide and show out-takes to the boys how they did the Duke brothers' car jumps using small Barbie and Ken dolls in toy cars. Since that time Michael has worked on over forty films, including ten for the Billy Graham Evangelistic Association.

One of the films he wrote and directed was *The Ride*, based on the story of Jan and me and Rawhide. Other films he directed were *The Ultimate Gift*, starring James Garner, Brian Dennehy, and Abigail Breslin, and *One Night With The King* starring Omar Sharif, John Rhys-Davies and Peter O'Toole. He recently hired one of the Rawhide alumni, Shawn Morrison, to work with him on movie projects.

Chuck Woolery started out as a singer with Elkin Thomas. During our first year at the ranch, they came to Rawhide to spend a day singing for the boys. They fell in love with the ranch and the boys, and for several decades they returned to visit for a few days each year.

Chuck went on to host the successful the Hollywood game show *Love Connection*. He volunteered his time as a celebrity host at several of the Rawhide telethons and has become a lifetime friend and promoter of the boys ranch. Chuck also donates his time as a guest fishing guide hosting disabled veterans and terminally ill youth as part of The Way Outfitters, the charity founded by Rawhide alumnus Roger Devenport.

Under the direction of General Manager Tom Hutchison, WLUK Green Bay TV station donated a twenty-hour telethon for several years. The station would bring in Hollywood celebrities who would visit the ranch and then participate in the telethon program. For several years the show was produced and broadcast from the ranch.

Over the years other Hollywood celebrities to visit Rawhide were Karen Valentine, Peter Breck, Bob Eubanks, Nick Barkley, and Harvey Korman.

Wisconsin Governor Tommy Thompson was a close friend of Rawhide during his four terms in office. He set aside a full day every summer to visit the ranch, and he didn't want the press to know of his visit. He just wanted to spend three or four hours with the boys and have a meal with them. On occasion, we needed his help dealing with complicated regulations for children's homes, and he always valued our opinion to improve the rules. We learned that when his health and social services department was proposing rule changes for residential youth care programs, his first question to them was, "How does Rawhide feel about this?"

Governor Thompson went on to become George W. Bush's

health and human services secretary. Rawhide staff and the boys had the chance to meet with him in his Washington office.

Governor Scott Walker has also been a guest at Rawhide. He and his wife, Tonette, have two sons, so they understand some of the challenges of raising boys. They appreciate the approach we use to redirect boys' lives at the ranch.

Other political visitors have included US Senators Herb Kohl and Ron Johnson. Members of Congress include Mark Green (who later became a U.S. Ambassador), House Speaker Paul Ryan, Congressman Mike Gallagher, and Congressman Reid Ribble. Reid's parents were Rawhide volunteers when we founded the ranch in 1965. When Congressman Reid was back in his home district, he rarely missed a chance to attend a Rawhide Fish Fry held every third Friday May through October.

As Jan and I were growing up, our parents took us to events where we had the opportunity to hear and sometimes meet interesting sports, political, or civic leaders. As kids, we were impressed with how personal and friendly they were.

Our grandson, Reagan John Gillespie, was named after President Ronald Reagan and me. When he was nine years old, his father, our oldest son, Steve, helped him send an eight-by-ten-inch framed photograph of himself that he had signed "From Reagan to President Reagan, my namesake." It resulted in an invitation from President Reagan's staff for our Reagan to visit with the former president at his Hollywood office. Reagan, his dad, and I made the trip. Because of President Reagan's advanced Alzheimer's disease, we were the second-to-last people ever invited for a visit. It made a solemn and gratifying impression on our grandson, and on us.

# "America's Team"

At the heart of this entire circle of contacts, the encouragement the boys got from Bart and Cherry Starr and numerous other Green Bay Packer players was invaluable. Several of the Super Bowl I and II players, like Jerry Kramer, Boyd Dowler, Max Magee, Fuzzy Thurston, Henry Jordan, Zeke Bratkowski, Carroll Dale, and Elijah Pitts, visited Rawhide many times. Some would come to Rawhide to bow hunt and then stop by the lodge for pie and ice cream while they visited with the boys around the table. Once a newspaper photo convinced the kids from school that the boys really did spend time with Packers players, they all begged to be invited to the ranch the next time Packers players visited.

Brett Favre and his wife, Deanna, have been longtime supporters of Rawhide through their Favre4Hope Foundation. In addition, Brett has donated time to attend several ranch promotion and fund-raising events, including an annual event called a "Chalk Talk" luncheon that has annually drawn up to 1,600 guests to Green Bay's K.I. Convention Center.

During the early years, Green Bay Packer quarterback, and later coach, Bart Starr, was able to provide tickets for Packer games for some of the boys. On occasion, as a special honor, they were invited to the Starrs' home to visit and share snacks after a game.

Bart and Chuck Woolery became good friends, volunteering their time to work together on several Rawhide events. Once when Bart was a player and Chuck had a record at the top of the charts, Bart asked Chuck to be involved in a prank on the first day of Packers rookie camp. It was the custom for a few rookies to be randomly called on during a meal to stand on their chairs and sing a song. They were always terrible, and they were met with a room full of "boos" from the veterans. That day, Bart introduced Chuck as a rookie from a Division 3 school no one had ever heard of. Asked to sing, he climbed on his chair with his guitar and belted out his hit song, "Naturally Stoned." It only took a few seconds for everyone to recognize the song and realize they had been set up.

The boys benefit from the opportunity to meet celebrities, but the celebrities benefit as well. Many have told us how blessed they felt to visit Rawhide and meet the boys. In some cases we had celebrities call us asking if they could schedule a visit to the ranch.

For the boys, the best part was realizing famous people actually cared about them. A great example was that they knew Bart and Cherry loved them just as they were, but wanted them to succeed in life.

Roy Rogers and Dale Evens gave the boys another example of how much celebrities could care when they visited the ranch. Dale had the opportunity to have a long visit with Dennis Green, featured in Chapter 11 with his horse, Frisco. Dennis was new to the ranch and still had a very recognizable chip on his shoulder. At the end of their visit, Dale asked Jan about Dennis. "I am going to pray for Dennis," Dale said, "that he will open his heart to the Lord," In the next few weeks, she called Jan twice to check up on Dennis, and on one occasion talked directly to him.

We all need people to care about us. Troubled youth especially need to feel accepted and loved. The spirit of caring is strong in the Rawhide family. It is very evident to the boys, that the staff, volunteers, and hundreds of donors do it because they know it provides an opportunity for them to turn their lives around.

# CHAPTER 17

# A BLESSING INDEED

## *John:*

Writing this book was an adventure and a blessing for Jan and me.

It all started in mid-2013, when I got a call from Dal Wood, a retired investment advisor and a longtime friend. He asked to schedule a time to share an idea with us. Dal arrived with a page of notes and a couple of books. He is an avid reader, and has an appreciation of good writing.

We sat down at the dining room table, and he made his opening statement. "John and Jan, what will it take to convince you to write a book about the vision, values, and success of the Rawhide Boys Ranch? If you don't there will be dozens, or even hundreds, of stories about the early years' challenges and blessings that only the two of you can tell." He continued. "If you write a book, I will help you."

This was not the first time somebody suggested that we write a book about the founding of the Rawhide Boys Ranch. My somewhat casual answer was always, "If we were convinced that a book would be a help to others, we would do it." We were never sure it would be worth the effort, so we procrastinated.

Over the next thirty minutes, Dal went through his well-thought-out notes in a very convincing way. He had years of experience motivating others as a colonel in the United States Marines, and his words definitely made an impression on us. After Dal's visit we took some time to make a list of the reasons we should write a book, and the reasons we should not. The "we should" list easily won.

Jan and I had used the Franklin Covey planning system well before founding Rawhide, so we had a record of what we did every day over our thirty-five years as houseparents at the ranch. I suggested to Jan that we go through our day-planners, from 1965 to 2000. It took over a month. We made notes on three-by-five cards of stories that might be of interest in a book, and we ended up with about two hundred cards, each with a few notes about memorable incidents.

I suggested we put up a large sheet of cork bulletin board in the living room, where we could pin the cards in the order they might appear in the book. Jan paused a moment and said, "How long would this board be hanging over my picture windows?" I said I thought it would just be a couple weeks. Well, it was up almost three months, during which time we added, moved, or deleted various story cards. Even our family and friends got into the act once they saw what was going on. It seemed that every visit turned into a chance to check out the "book board."

The day finally arrived when we had exhausted the story-search phase, and 157 stories had made the cut. Now it was time to start writing each one in detail.

Jan had previously been diagnosed with a bone cancer called Multiple Myeloma, so with weekly doctor appointments and treatment days, the writing process took longer than expected. However, this was a wonderful time for both of us to share in the writing of our stories and to spend many hours recalling the details of each one. On the many days Jan had to spend three hours at the oncology clinic getting chemo treatments, I would sit with her, and we would go over book notes. Recalling the blessings and challenges of our first thirty-five years at Rawhide made the time go quickly.

As the book came together, we were convinced that our experience working with boys and families in conflict could be a help to others. We knew that the approach we followed at Rawhide helped motivate teenage boys to set and follow new goals for their lives.

Jan and I met in second grade, and were best friends for the rest of our lives. We were excited about our future, and we wanted to honor God. Little did we realize that He had a very unique direction for us that was even more exciting and rewarding than we could imagine. The first twenty-five years of our lives involved summer jobs, college, military service, athletics, involvement with horses, founding a successful business, and work with church teenagers; our compassion to help others provided a good foundation to lead Rawhide Boys Ranch. Jan and I both had a sense of humor that helped us find something funny in unusual or trying situations and the ability to laugh at the boys' antics, and our own. Giving to others sustained our efforts. Giving up was never a consideration.

Over the thirty-five years after we founded the ranch, we monitored the progress of our young alumni for up to five years after their discharge. We found that among boys who had completed at least three months with us, eight out of ten had no future police contact for any offense. Our follow-up showed that for those who did have police contact, half of them committed only minor offences, like traffic violations.

There are a variety of character traits we have been able to strengthen, in a relatively short time, in the boys we were privileged to work with. We have listed our top eight factors for successful character development in the hope that they may be a help to parents and youth workers.

## 1. Male Mentor

Over half the young men sent to live with us at Rawhide had no positive adult male mentor in their lives. Many of the boys did not even know who their fathers were. However, most would likely become fathers themselves, without first-hand knowledge of what a loving, encouraging father can and should be. We wanted the boys to experience the value of a nurturing father.

In each of the homes, we had a married couple, usually in their 50s, who had already successfully raised children of their own. Each home had an apartment for the houseparents, providing privacy that was important for time off. They lived in the home full-time, and did not work a shift. In most cases, the housefather became the boys' first example of what a father should be. This was a new experience, and they quickly bonded to their houseparents, especially their house-dads.

We encourage a single mom who does not have a male mentor for her son(s) to take steps to find one. Big Brothers Big Sisters of America is a national organization that matches mentors with boys just for this purpose. Another excellent way to find a male mentor is to become active in a local church and ask the minister to help find a substitute dad.

## 2. Encouragement

All children, youth, and adults alike need praise. We all appreciate rewards for our accomplishments, no matter how trivial they might be. Youth growing up in dysfunctional home situations, failing in school, and clashing with authorities have been told many times they are "losers," and they believe it.

When a boy arrives at Rawhide, we ask that he put his past behind him. We don't want him to talk about his failures; we want him to concentrate on his abilities and learn how to use them to focus on an exciting future. The whole program at the ranch is built around daily rewards for modest accomplishments and positive correction to encourage improvement.

It is important for parents to praise and compliment children from early on, many times more frequently than correcting them. It is difficult for parents, especially single moms, to have the energy and innovation to look for things to praise. It is even more challenging to calmly and patiently correct children while communicating that they are still loved. It is important that children understand that parents are in charge, even though the children will constantly press for more freedom.

## 3. Discipline and Correction

Children automatically resist rules, but they are never satisfied if their parents give in. They become frustrated if they realize the parents have given up and that they, the kids, have won the rules battle.

When most of the boys arrive at Rawhide, they resist the rules. But after a few weeks, or at most a few months, when they realize their houseparents and other staff mean what they say, they learn that there are always consequences for disobedience. Then they relax and actually start to enjoy being at the ranch. Our policy is always "Praise in public; correct in private."

We encourage parents to seek professional help if they start to lose control. Many times parents are reluctant or embarrassed to ask for help until problems in the home reach a dangerous level. We encourage them to seek counseling help as soon as serious conflict becomes a pattern. Rawhide has chosen to expand its professional counseling offerings by opening centers around Wisconsin (and eventually in other states) that offer practical guidance to help families in turmoil. These centers are available to our alumni, their families, and any youth or adults needing help. A list of centers can be found at www.rawhide.org.

### 4. Adventure, Excitement, and Risk

Children of any age enjoy activities that provide excitement, such as climbing a tree, jumping off the garage roof, and building a ramp to see if they can jump it with their bike—or, unfortunately, things like stealing cars or experimenting with drugs.

Driving outboard hydroplanes on the Wolf River, successfully skiing all the black-diamond runs at White Cap Mountain, and serving on a fire department are just a few of the things that allowed teenagers to fill that need for adventure at Rawhide. They found out that wholesome activities like these are even more fulfilling than the destructive things that had been part of their young lives.

We encourage parents to plan activities like camping or hiking, building a go-kart, or training to participate in family fun runs or races. And there are many other community programs that provide these kinds of activities, such as high school service clubs, Boy Scouts, YMCA sports leagues, and martial arts classes, to mention a few.

### 5. Serving Others

Children and youth who grow up demanding things for themselves are never satisfied. They usually grow into selfish adults who continue to want more, without concern for others.

Many of the ranch activities are designed to allow the boys to experience the gratification of serving others. These might include delivering large loads of firewood they had split to families in need, hosting visiting groups that take tours and enjoy meals at Rawhide, or providing community tornado or flood cleanup.

Parents are encouraged to seek out opportunities to serve others as a family. These might include ringing the Salvation Army bell during the Christmas season, volunteering at a food pantry or nursing home, or caring for an elderly person's yard and visiting him or her once or twice a month. If children experience the joy of serving with their parents, it may become a lifetime activity and a great character builder.

## 6. Self-Confidence

Boys arriving at Rawhide try to put on an act that shows they are cool, in control, and self-confident. The opposite is true. They feel like they are failures and need to hide that image. They really do not believe in themselves, and they are not excited about their futures.

Building self-confidence starts the day the boys arrive at Rawhide. They are treated with respect, and they may realize for the first time that the adults around them, their houseparents and the other staff, really care about them. Many young men living with us had dropped out of high school, but within a few months they wanted to get their diplomas and even go on for more schooling.

Parents can create an atmosphere of encouragement and assurance the children need to believe they are valuable. It is important to build them up by pointing out their unique qualities and abilities.

## 7. Belonging

Everyone wants to belong, to be part of a group or organization. Many of the young men coming to live with us had been involved in gangs for that reason. They may feel like losers, but know their friends are just like them and accept them. The gangs become their families.

It takes a few weeks at Rawhide for a new boy to accept his household of boys and staff as his new "gang," But as it happens, he realizes it is a more fun and a more secure group than his previous gang.

Parents need to help youth find and become involved with wholesome groups that match their interests and abilities. These might be a community youth activity group like a Scout Troop, a church youth organization, or a sports team.

## 8. Faith

We believe all of us have times in our lives when we wonder if this is all there is, or if something happens after we leave this life. This falls under our need to believe in a higher power. Most of the boys come to us with little hope and no faith, wishing there was more to life. Their lives have not been very purposeful.

Houseparents and staff at Rawhide come from a variety of church backgrounds, but they all share a strong Christian faith. Few boys coming to us have previously attended church. We always get parents' permission for their sons to attend church with their group and houseparents, and the boys soon enjoy the experience. Many develop a personal relationship with the Lord that becomes a lifetime partnership.

We encourage parents to find a church that they are comfortable attending. Church members and staff can provide a variety of support for many family challenges.

# A Closing Comment

We know our efforts, along with the support from Bart and Cherry, and all the other people who have partnered with us, have made a difference for thousands of young men and their families. Now it is our hope that this book will continue to be an encouragement for parents, professional youth workers, our alumni and their families, and all of our readers. It was a blessing for Jan and me to write this book. It is our prayer that God will use it to help others.

# ACKNOWLEDGMENTS

Jan and I owe a huge "thank you" to many people in addition to those already mentioned in the book. Our apology to those we may have missed in this acknowledgment list.

## Getting the Stories on the Computer

Once Jan and I had selected and written the stories, many hours were spent sitting by my grandson, Reagan Gillespie, at the computer typing in 157 stories, comprising 90,000 words. His computer skills and patience with me were essential to constructing the book.

## Editing

A first read-through and basic editing was provided by Bobbye Hartzheim, a retired teacher and close friend. Next came several months of editorial support and rearranging the story line by John Paine of John Paine Editorial Services, and our book encourager and mentor, Dal Wood. Considerable attention was needed to revising, adding and deleting some of the stories. Additional editing was provided by Paul Thomsen and Dennis Meredith, both authors themselves. Others that did draft read-throughs and added great suggestions were Tony Walter, Jo Pulido, Shannon Gillespie, Shawn Morrison, Reagan Gillespie, Marian Koepke, Betty Able and Debra Vandalen.

**Rawhide Theme Song**
David Claus is one of our alumni. In his sixties he wrote, directed and sang the song that has become the boys ranch theme song, "I'm a Rawhide Guy." You can listen to it on the book website, www.Our351Sons.com.

**Rawhide Board and Staff Support**
Throughout the writing process the Rawhide Board of Directors were encouraging and offered valuable suggestions. The Staff assisted with story and photo selection, and the Executive Director for seventeen years, John Solberg, provided words of wisdom and encouragement throughout the process. Our current Director, Alan Loux, took over Rawhide in 2018, and his past book marketing experience helped develop and lead the ranch book sales efforts.

**Video Support and Website**
Craig Smoll, a founding partner in Webouts, a national company headquartered in Appleton, provided various video support. The book website, Our351Sons.com, was developed and managed by NuTerra, LLC, led by Brian Stedl and Frank Sterzinger, of Neenah, Wisconsin.

## Baer Printing and Design
Jim Baer and John Gillespie became friends when Jim founded his printing and design business in 1962. When the Gillespie's started Rawhide, Jim's company began fifty years of providing printing and design services for the boys ranch.

## The Fedd Agency Support
After evaluating numerous publishing agencies we selected The Fedd Agency, of Austin, Texas, founded by Esther Fedorkevich in 2003. The agency represents authors in both faith and secular markets.

## LSC – Communications
The final layout and printing of the first 10,000 copies of this book was done by LSC-Communications. Steve Williamsen, the LSC senior sales representative, was our coordinator and provided excellent support to help us produce a high-quality book. He was excited to work with us, having growp up just a 20-minute drive from Rawhide.

## Program Challenges
Our approach for teenage boys placed with us by the juvenile courts to be involved in numerous community support projects. Many of the projects were covered by newspapers and television stations, and they liked interviewing the boys, and the boys loved getting back to the ranch in time to see if they made the evening news. It was great for their self-esteem. But we needed legislative support and rule changes to allow the boys to be interviewed as they worked on community projects.

## Jerry Monson

This book opens 1965 with thirteen-year-old Jerry Monson "spending the day" with Jan and me, and staying almost two years. As we were expecting our second son our rented two-bedroom farm house was going to be too small. We started our search for a larger home, and that search turned into the founding of Rawhide Boys Ranch.

Jerry is in his seventies now and continues to be a close friend. He was a helicopter mechanic serving in combat in Vietnam, and suffers with COPD from exposure to Agent Orange, which now prevents him from holding a job. He was living in rural Appleton on a city lot he owned in an older mobile home that developed a minor roof leak. He had no savings and was living on Social Security of $650 and $425 veteran's benefits a month, when he found out he qualified for a federal home repair program. The agency sent three men to tar the roof but they caved in the area above the living room, and then said they were not authorized to do any repair carpentry work. He had no money to fix the roof, and after a few days of rain he was required to move out due to mold growing in several rooms.

The insurance company for the federal agency agreed the damage was their client's fault and agreed to pay for a used mobile home of the same size. But the city stepped in and said his lot had been annexed into Appleton some years earlier and they have a no-mobile-home zoning restriction. We spent three months trying to get Jerry qualified for a Habitat Home, but his income was too low, and they could not help him.

In desperation I called Ross Giordana. Ross had worked for me at Rawhide for ten years directing our building programs, then left and started Giordana Home Builders, in Kaukauna. He had an excellent reputation building top-quality homes. I shared Jerry's plight. Ross said he would send an email to a couple dozen of the subcontractors who worked with him to see if they would be willing to donate time to put up a home for Jerry. Everyone agreed to donate their time, and several said they would also get the materials they would need donated. The next six months were a miracle watching Jerry's three-bedroom, two-bath home with a full basement take shape on his lot.

The construction team consisted of over fifty support companies and others: A-1 Cartage, Arn's Cabinets, Absolute Asphalt, A & B Tree Service, Able Distributing, Brenda B Interior Design, Bay Therm Insualtion, City Disposal, Conrad Price, Decorative Curb & Concrete, D & D Excavating/Landscape, Faith Technologies, Fox Valley Veterans Council, Giordana Home Builders, Goodwill Industries NVW, Gabriel Furniture, Hoffman Planning & Construction, Hallman Lindsey Paint, Harris Construction, H.J. Martin Flooring, Hoheisel Painting, Keller, Inc. Builders, Kolosso Toyota, Leo Harke Plastering, Leo Van de Yacht Wells, KSG Gutters, MCC Concrete Division, Modern Heating, Machine Shed Resturant, Neterrallc, Northern Asphalt, Northtown Lighting Group, Outagamie Housing Authority, Price Home Services, Ric Huss Excavating, Romenesko Cran, Rawhide About Face Team, Senator Roger Roth-Wisconsin, Roger Williams-Sheet Rock, Representave Dave Murphy-Wisconsin, Signarama Appleton, Sommerville Flag, Watters Plumbing, Welch Builders, Wisconsin Building Supply, Werner Electri, Van Vreede's Appliances, and Vander Loop Construction.

## Dal Wood

Dal Wood served as a Marine Corps officer for twenty-five years, attaining the rank of Colonel. He is a veteran of the Vietnam War. After retirement from active duty, he and his wife, Lorna, moved their family to Green Bay, Wisconsin. In a second career, Dal was an investment advisor and tax consultant for his company, Wood Financial

Services. Dal and Lorna have been devoted volunteers for Rawhide for more than thirty-five years, and helped start the Green Bay Friends of Rawhide group, which grew to 140 members. Dal asked to meet Jan and me to urge that we write a book about the founding, building and blessings of Rawhide Boys Ranch. He said he would help, and he did . . . throughout the entire project. *Without Dal's persuasion, literary ability, and friendship, this book would not be a reality.*

### Terry and Mary Kohler

The Kohlers, from Sheboygan, Wisconsin, have been close friends for many years, and have provided unwavering support for Rawhide. Terry was an Air Force Captain, piloting a B-47 Bomber on determent missions over the Soviet Union during the Cold War. Terry and Mary have been active in conservative political activities and have owned several successful businesses. Terry fervently wanted Jan and me to write this book, and generously offered to fund the research, writing, and editing costs. *Without the Kohler's guidance and financial support, we could not have completed this book.*

### Bart and Cherry Starr

Many wonderful stories of Bart and Cherry Starr agreeing to partner with Jan and me are shared in the book. But it is important we offer one more "thank you" for their decades of dedicated support. It all started with Bart taking my phone call at a very busy time in their lives. *Without the Starr's help there would have been no Rawhide, and no book.*

**And I especially want to thank my family for their support as God led them to play various roles in Rawhide Boys Ranch becoming a success.**

Steve was a second grader and Tim not yet ready for school, on that December day in 1965, when we moved from our little farm house to the "mansion," as Jerry called it. This was the start of our lifetime journey with Rawhide Boys Ranch.

Both of our sons grew up on the ranch, with many big-brothers in our home. Then followed several years with the boys as their peers. And lastly, there were more years as they continued their schooling and held various jobs at the ranch. They played an important role in helping with the boys, and offering Jan and me a variety of great suggestions.

And especially, I am grateful to God for allowing me to have an amazing wife and partner. She was a great mother, grandmother, and great-grandmother, and still had the capacity to love 351 other boys. Her spunk and tenacity was essential to our being able to found and lead the Rawhide Boys Ranch.

Jan lived by the motto that hung inside her cupboard for thirty-five years . . .

**Those who deserve love least, need it the most.**

# IN MEMORY OF JAN
## MY AMAZING PARTNER AND WIFE

I received many blessings in my life, but the best was God giving me a wonderful wife for sixty years. Jan was a dedicated mother, grandmother, and great-grandmother. She had the capacity of loving every foster boy the instant she met them. The more defensive they were, the more she knew they needed our love.

Jan was self-confident, strong-willed, and had an abiding faith in the Lord. She always had a positive attitude even during the ten-years she struggled with multiple myeloma (bone cancer).

She woke up on January 25, 2017, with what seemed like the start of a cold, but as the day went on it got worse. I said, "We need to get you to the emergency room." Jan said, "I'm so tired; I'll lie down for a few minutes first." As her head touched the pillow her heart gave out and she passed away.

I had a minute of disbelief, but then realizing she was with our Lord . . . God's peace flooded over me.

We had selected as our life-verse, Proverbs, 3:5-6:

> *"Trust in the Lord with all your heart, lean not unto your own understanding; In all your ways acknowledge Him, and He shall direct your paths."*

God has directed our paths, and provided bountiful blessings. We will be united in Heaven; but until then, I have this book we wrote together to share with others.

Jan, I love you and will be with you soon. *John*